PENGUIN BUSINESS
BELL THE CAT

A self-proclaimed standardized test junkie—having taken the CAT more than fifteen times, with scores of 750/800 (2008) and 770/800 (2017) on the GMAT, and 333/340 (2011) on the GRE—Tony Xavier is an alumnus of IIM Lucknow. Following a short stint with the Aditya Group after his MBA, Tony joined IMS Learning Resources in 2006.

Founded in 1977, IMS is one of India's oldest test-prep firms, mentoring around 75,000 aspirants every year to get into elite institutions such as the IIMs, Harvard Business School and MIT, to name a few. Over the course of his career with IMS, Tony has taken on roles across the entire breadth of the business. Having started with designing content and curriculum, he eventually went on to head the academics department, run the IMS franchise in Chennai for four years—actively training close to 3000 students—and is currently the chief learning officer at IMS. In this role, Tony heads the learning management department, which manages pedagogy, technology and all the post-enrolment services delivered by IMS across all exams, including GATE—from designing the learning app and introducing AI across curriculums to recruiting mentors and handling customer care. Tony still loves teaching and takes full-day in-person masterclasses across various cities and online for all aspirants preparing with IMS. He keeps telling them the same thing—taking a test is like playing a sport.

YOUR FRIEND,
PHILOSOPHER & GUIDE
FOR **CAT** PREPARATION

BELL THE CAT

TONY XAVIER

PENGUIN
BUSINESS

An imprint of Penguin Random House

PENGUIN BUSINESS

Penguin Business is an imprint of the Penguin Random House group of companies
whose addresses can be found at global.penguinrandomhouse.com

Published by Penguin Random House India Pvt. Ltd
4th Floor, Capital Tower 1, MG Road,
Gurugram 122 002, Haryana, India

First published in Penguin Business by Penguin Random House India 2024

ISBN 9780143469087

Typeset in Adobe Caslon Pro by Manipal Technologies Limited, Manipal
Printed at Replika Press Pvt. Ltd, India

www.penguin.co.in

To all of my students
for teaching me
how to teach

Contents

Preface

The Origin Story

By the summer of 2014, I had spent more than two and a half hot and humid years in Chennai running the IMS franchise for the city. I had mentored more than 2000 students across four centres and I was busier than ever. My office in the evenings resembled a doctor's clinic. From about 5 p.m. every day, there would be a line of students waiting for a chat with me about their prep, their career plans, their dilemmas and their fears, and on most days, I would end up shutting shop—literally pulling the shutters down—by around 10 p.m.

Any MBA worth their salt will always try to simplify things and I saw that most of the students ended up having the same doubts, dilemmas and fears. That is when I thought that a blog handling all the typical queries I have heard over the two years would make things mighty easy for everyone. Students would not have to travel far to meet me; I would not need to explain everything from scratch to every single student.

Once I decided to do it, I drew up a list of titles for all the posts I would do and the sequence in which I would do them, and set about writing one post a week. When I look back now, it was one of the best things I did for myself and for my students. Thus, once a week, instead of going to the centre in the morning, where I would get sucked into things, I stopped at the coffee shop on the way, sat down for three to four hours at a stretch and finished a post.

Why did I say it was good for me?

Because it gave me what I like most: to recharge in the middle of the busyness of running a business—a few hours by myself, immersed in a task, usually writing.

Sometimes, we do not realize the good times or the good moments when we are in them; so it was with me in Chennai. It is only after I left Chennai that I realized that some parts of life there were really good. Especially the mornings spent at the coffee shop overlooking the little beach—Bessie, as it is affectionately called—mornings spent absorbed in writing and the occasional raise of the head to watch the sea—indigo shimmering under a blazing yellow, with scarcely a soul moving about both outside and inside.

The core of this book was written on such mornings.

Since then, what was intended to make my job in Chennai easy has taken on a national life, with aspirants across the country reading and reaching out to me to help them with their queries (no number of blogs or videos can ever stop that).

I found that a few aspirants either read a post relevant to them a bit too late and ended up wasting a year, while many others just read one post that they came searching for or discovered by accident and were too lazy to browse through the blog to read other posts that would definitely help them.

This book is intended to make life easier for readers of the blog, and other aspirants too, in that they can find everything they need in the order they will need it.

I hope, dear reader, that it plays a part in what will hopefully be a successful campaign to enter your dream institution (or one close to it).

Introduction

CAT and Cricket Are Two
Sides of the Same Coin

What do they know of cricket that only cricket know?

—C.L.R. James

We succeed at a particular project not merely because we are good at it but because intuitively or through guidance, we understand all things beyond the merely obvious that go into being successful at precisely such a project. Notice that I have used the phrase 'a particular project' and not success in general. This is because this is not intended to be a generic book but one that really understands what it takes to succeed at high-stakes exams such as the CAT.

Every year, around 2,50,000 youngsters between twenty and twenty-five years of age prepare to take what is arguably the third-most challenging entrance examination in India after the JEE and the UPSC—the Common Admission Test, or the CAT, the gateway to securing a seat in one of the prestigious IIMs, apart from premier private business schools in the country.

What are the odds of making it? 1 in 100. Not very different from becoming a top-flight cricketer. And what does it take to become not just a successful cricketer who represents their country for many years but to become successful at any sport?

Merely knowing how to bat or bowl or keep wickets does not suffice. The biggest requirement for success is mental strength. We know of many a great talent who lost their way because they did not know how to get their minds under control—as much off the field as on the field. We also know of another breed of sportspersons—those who are fairly sober on and off the field but never realize their true potential at the highest level because they are never able to strategize well enough to convert talent into success on the field. One loose shot, the odd lapse in concentration at a crucial time keep happening time and again, leaving their entire careers as one great question—what could have been?

Then there is a third breed of sportspersons—those who change at just the right time. They start off as super-talented, wowing the world with their initial displays, lose their way a bit and then, in the nick of time, find the right mix of strategy and mental strength to build a great career.

Rohit Sharma is a great example of this kind of cricketer. Aravinda de Silva, the gifted and mercurial Sri Lankan cricketer, found this right mix in the final stage of his career and at the 1996 World Cup no less. Legend has it that his skipper Arjuna Ranatunga had a chat with him before the World Cup, telling him that he was the greatest talent his country had produced and that he would have to take his country to the Cup—everyone else would play around him.

What about the only breed that we have not spoken about—the Sachin Tendulkars, Rafael Nadals and Iga Świątek of the world—who appear fully ready right from the time they step on to the field? Were they just born that way? Absolutely not.

Sachin has acknowledged feeling a lot of stress and having sleepless nights before major matches, but he managed to find a way to shut things out—remember him having his headphones on all the time? He even had a brother who had professionally played cricket and a super supportive family. Rafael Nadal's uncle's role in making his nephew mentally strong is legendary. There is an anecdote that is particularly insightful. When Rafa won a prestigious tournament as a youngster, the family decided to celebrate. His uncle walked in during the party and threw them a piece of paper with a list of names. The family was puzzled as to who these people were. Exactly the point his uncle wanted to make—no one knew these people and all of them had won the same tournament previously! A lot of successful sportspeople come from a family background of sport and a set-up that teaches them the right things from a young age. Kylian Mbappé's father is a football coach and his mother is a former handball player. Carlos Alcaraz's father was a tennis player. We also know of parents who traumatized their kids to make them famous champions!

The younger generation is now coming into sport knowing that it is not just skill but great physical conditioning and diet as well that play a crucial role. But some of them know that more than all of these, it is the mental conditioning part that is most important to maximize. Iga Świątek travels along with a psychologist!

Succeeding at elite exams such as the CAT and getting into an IIM is no less difficult. In fact, it is more difficult because there is an added element: information. What makes this test different from the JEE or UPSC exams is that selection is not based on the test alone but on the academic and professional profile of the applicants as well.

How many aspirants have a background where they have been trained since childhood to succeed at this? A very, very small proportion—those whose parents or close family themselves have studied in elite institutions.

Another small fraction who graduate from elite schools also end up getting the right information. In contrast, the majority only have a vague idea of what it takes.

This book intends to fill this precise gap and help every aspirant, irrespective of their background, to do three key things:

1. Build their profile, align it to an MBA and plan their long-term career goals
2. Apply precise strategies at an area, section and test level to handle any sort of paper that turns up
3. Condition their mind to manage the stress and anxiety of preparation and achieve the mental clarity required to perform to the best of their ability every time they sit down to take a test

I feel that CAT and cricket are two sides of the same coin since facing a question is like facing a ball bowled in cricket. Every question is in some way unique from the many questions you would have solved in practice. Just like every ball a cricketer faces is different from the millions one faced at the nets.

Unlike international exams like the GMAT and the GRE, the CAT is not a standardized test; the paper keeps varying in some way or the other from year to year. Not very different from cricket—no two pitches are the same and even the same pitch behaves differently in different weather at different times of the day with different states of the ball! No other sport offers a similar analogy.

Over the course of this book, I will use cricket and sport analogies to help you build the three things I spoke about: profile, strategies and mental strength. Apologies to those among you who do not follow any sport. I assure you that it will not detract you from your learning one bit!

How to Use This Book

This is not a book that needs to be read in one go.

I would suggest using the book in the following way. Parts I and II are intended to set you up to plan your whole prep journey—not just test prep but also profile. Thus, you should complete reading Parts I and II within the first week of buying this book and draw up a personal plan based on it.

Parts III, IV and V focus on each of the three sections covered in the CAT. You can choose the order in which you want to take up each of these parts based on your own strengths and areas for improvement, starting from your weakest section to your strongest.

Do not take any mock test before you read Chapters 1 to 8 of Part VI, which is all about test-taking strategies. The rest of the chapters in Part VI should be read during the testing phase. During this phase, you will also benefit a lot from revisiting the relevant portions of Parts III, IV and V.

Part VII, which is about mental preparation for the CAT, is best taken up as you get a bit closer to the test. October is the best month to get started on this. I would advise not reading all chapters of Part VII in one go. Reading one chapter a week will work best. The CAT is conducted in the last week of November. The seven chapters will align perfectly when done one a week, starting in the first week of October.

Parts VIII, IX and X are for the second phase of the whole process—WAT-GD-PI and college selection—and are best read from December to April.

The epilogue can be read any time.

To help you have a more immersive experience and understand the content better, we have put together videos related to the text in various chapters. These videos are available on the Bell the CAT YouTube Page. The QR code on page 332 will take you to the same.

Part I
MBA, not CAT

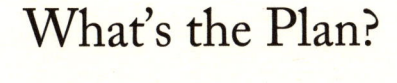

What's the Plan?

1

Why Do You Want to Crack One of the Toughest Exams in the World?

Why do you want to put yourself through this?

- Appear for a test for which about 2,50,000 aspirants register every year
- A test that only a small fraction of test-takers clear at the first attempt
- A test that is part of the admission process for an education that will cost you anywhere between Rs 15 lakh and Rs 25 lakh—an amount that is maybe, in most cases, higher than what you have spent so far on your entire education

What prize stands at the other end that you want so badly? Do you really want the prize, or are there other reasons?

- A ton of money
- A name tag with two *II*s that in India will give you a lot of respect
- The chance to undo the loss of not cracking the JEE
- A shift away from all the mistakes of the past that led you to where you are right now
- A shift away from IT
- A feeling that you will be better at management
- A way to buy some time to figure yourself out and have a good brand on your resume in the process
- You got ditched and want to show *that* person what you are capable of
- Buy a few more years from your parents before they start suggesting marriage
- More than one (or all) of the above

There will be a few aspirants—when I say *few*, I mean in terms of a percentage out of 2,50,000—who will have answers such as these:

- I have beginner-level experience in a consulting firm and an MBA will help me become a full-fledged management consultant with one of the leading consulting firms

- I have operations experience with an automobile manufacturing firm and am now looking at taking up an MBA in operations to take on larger roles in the domain
- I am a CA with a commerce background and want to build a career in finance
- I am an engineer with two years' experience and have cleared CFA Level 1. I want to take up an MBA in finance and clear CFA L2 as well in due course to build a career in finance
- I am a graduate from a great college and have stellar academics—9/9/9 and want to get into consulting
- I am a fresh graduate with a profile aligned to marketing—lots of positions of responsibilities through school and college, and enough extracurriculars

The tragic part is that even those who crack the CAT and get admission into a good business school do not have a clue as to what the outcome of their MBA should be in the long term. Very few have a clue as to what they would do with a degree they will spend more than a million rupees on.

Sample a few of the answers that I heard when I posed the question—what should be the end outcome of your MBA?—at a felicitation function we held recently for all our achievers, aspirants who secured admission into the top thirty business schools in the country:

- to learn time management
- networking
- to learn stress management
- to find the right career path for me
- last chance to study in a good college and get good marks

The less I say about the above reasons for paying Rs 20 lakh to do an MBA, the better. None of them had what should have been the real outcome of their MBA—*to become the CEO of an Indian or international firm, or to start a firm of their own.*

Some of you might think—*but I might have other plans, and the MBA is just a pit stop.* Yes, you can have other plans but the entire course—the subjects you will learn, the skills you will develop, the brand that you will have on your resume, the network you will build and the fee that you will pay—is geared towards making you a business leader in the future.

In a relatively poor and still developing country like India, a job has always meant security, not a way to make the most of one's skills. This leads to an erroneous focus on exams and not careers. JEE, NEET and CAT become ends in themselves and not one step towards the larger goal of building a great career by making the most of our skills and talents.

Our strategy is simple—first crack the test, then see what is the best college your percentile can get you and then finally start thinking about specializations.

The funny part is that we do not seem to learn from our mistakes—this is the same policy we followed for our graduation as well, and we now want to do an MBA so that we can undo the mistakes of our graduation, without having changed our standard operating procedure!

This is something that is best reflected in the question that I have heard and continue to hear from all and sundry—*In which field is there more scope?*

Imagine someone asking a former cricketer, *in which field is there more scope—batting, bowling or wicket-keeping?* The absurdity of the question is manifest! It assumes that the aspiring cricketer can become anything he or she wants!

You might say, but what they really mean by scope is which field has more money.

A student had once posed this same question: *Sir, what should I choose, an MS or an MBA? Which one has more money?*

My answer? Why should anyone pay you money? No course guarantees you even a single rupee!

If we look at the vast array of careers on offer, is there any field where there is no scope to make good money? Every single field, including the movies, offers the chance to build a great career—*if you have the right skills, the right profile and go to the right college*. Some might do it without the right college and profile, but no one can do it without the skills.

So, unless you are sure that you have the right skills and the right profile for a career in management and know which domain(s) you will specialize in, you are not getting off on the right foot towards building a great career.

The next chapter will tell you why you should choose your specializations right now, what each specialization is about and what sort of profiles recruiters from different domains look for. This should help you get some clarity on which specializations might be a better fit for you.

2

You Need to Choose Your Specialization RIGHT NOW!

Why do you need to choose your specialization right now?

Don't you have the luxury of joining an MBA programme, getting to study basic subjects from all specializations in the common course of the first year, and then choosing your specializations in the second year?

Well, fifteen or more years ago, when information was scarce, the fee was low—I paid Rs 2.4 lakh for the top-drawer education I got at IIM Lucknow—and recruiters were not as picky as they are now, so it was okay to take this approach. In fact, it was a common answer that many, including me, had in mind in case the interview panels asked us what specializations we intended to take up.

But today, it is a strategy that will set you up to make the least initial return on investment on your MBA.

All the premier B-schools have great placement statistics—great average salaries, astronomical highest-pay packages, 100 per cent placement in three days and so on—but these statistics do not mean that everyone has an equal shot at all the jobs.

Every candidate who is sitting for placements and looking to land a job in a domain, say marketing or finance, has taken the same courses in their MBA. How, then, do recruiters choose between one candidate and the other? CGPA? Wrong.

CGPA is only one of the factors and, in some domains, not a factor that recruiters use to differentiate between candidates. What matters most is the alignment of your profile to the roles offered by an MBA.

A profile is made up of the following components:

- Academic background (the graduation degree)
- Academic profile (marks)
- Academic pedigree (brand of graduation college)
- Work experience
- Professional certifications (CA, CFA, etc.)
- Positions of responsibility (PoRs)
- Extracurricular activities (ECAs)

Recruiters from different domains visit campuses—sales and marketing, finance, operations, general management, management consulting, human resources and information technology.

Each domain requires specific skills and traits demonstrated through specific profile aspects. PoRs and ECAs become very important in some domains, whereas in others, academic profile and brand of graduation college trump everything else. In a domain such as finance, there are so many sub-domains that each sub-domain has a different profile requirement.

So, the equation that has to make sense is this:

Profile + MBA = Roles offered by recruiters in a domain

Getting into an IIM does not guarantee a great job. It offers everyone an entry into a sumptuous banquet that has a spread of great jobs. The candidates who get their dream jobs are those who know what they want and have built their profile for the same even before they entered the B-school.

If you wait until the end of your first year of MBA to decide which specializations to choose and which domains to work in, you will be lagging way behind those who have been building their profile since the first year of their graduation. Even if you start building your profile in earnest right from the time you step into an MBA programme, which offers great avenues for profile building, you will be much better off than starting at the end of your first year.

More importantly, knowing what you want to do and having your profile aligned to the same will be a great advantage in the personal interviews (PIs) you have to crack later, for acing the CAT. Imagine going into an interview and speaking about career goals—*I want to get into investment banking (i-banking)*—with a profile that an i-bank will not even shortlist! The panel will not reward that ignorance with marks!

This is the best way to look at it: if two people with more or less the same ability have the same goal, the one who starts earlier will have a head start.

Many people aspire to get into a good B-school, but very few have the ambition. An aspiration is a desire to achieve something, an ambition is the determination to do whatever it takes to achieve the desire. That is the reason why the word 'ambitious' can sometimes have a negative connotation.

So, if it is your ambition to build a great career, the time to decide on your specialization, if you haven't already, is right now.

3

How to Choose the Right Specialization

Finance is more than just watching *The Wolf of Wall Street*; marketing is beyond I-can-make-better-ads-than-these; operations needs more than being a mechanical engineer; and human resource management is not just about loving to interact with people.

One of the sessions I love to take and my students enjoy is called 'All About Specializations'. It covers what a career in each domain means—what your first job will be like, what skills and traits you will need, and thus what profiles recruiters select. The session is obviously not theoretical but built around anecdotes and case studies.

A video of the session is available on the Bell the CAT YouTube Page. The QR code on page 332 will take you to the same.

Once you watch the videos, your aim should be to determine which domain you will be good at. Any above-average person can be a six out of ten on most things, but a six out of ten is not good enough for you to be really successful in the long run. You should try to find the area where you can be an eight out of ten.

If you want to learn more about each domain, you can do so by going through some great books.

The Finance List

Before one gets into finance, one needs to understand the basics of economics and these are covered in an easy-to-understand manner in these two books: *IIMA: Day to Day Economics* and *IIMA: Why I Am Paying More: Price Theory and Market Structures Made Simple*—by Professor Satish Deodhar who teaches economics at IIM-A.

While learning the technical aspects of finance can be left for later, you can pick up a real-world flavour of the workings of hedge funds, investors and quantitative finance by reading these two books: *The Big Short: Inside the Doomsday Machine* and *The Quants: The Maths Geniuses Who Brought Down Wall Street*, which narrate real-life events pertaining to the financial markets.

Both of the books above are very entertaining reads and the first one, as some of you would know, has also been made into a movie.

For anyone interested in trading, *The Intelligent Investor* by Bill Graham and *The Alchemy of Finance* by George Soros are must-reads.

The Sales and Marketing List

Maybe seemingly the least bookish of all disciplines and yet it poses the toughest challenge for all firms—*how do we sell what we make* or should it be *should we make something that sells* or should it rather be *what do people want?* Not too many books directly explain the nitty-gritty of marketing but these three should do the job:

- *Selling the Wheel: Choosing the Best Way to Sell for You, Your Company, Your Customers* by Jeff Cox and Howard Stevens
- *Positioning: The Battle for Your Mind* by Al Ries and Jack Trout
- *Buyology: How Everything We Believe about Why We Buy Is Wrong* by Martin Lindstrom
- *Hooked: How to Build Habit-Forming Products* by Nir Eyal

The Operations and Project Management List

The Bible for operations and a part of the syllabus in most of the IIMs, *The Goal*, uses a fictional story to help you understand the core concepts of operations and systems management. The author, Eli Goldratt, has used the same concepts to write a few more books to cover the entire domain of operations; the last book in the list below covers project management. Read him and you will not have imagined operations can be taught in such an engaging and insightful manner: *The Goal, The Goal–2* and *Critical Chain: A Business Novel.*

The Human Resources List

Work Rules: Insights from Inside Google That Will Transform How You Live and Lead by Laszlo Bock, *Kingdomality: An Ingenious New Way to Triumph in Management* by Sheldon Bowles and Richard and Susan Silvano, and *Thinking, Fast and Slow* by Daniel Kahneman and Amos Tversky (if you read this book well, you will understand why you tend to make silly mistakes on most problems and why, more often than not, you are unable to find unorthodox solutions that seem so obvious to a few others).

Read to get better, read with a target

The first thing to do is to approach these books with the right mindset. DO NOT read to:

- use information from these to build answers in your interviews. That can be the most stupid thing you can do since you will be showing the panel you are doing what the Indian system has taught you to do—memorize and regurgitate
- show off that reading is your hobby. If it is, you should already have a list of favourite authors and books

Treat these books as stepping stones to learn more about the vast world of business management.

Do not look only at books that deal with your specialization because if you want to be a business leader, you can't just be a finance person or a marketing person. You need to be curious to learn about everything that contributes to building a great organization.

The ones among you who should read all of this at any cost are those who, one year from now, when faced with the interviewer asking you—Why MBA?—are ready to say—*I want to start my own firm in the future.*

These books will cost you, some a little and some a bit more, but think about how much you spend on watching a stupid movie or on an evening out with friends. If you have your priorities right, you will find a way to acquire and read them even it means making a few sacrifices on other fronts.

A good target to set will be to choose twelve out of these sixteen and finish them before starting your MBA programme.

And before you sigh, thinking 'I don't have the time for this' or 'I wish I had the time for this', you will rarely have more time (and more hair) than you have today. Maybe more time after you retire!

Look at your day, look at the apps on your phone, and look at your browsing tendencies. Whenever you make a choice to do one thing with your time, you are not doing something else with it.

Your current consumption of entertainment might seem much more interesting than this reading list but that is not very different from eating potato chips—absolutely irresistible to eat but totally useless for your health.

So it is time to weed out the potato chips you are feeding your mind and give it something that is aligned with your long-term goals.

Want more information?

The IMS YouTube Channel hosts a segment of videos called *Future You*. Each episode of *Future You* is an interview with a working professional in a particular field, say an i-banker with two years' experience or a brand manager with five years' experience. The objective of the segment is to give you a ringside view of what different roles in a particular domain are like and help you determine whether you will be fit for the same.

Now that you know that profile + MBA = roles offered by corporates, you are primed to segue into the next section—Profile Matters—that deals with all things related to your profile: the chances of you getting a call from the IIMs and how you can build your profile before you get into a B-school.

Profile Matters

1

The Elements of a Profile

Before we get into what makes a profile great, we need to get past the boring technicalities that often create a lot of doubts in aspirants' minds.

Let us dive deeper into each of the elements that comprises a profile.

- Academic Profile

  o Your Class X, Class XII and grad marks and/or CGPA constitute more than 90 per cent of your academic profile.
  o You need not worry about the fact that your board is stingy with respect to awarding marks vis-à-vis another board, since most MBA colleges have a way of normalizing the marks/ CGPA across boards.
  o Since students from various boards and universities have been applying to the IIMs for ages, they have done enough data mining to know that 85.XX in Board X is equivalent to 95.XX in Board Y.
  o Ranks in Olympiads, NTSE, paper presentations, journal publications and any other academics-related contests outside of regular school and college work.
  o City/state/national level ranks secured in school, college, university and/or entrance exams such as JEE, NEET, CET, etc.

- Academic Background

  o The academic discipline of your graduation degree—commerce, arts, engineering, media studies, psychology, agricultural sciences, etc., plays a minor role in the whole selection process.
  o Some schools, such as the eminent SPJIMR in Mumbai, ask you to apply to particular domain—marketing, finance, operations or information management—and not to a common MBA programme, like the IIMs and a majority of other schools do. So, it becomes imperative that your graduation degree is aligned to the domain you are applying to. A commerce grad

applying to the operations domain is very unlikely to get shortlisted and so is an engineer applying to the finance domain.

- o To ensure that their batch comprises individuals from diverse educational backgrounds since recruiters have roles in diverse domains, some colleges, such as IIM-A, give extra weightage to those from non-engineering streams (more on this in the next chapter).

- Academic Pedigree

  - o The brand of the college you have graduated from: elite national-level brands such as the IITs, NITs, BITS; elite state-level brands such as VJTI, DCE, Stephens, COEP, CEG.
  - o Please note that *this DOES NOT play any role in the admission process* into a B-school since no marks are awarded for the same.
  - o This plays a minuscule role in campus placements with a very small cohort of companies, which hire in small numbers, shortlisting only those who graduate from elite schools.

- Work Experience

  - o This is quantified in terms of number of months of full-time professional work experience after your graduation.
  - o *Internships (done during or after graduation) DO NOT* count towards work experience.
  - o Experience in your own start-up is counted but only the months after graduation and provided your start-up has been registered and you have proof such as incorporation statements and bank accounts to validate the same.
  - o Family business work experience is considered, provided you have an offer letter/appointment letter, salary slips and/or bank statements as proof. Basically, work in family business will also be treated as professional experience if you have all the documents.
  - o So, if you plan to join your family business and prepare for the CAT or if you have your own start-up, ensure that you have the necessary documentation. The panel will not take your word for it.

- Professional Certifications (CA, CFA, CS, etc.)

  - o Apart from one's graduation, professional certifications such as CA, CFA and CS play a huge role in a domain such as finance (more on this in the next chapter).

- Positions of Responsibility (PoRs)

  - o Official posts held at a school, college and university-level, or bodies such as AIESEC, Rotaract, etc.
  - o Please ensure that you get letters/certificates for all such PoRs.

- Extracurricular Activities (ECAs)

  o Any extracurricular interest pursued out of passion both with or without achievements—reading, writing, sports, games, singing, dancing, painting, trekking, photography, short-film-making, among others.

- Gender Diversity

  o Just as colleges want their batches to have students from a diverse set of educational backgrounds, they also want enough gender diversity within each batch.
  o Gender diversity is now mandatory on the boards of large corporations. This cannot be fostered if there is no gender diversity at the management education level.
  o Also, there are many product categories where the decision-makers are women, so it goes without saying that having women business managers in companies that manufacture and market these products makes business sense.
  o Some schools, such as IIM-K and IIM-B, give extra weightage to gender diversity.

Without education and gender diversity, management schools will churn out the most vanilla profile year after year after—Male Engineer with IT work experience. (I know it hurts but the truth always does.)

Why diversity *versus* meritocracy is a false binary

Some of you might ask—but why should diversity come at the expense of meritocracy?

Well, it actually does not. Given the way the tests are structured, getting one or two questions wrong can drastically make a difference to the percentile a candidate gets, excluding them from having a shot at a management career.

One or two questions is not a statistically valid sample to say that X will definitely be a better candidate for a career in management at the expense of diversity. Making diversity a part of the selection process—and we are taking about a very small weightage—ensures that both aptitude and profile go hand-in-hand to create the kind of batch that will both foster better learning and also meet the expectations of recruits and corporations at large.

2

What Makes a 'Great' Profile?

A good profile is one which would rate as 'average' or 'above average' on most of the elements listed above and has a *spike* on at least one of the elements. A spike is a level of achievement on an element that indicates you are really better at it than most other people in the fray.

A few examples of what spikes are:

Academic Spike: Someone who has above 90 per cent in Class X, Class XII and graduation will be considered to have a huge spike in academics. The key is the 90 in graduation since most aspirants (at least in this part of the world) tend to have 90 per cent in Class X and Class XII, it is the 90 in your graduation that will put you in the outlier category.

Sports Spike: Those who have participated in individual or team sports or games at a district, state and national level will be viewed as having a spike since most aspirants will have played but not professionally. A student I met recently told me that the moment he put forward his national-level badminton at the under-13 level in front of the NMIMS panel, the interview changed (he made it despite the fact that he had just cleared the cut-off). Even running the marathon or cycling if done seriously with achievements to speak about can be a major spike.

Similarly, you can have a spike in any one area—it can be a leadership spike if you have always held positions of responsibility. It can be an extracurricular spike if you have participated in a lot of dramatics, singing or dancing at college level. It can be an ECAs spike if you have formally taken up dancing, singing, painting, languages or any other interest and are pursuing it seriously.

How does your profile impact your MBA aspirations?

Your profile plays a major role in three things:

- Getting a personal interview (PI) call from premier B-schools
- The conversation you are going to have in your PI
- Campus placements: summers and finals

But all the elements listed in the profile factors do not equally influence the three things mentioned above.

Getting a personal interview (PI) call from premier B-schools

Since B-schools cannot be vague about the definition of 'good', opening themselves up to court cases in the age of Right to Information (RTI), all colleges have their own mathematical equation for sending out calls for the second stage: essays–group discussion–personal interview round after the exam—be it CAT, XAT, NMAT or SNAP—results are out.

The major elements that come into play are **CAT score, academic profile** and **work experience.** The minor elements that are not considered by all schools are **educational diversity** and **gender diversity.**

Each B-school gives each of the three components a different weightage and in some cases, no weightage at all to calculate a composite score (they might use a different name).

For example, college X can have: 70 per cent CAT score, 15 per cent academic profile, 10 per cent work experience, 5 per cent educational diversity, 5 per cent gender diversity.

This college will give a score out of 100 to each candidate. For example:

- The 15 marks for academic profile can be divided into 5, 5 and 5 for Class X, Class XII and graduation, respectively.
- The 10 marks for work experience will be based on slabs: 36 months and above—10 marks; 24–36 months—8 marks; 12–14 months—5 marks; below 12 months—0.
- Female applicants get 5 marks for gender diversity.

We can get into the detailed computation of the same but that will be futile beyond a point since each college has a different criteria. IIM-B gives weightage to work experience, IIM-I gives more weightage to Class XII marks, etc. What is important to note is that these criteria might also change from year to year!

The conversation you are going to have in your PI

After the test, most top colleges send out an online form to those who clear the cut-off, to be filled out and submitted well before the interview. You will be asked to provide not just details about your academic profile and work experience but also:

- list achievements—co-curricular, extracurricular and work-related (if applicable)
- write answers to questions such as:

  o Why do you want to do an MBA?
  o What are your career plans?
  o What are your strengths and weaknesses?
  o What is the biggest challenge you have faced in your life so far?
  o What is your biggest failure and what have you learnt from it?
  o What are your hobbies and interests?

The panel will have your completed form when you go into the interview and you will be asked questions based on what you have filled up. This is where the academic achievements, professional certifications, positions of responsibility, extracurricular activities, etc., come into the picture since these have no weightage in getting an interview call.

Even if the panel does not have a form and starts off with a 'tell us about yourself', the interview will be based on the things you can say about yourself that are not captured in the CAT application.

The more you can have a conversation about these things and the more well-rounded your profile seems, the higher your PI score is likely to be.

The two elements—brand value of the college where you pursued (or are pursuing) your bachelor's degree and the brand value of the firm that you are working for—are not evaluated quantitatively, which means that no marks are allotted to the same separately, based on any criteria, during the admission process.

The panel will make it a part of the overall marks it awards you in your PI, based on how you perform in the PI. So, a good college brand by itself does nothing unless you do a good job in the PI.

Campus placements: summers and finals

You will be having your summer placements three to four months into your MBA. This means that your resume will not have changed at all. So, the profile you have before getting into the B-school is what you will have while applying for summer training.

The elements that take precedence, though, are completely different from the admissions process. In addition, each domain gives importance to different elements in the profile, based on the traits and skills required in that domain. I deal with this in detail in the *All About Specializations* videos. **These videos are available on the Bell the CAT YouTube Page. The QR code on page 332 will take you to the same.**

This is a table that summarizes the importance of various elements across domains.

Please note that gender diversity is not a domain-specific criteria. It is firm and role-specific.

DOMAIN	Academic Profile	Academic Pedigree	Academic Background	Professional Degrees (CA, CFA)	Work Experience	ECAs	PoRs
MARKETING	Not Important	Not Important	Not Important	Not Important	Bonus	Very Important	Very Important
FINANCE	Very Important	Important	Important	Very Important	Bonus	Not Important	Not Important
OPERATIONS	Important	Not Important	Important	Not Important	Very Important	Not Important	Not Important
HR	Not Important	Not Important	Bonus	Not Important	Bonus	Very Important	Important
IT/TECH/ e-COMMERCE	Not Important	Not Important	Not Important	Not Important	Very Important	Not Important	Bonus
GENERAL MANAGEMENT	Important	Important	Not Important	Bonus	Bonus	Important	Very Important
CONSULTING	Very Important	Very Important	Not Important	Bonus	Bonus	Very Important	Important

It is at this stage that the brand value of the college where you pursued your bachelor's degree and the brand value of the firm that you worked for become important in some cases.

Some firms, especially those in finance and consulting, are so sought after that they will have loads of resumes to choose from. These firms also end up having elaborate multi-round selection processes that are very time-consuming. They tend to make their jobs easier by giving out shortlists to those with big brand names on their resumes. So, this is where the real value of the brand name kicks in! Thankfully, only a handful of firms do this.

Are freshers at a disadvantage when compared to working professionals?

Freshers need not worry since most B-schools take in a healthy percentage of freshers (about 30–40 per cent). The weightage for work experience will make it easier for working professionals to get a call—they can get in with a lower percentile when compared to freshers. Also, for the first call, it is only the quantity of work experience that will play a role and not the brand of the firm that you are working with.

Do not worry about what you cannot change, focus on what you can

Some of you might worry that not having a big brand on your resume might hurt your chances of getting a shortlist from an investment bank. Others might worry that their poor academics are a hindrance to getting into one of their dream schools.

These are not in any way hindrances towards building a great career. For example, while companies might prefer graduates from IITs on campus placements, they might not do the same off campus. In fact, while some firms might visit only certain IIMs for campus placements, off campus they recruit candidates who graduated from any of the premier B-schools. So, you might find yourself working for a major consulting firm even though you did not crack the CAT but one of the other exams—XAT, SNAP or NMAT!

The same thing applies in the case of your academic profile not being up to scratch. Yes, you will find it tough to get a call from IIM-A, but that does not mean that you cannot have a great career! IIM-C gives a very low weightage to the same; so get a good CAT score and you could be in!

What you can change and work on though are the other aspects of your profile from now until you get into a B-school. You can take up various things to align your resume to the roles and domains you want to get into.

The importance of planning ahead

I'll leave you with a story of one of the best students I have had in recent times. A fresher in his third year of engineering, he had enrolled for the GMAT with us and attended most of the classes diligently. Each and everything I told him, right from reading the GMAT blog to planning the mocks, he followed diligently. After every mock he brought his laptop along to discuss how he could get better (he was not late even for a single appointment).

He was taking the exam in Bangalore and so before he left for the exam, he came to me to discuss the mental part of test-taking (he said he would get tense when he was unable to solve a QA problem and I had sorted out the issue for him).

Three days later, he texted me saying he got 760!

I asked him whether he was applying to the ISB Young Leaders Programme and he said he was planning to work for three years and then apply to premier MBA programmes abroad; he was not looking at any school in India!

For some reason, throughout these three or four months, I had not asked him which college he was from. Listening to his career plans, I asked him which college he was studying in and he replied that he was from IIT Madras!

Given the stereotypes surrounding IITians' ability and their attitude, it had not even remotely occurred to me that he might be from IIT-M. I thought he was a bright student from CEG, SSN or SRM (the biggest colleges other than IIT-M in Chennai).

More than being gifted mavericks, the IITians we see rising to the top of corporations across the world are diligent, organized and focused. That is why they do so well.

The way this student went about his prep for GMAT was exemplary. I recommend that those of you reading this book should also do the same.

In the next chapter, we will look at all the things you can do to build your profile.

3

How to Build Your Profile for an MBA

As we discussed in the previous chapter, you need to focus on what you can change—your present—and not what you cannot—your past.

And since by now you would have already decided on the domain(s) you want to work in and the specializations you want to take up, we will take up different profile-building activities and discuss their relevance for each domain. It goes without saying that some things might be possible only for those still in college and others for working professionals.

Professional degrees

As discussed in the video series called *All About Specializations*, the first and foremost requirement for finance is the relevant education background. But there will be so many people with a commerce or economics background! So how do recruiters in this domain whittle down the list of applicants? By giving first preference to those with a professional degree.

A CA or a CFA degree has become a must-have if you want the best roles in finance, especially investment banking, trading and the like. But it might not be possible for everyone to do their CA now. Enter the CFA.

CFA stands for Chartered Financial Analyst (CFA) and it is a postgraduate professional certification offered internationally by the US-based CFA Institute to investment and financial professionals. To put it simply, it is the international equivalent of a CA and it can be taken up at any stage of your career, irrespective of your educational background.

The CFA has three levels—L1, L2 and L3—and each of these can be taken with any amount of gap between them.

You might ask: But isn't an MBA in finance enough? Well, yes and no.

Yes, an MBA in finance will have subjects overlapping with the CFA programme, but then on paper there will be no differentiation between your profile and those of your batchmates who have also done an MBA in finance.

The CFA degree thus ends up being the differentiating factor.

Commerce and engineering grads without a CA or a CFA will lose out to those who have one. IIM Calcutta is considered the mecca for finance jobs in India. On average, there are a minimum of 100 engineers in every batch with at least a CFA-L1 degree. Firms do not require you to have cleared all three levels. Clearing CFA-L1 suffices for you to get shortlisted for some roles.

More than anything, a CFA is a signalling device from candidates to recruiters that they are very, very serious about building a great career in finance.

Why is it such a strong signalling device? Is the exam very tough?

The exam is not as tough as the Indian equivalent, the CA, but it does take quite a bit of studying to clear. L1 and L3 are relatively easy and L2 is the toughest of the three levels. But the exam is very expensive. It costs anywhere between $900 and $1250 to register for every level, depending on when you register. They give out official material for each level that costs $250. There is a one-time registration fee of $350.

Each level is conducted more than once a year, with L1 being conducted at least three or more times. The months when they are conducted and dates may change annually.

How to plan for a CFA

Most readers of this book will either be in college or working. This means that a good eight to twelve hours of your day are already pre-booked. Once you enter an MBA programme, you will be in the most demanding academic phase of your life. How does one fit a CFA into all of this?

Since firms look at candidates with at least an L1, most people aim to enter an MBA with an L1. They then aim to clear L2 as soon as they finish their MBA programme. L3 is then icing on the cake that professionals take at a later stage.

So, your goal should be to clear L1 before you enter an MBA programme. This means that you should plan to take the test a few months after the CAT and other exams get over.

Since it takes a lot of time to prep for the CFA alongside your CAT, you will be required to balance both preparations side by side, with CAT and other exams taking the lead until December and CFA from January onwards.

Those who have just graduated or begun working can choose to first knock off CFA-L1 and take up CAT the following year since there is no rush to join an MBA immediately after your graduation.

Is CFA-L1 a must before an MBA? What if you cannot take any level of the CFA before you complete your MBA?

When I said that candidates without a CFA will lose out, all of this is in the limited contest of campus placements. What we are aiming for is a career in finance, not merely campus placements.

A lot of my students, especially freshers, wisely chose to ace the CAT first, get into a good school, and work like crazy to get a CGPA on campus. This ensured that they got decent jobs in finance if not their dream i-banking job.

They finished their CFA L1 and L2 in the first two years of working and got their dream i-banking jobs.

Certification Programmes

The biggest reason to take up profile-building activities is to show that you are not just saying that you want to build a career in marketing, finance, operations, etc. Because talk is cheap; it does not cost anything. You have to show that you have taken concrete—even if they are small—steps towards building your career in a particular domain.

This is where certification programmes come in.

NSE Certifications for Finance

For those keen on pursuing finance, taking up National Stock Exchange (NSE) certifications is a good idea. They will make you knowledgeable about the basics, do not require a lot of prep, are easy to ace and are very affordable. They range across various sub-domains within finance, and so you can choose the ones that are your area of interest.

Online Certifications for all other Specializations

Platforms like Coursera and Udemy offer certification programmes across various domains. The task is simple—shortlist certifications by the domain—marketing, finance or operations, and choose the ones offered by premier international schools such as Wharton. These courses are again easy to complete, affordable and will equip you with foundational knowledge.

Analytics is used across domains, so it is an additional certification. Instead of taking up generic analytics courses, take up courses tailored for the domains you are interested in—marketing analytics, etc.

Positions of Responsibility

This is one thing that freshers should really go after in the next semester. Forget about publishing a paper as part of a symposium, organize the symposium! Paper publications make sense if you want to do an MS, not an MBA!

There are loads of committees and clubs on campus. You need to get into at least one of them, actively organize events as part of the committee/club and ensure that you get a certificate for the same.

Social Impact Activities

While both freshers and working professionals can take this up, it is easier for the latter to become an active contributor to the CSR initiatives in their organization. You can also sign up to do volunteering work for an NGO working in the field of your interest—education, healthcare, environment, etc.

One specific thing that freshers can look at is applying to and joining student organizations such as AIESEC (they have city-wise chapters) or take part in their initiatives.

ECAs—Achieve something with your passions

If you are not interested in organizing, then take part in inter-college events based on your interest, be it case study contests, B-plan contests, singing, dancing, acting, sports—whatever you are passionate about. The idea is that you should come across as someone who does more than just going to college and back home.

Your IIM interview can revolve entirely around your passion or interest. So, take whatever interest you have and explore it seriously. If you like languages, then start learning a language and clear at least a level. A student of mine liked to read manga (Japanese comics) and she ended up learning Japanese and clearing a few levels.

If you like outdoor activities such as trekking or cycling, join a trekking club. If you have always wanted to train for a marathon, then train to do at least a fraction of it.

Take an interest in the entrepreneurship cell of your college

A lot of people keep saying they want to become entrepreneurs some years down the line when asked about career plans or why MBA. But mostly, the line is similar to 'and they lived happily ever after'; nobody knows how we are expected to take it at face value. So, show some interest and become a part of the E-Cell if your college has one!

Improve your public speaking skills by joining Toastmasters

If you ask me what the biggest fear of aspirants is, I think, beyond Quant and Verbal, it is public speaking and communication skills. Students who are completely free and articulate in their mother tongues go into a shell the moment the language shifts to English.

You can overcome this weakness and add to your profile by joining Toastmasters. Toastmasters is a not a training institute but a club for people to improve their spoken English. A student who had a mild stammering issue benefited a lot from this exposure. Once you become a member and develop some skills, you can also take up positions of responsibility within the local chapter that you attend—such as moderating a chapter meeting, etc.

This is possibly one of the best things you can do since it ticks all the checkboxes—it transforms your skills, gives you a position of responsibility, and helps you develop confidence by discharging the duties in that position.

Do you do more; do you stand apart from the crowd?

As aspiring management professionals, you need to display that you are capable of doing much more than others. You need to show that you do more than just go to college or work and back home. You need to show that you are passionate about things apart from what is required. You need to show that you have the potential to perform on a much larger canvas.

So pick a few things from the list above and get started.

Choosing the Programme That Is Right for You

1

A-B-C or Nothing: Possibly the Worst Goal Ever!

Whenever we are preparing for something, we are always told to aim for the peak, for the very best. We are told to never settle.

I always had a small motivational plaque on my study table. It said: *Aim at the sun; you may not reach it but you will fly higher than if you never aimed at all!* I took it to mean that I am supposed to put all of my efforts into flying as high as I could.

This is also possibly what everyone in the motivational industry pushes. But every teaching, even the best, is bound to be misunderstood by the students. And the misunderstanding takes one form—a very, very narrow interpretation of the original guidance or message.

In the CAT prep industry, this exhortation to aim for the top has taken on a particular form among some aspirants—A-B-C or nothing! By A, B and C, I mean IIM Ahmedabad, IIM Bangalore and IIM Calcutta.

This is possibly the worst strategy ever for CAT prep since the downside of this strategy beats the upside. The upside is great; why not get into A, B or C? Nothing like it. But is it really that great?

Firstly, A-B-C or nothing has to yield a benefit that few other schools can give. But from a placements and career perspective, they offer a very limited benefit. There are just a handful of firms that hire in very small numbers, who recruit only from A, B and C and no other schools. What's more is that this is true with respect to campus placements. Off campus, people find their way into these firms once they have built a good resume and network. These roles are most likely to be very niche finance roles. These firms are so selective that they only ask a small cohort of aspirants to apply, say JEE AIR 400 and below!

I had once told a student, who was obsessed with A-B-C and i-banks and was turning down a top thirty admit after a gap year for his third attempt, that the i-banks might not even take a second look at his resume. So what is the point?

In short, A-B-C or nothing makes sense only if you are looking for these very niche roles and already have a super stellar profile that these firms look for on these campuses.

Because this narrow focus is likely to meet with failure, aspirants who are fixated on them tend to always be in a constant state of disappointment. Nothing in the world seems to even come close to this one campus, this one firm, this one role. Having such a narrow goal at such a young age is counterproductive for three reasons:

- You shut out what can offer you the whole world for one or two roles and firms
- You might not yet be aware of your skill sets and interests and what those roles and firms are actually like
- You end up thinking of yourself as a failure rather than setting up a platform for success

Apart from a handful of roles, every other role that is available at A, B and C is also available at most of the other top schools. In fact, the better the job market, the longer the list of schools top firms will visit!

You might say: But what about the network? All the big schools apart from A, B and C have now been around long enough to have a huge network of successful alums. The biggest thing in this whole career game is that it unfolds over the longer term.

If only the A, B, Cs, the Ivies and the McKinseys are worth striving for, then every single person from every other school and firm must be worthless, but that is not the case. Satya Nadella, the CEO of Microsoft, did not graduate from an IIT! He did not do his MS from a big-brand university. Yes, he did earn his MBA from a top school—Chicago Booth—but that was nine years after he graduated! Many of my students who obsess over A-B-C or nothing would not have had the patience or the ability to make the most of their opportunities over a nine-year period.

Don't use the CAT to cure your JEE hangover!

The underlying reason in the case of some candidates is the disappointment with not having cracked JEE and made it to an IIT—the graduate dream. This leads them to double down even more when it comes to their post-graduate dream—the CAT and the IIM. Not just any old IIM but A-B-C or nothing.

Elite schools can give you a platform but do not guarantee success. It is your skills and capabilities that guarantee success. What you are, what your skill sets are, are better revealed over the course of a career in different workplaces rather than in exam and college settings. And great careers are built over a period of time and not by merely getting into a great college.

I hope I have written enough to not have to explain why this is an unhealthy fixation. It has to do with psychological or social validation and has nothing to do with setting up the foundation to build a great career.

2

How Should You Choose Which Colleges to Apply To?

Now that we have got unrealistic expectations out of the way, we can focus on how to put together a good realistic set of schools that will gear you up for a great career.

The first thing to assess is your current earning potential. If you are in college, you can measure it by the average salary that you are likely to earn when you graduate. If you are above the average of your graduating class in terms of your profile, then you can estimate your earning potential to be higher than the average or median salary from the previous year's placements. For working professionals, it is straightforward—the salary you are earning is your current earning potential.

Depending on what the base is, you should look at a post-MBA average salary that is two or two and a half times your current earning potential. Any school that offers this should be in your consideration set.

You might think: The college I am studying in or my current workplace is not a good reflection of my talent; I feel I can crack the CAT—why should I aim low?

You will not be in a very different situation from me during my graduation. The first time I took an old CAT paper, I felt that it was right up my alley—*I can easily crack this, no big deal; why do people think it is tough to crack?* But this did not mean that I was aiming only at the IIMs. Despite my supposed potential on the CAT, my resume or profile was not one that merited only IIM or nothing. I applied to the other top national schools as well. I knew I was very good but I also knew that national institutes of great repute, such as MDI-Gurgaon, were also very good and could give me the start I needed.

For specialized interests, choose specialized schools

All the flagship MBA programmes at IIMs and other premier institutes offer some variant of a post-graduate diploma in management (PGDM). By variant, I mean that every college will have a slightly different name for it: post-graduate diploma in business management (PGBM), etc.

All of these premier programmes will provide you with an MBA degree. During the course of your programme, you will choose more than one specialization to finish your curriculum requirements based on the domain you want to work in. For example, those who want to get into consulting will choose a combination of marketing, operations and strategy. This will not be mentioned on your degree since the ultimate goal for all MBAs from premier schools is to become a CEO and not stop at being a chief marketing officer or chief operating officer.

Those who are very clear about building careers in a specialized field, such as HR, should focus on colleges and programmes (and exams that those colleges accept) dedicated to HR. The flagship MBA programmes at the IIMs and other schools do not attract HR recruiters. This is because while the IIMs offer subjects in HR, they are not enough to create full-fledged HR professionals. If both programmes are the same, then XLRI—the mecca for HR aspirants—will not have two separate programmes called Business Management and Human Resources. The specialized HR programmes at XLRI, MDI, NM, TISS or Symbiosis will have the entire two years dedicated to HR.

So, it goes without saying that for those aspiring to build a stellar career in HR, the CAT is only one of the exams to take. In fact, it is of lesser importance than XAT, SNAP and NMAT.

3

Should You Consider an International MBA or MIM Programme?

When aspirants ask me to evaluate Indian versus international programmes they do not realize that they are not comparing apples to apples. What you are choosing is not merely between the quality of programmes but on two different career trajectories.

Why do I say this? Because everything about these two choices is drastically different.

You will be spending way more to apply to a programme abroad

Right from the test, everything about applying for a programme abroad is expensive. The CAT costs around Rs 2400 or ~$30 and the GMAT/GRE costs $300 or Rs 24,000. The application fee to the IIMs is free along with the CAT; for other programmes, the application fee is Rs 1200–2500. The application fee for international schools is $200–$300 per school. So, purely on applications, you should be prepared to spend around Rs 1 lakh to Rs 2 lakh depending on the number of colleges you apply to.

The fee for an MBA programme in India ranges from Rs 12 to Rs 25 lakh. You will be spending anything from Rs 50 lakh to Rs 1 crore or more for a programme abroad.

Obviously, it goes without saying that the average salaries in US dollars will also be commensurate. You will start with salaries of Rs 50 lakh to Rs 1 crore and above. Basically, the fee and salaries go hand in hand, more or less.

There are no 'campus' placements

Unlike Indian schools, colleges abroad do not have a campus placement programme where companies visit campuses and recruit students. Firms visit campuses and make presentations. It is your job to decide which firms your profile and interests align with and apply to them. The placements office and alumni network will assist you with the same.

So, you will have to be very resourceful, and have good communication and networking skills to be able to build a great career in management there.

If you want to emigrate and build a life abroad, choose an international MBA programme

As good as the IIMs are, they are not agencies for foreign placements. The IIMs offer jobs in different sectors. Whether and when you get to go abroad depends upon the companies and the sectors in which they operate.

All the post-MBA roles in IT offer a very high likelihood of moving abroad quickly. This is because most of the IT roles involve IT services and since most of the clients are abroad, the post-MBA roles in business development, project management and IT consulting tend to require moving abroad quickly.

In all other sectors, the chance to move abroad, if it arises at all, that is, comes up much later. For example, if you are working in HR with a multinational corporation, you will get a chance to manage the Asia-Pacific region from Singapore. But this will happen only after you have worked for more than ten years in HR. Some firms such as Amazon put up internal postings for openings across the world to which you can apply.

So, if your goal is to emigrate abroad, then it makes a lot of sense to take the GMAT/GRE and apply to MBA programmes abroad.

What if I want to study abroad and return to work in India?

Given that we have discussed how high the costs of applying and studying abroad are, it makes no sense to return to India immediately if you want to recoup the money spent. You will have to work there, make a good return on investment (RoI) and then come back to India.

There will be no special value here for an MBA degree from abroad. You will have to sign up on job portals to hunt for a job. The alumni network from abroad will be of no use here. In India, for example, most graduates from top schools find jobs using platforms like iimjobs.com and their own college alumni network.

Thus, returning to India immediately after an MBA abroad makes no sense unless you have a thriving family business to join.

What is the difference between an MBA and an MIM?

It is only in India that freshers and graduates with very little work experience get to do and apply to an MBA programme as well. Abroad, an MBA programme is taken up after one has gained solid work experience, recouped the cost of the graduation degree, and is ready to make the next career jump. The average age at a Harvard or Wharton is likely to be around twenty-seven to thirty years, whereas at the IIMs it is likely to be around twenty-three or twenty-four.

Without requisite work experience, MBA programmes cannot give candidates the kind of senior roles that are offered post-MBA. MBA programmes thus accept applications from those with more than two years of work experience.

Those who have less than two years of experience but still aspire to entry-level roles in management apply to Masters In Management (MIM) programmes. MIM programmes are a recent phenomenon, which have taken off in the last ten years or so. Since they offer entry-level management roles, MIM programmes cost less than MBA programmes and offer lower starting salaries.

If you do an MIM, is an MBA mandatory later?

It depends on how your career pans out. Those who excel and manage to catch the right breaks might not need an MBA later. But most others might need to do another MBA around eight to ten years later.

4

How to Choose Between a One-Year or Two-Year MBA

All schools attract recruiters for roles aligned to their batch profiles. The premier two-year MBA programmes in India on average have batches with a work experience around twenty-two to twenty-four months. Those with more than forty-eight months of work experience will be a minority.

Recruiters visit campuses of premier schools offering two-year programmes to recruit those with zero to forty-eight months of work experience depending on the roles on offer. Those with forty-eight months or more of experience are likely to not have too many takers for their profile. This does not mean that you will not get a job at an IIM. It only means that all the items on the buffet might not be relevant for you. You are likely to find fewer people in the batch with your experience, and fewer roles on offer for your experience.

It thus makes a lot of sense to take the GMAT and apply to the premier one-year programmes in the country, in addition to taking the CAT and applying to two-year programmes.

How good are the one-year PGP-X programmes at the IIMs?

These programmes attract a different profile when compared to the two-year programmes, with candidates on average being above thirty years of age. They offer great career advancement opportunities within your specific domain. You will get that 2.5x jump in salary and a role within your domain. Domain shifts are usually rare but not impossible. The programmes at all the old IIMs and the premier private schools, such as XLRI and SPJIMR, offer good outcomes.

What about the ISB programme?

When it comes to one-year programmes, it is not the IIMs but ISB that offers the best outcomes. Recruiters looking for those with good work experience in particular domains recruit from ISB instead of the IIMs. ISB offers a lot of domain-specific consulting roles compared to two-year programmes. The average age at ISB is around twenty-seven years, skewing closer to that at international programmes.

ISB was set up along the lines of international one-year programmes that can be completed under twelve months. The reason for this is that those with good quality work experience will be losing their income for every year that they stay out of their job. Also, having work experience means that some of the basic topics need not be taught. The courseware is also designed along the lines of an international MBA.

This does not mean that ISB is not for those with less than two years' work experience. The ISB programme is for freshers and those with less than two years' experience as well. But for candidates with less than two years of work experience, ISB offers a deferred admission through the early entry option. ISB has a separate application process for this group of students so that they are comparing apples with apples during the admission process. Around 20 to 25 per cent of the batch at ISB has zero to twenty-four months of work experience.

Many candidates are scared away from ISB because of the fee, which is higher than that at the IIMs. They fail to subtract the first year's salary from the fee before comparing the fee with that of the IIMs since they will be graduating in under twelve months.

Who is the ISB programme for?

Given that the average work experience is above four years, ISB attracts recruiters who are looking for domain specialists—consulting or senior business roles within a particular domain, etc.

To give you a typical example, a student of mine graduated from a good college in Tamil Nadu, with stellar academics, worked for more than four years in Ashok Leyland in bus body design, got into ISB, and graduated with a business head role at Ashok Leyland itself for an entire vertical.

ISB, as I mentioned earlier, is built along the lines of an international programme and its selection process reflects the same. You should definitely consider ISB if you have a good profile:

- graduation from a premier college in your state and/or
- work experience in a brand name firm
- 8-8-8 academics
- excellent written and verbal communication skills, and/or
- do not prefer the CAT for some reason (once a year as opposed to round the year, paper that does not play to your strengths)

To summarize, given the course fee and the GMAT exam fee, the ISB programme ends up attracting older candidates with more spending power than the other Indian programmes who do not want to get into the madness of the CAT rat race.

So if you have two or fewer years of work experience, the options that ISB will open up for you will not compare to the ones that will be available in the regular two-year programmes.* Also, the longer duration of the two-year programme might be a much better learning track for those with less than two years of experience. This does not mean that you should consider ISB. Please do so if you feel that the GMAT is more aligned to your skills than the CAT!

---

* ISB has also launched a two-year programme starting 2025.

Part II

Learning to Learn

What Is the Prep Plan?

1

How Many Hours of Prep Are Required to Crack the CAT?

This is possibly the one question that I like to answer the least since there is no one answer that applies to all aspirants. While everyone has the same finish line, everyone has a different starting point. This in itself makes it impossible to define a standard number of hours for all students.

However, to give some structure to analyse this question, I will go from the basic prep requirements to the highest prep requirements. Also, the big three end-to-end brands in this particular segment are IMS, TIME and Career Launcher. I call them end-to-end because they offer everything from classroom coaching, live online classes, self-learning programmes to test series programmes. There might be other niche brands but none of them will have a test series that will be of the same benchmarking capability because of the small number of test-takers.

How do you know which bracket you fall into? Take a mock test from any of the big three brands. Each of them has a free variant.

Test Series Only Prep: April–November, eight months

The shortest prep needs are of those aspirants who will need to take only mocks tests to crack the CAT.

If you score 95 percentile or above in each section on the free mock, then you definitely do not need any prep beyond taking mocks and analysing those mocks well. A 95 percentile and above on each of the sections means that you have all-round skills to ace the exam by taking mock tests alone. All brands offer video solutions and analyses, and some also discuss alternate methods of solving the questions. These should suffice to help you prep well.

But the key to a successful prep is the quality and quantity of time spent in analysis. This analysis itself will comprise two parts: test-taking skills and conceptual skills. I will take up how to analyse a mock test in subsequent chapters. At the bare minimum, you will need about four to eight hours of analysis, prep and practice following every mock. All in all, it would mean about six to ten hours of time spent around taking, analysing and prepping a mock.

For your first serious attempt, you will need to solve thirty to forty mock tests. This would mean about 180 hours at the bare minimum to about 400 hours at the maximum.

All brands start with their first mock test or simulated test around the last week of April. From the last week of April to November means around eight months or thirty-two weeks of prep. This would mean a prep of six to twelve hours per week. Please note that these hours need not be divided in equal parts of daily prep. Just hit the six to twelve hours a week and you should be good.

So, on average, the bare minimum prep required to launch a successful campaign with a balanced amount of weekly prep is around eight months or ~300 hours of prep.

Test Series + Self-Learning Prep: January–November, eleven months

If you take a mock and score an overall percentile of 90, it means that you have some learning needs on each of the sections. This means that you will need more than just solution videos but concept videos as well to launch a successful campaign.

Most of the big brands have good self-learning programmes with pre-recorded video content and ample practice material. Ideally, you should finish your concept learning phase from January to April, so that by the time the first mock comes around, you have the ability to score a 95 on each section. From here onwards, your prep remains the same as those taking only test series.

This concept learning and practice phase from January to April will require about two hours every day from January to April. Considering a day off a week and the festivals, this period of four months will entail around twelve weeks of two hours a day prep or ~150–175 hours of prep.

Full-Length LIVE Classes Prep: fourteen to twenty-four months

For those who score around 85 percentile overall on their first mock, a good time to start preparing will be in October the year before your CAT exam. You will need the regularity of a LIVE learning programme—be it Online LIVE or Classroom LIVE.

For those who score below 85 percentile overall on their first mock, a good time to start preparing will be in June the year before your CAT exam. You will need the regularity of a LIVE learning programme—be it Online LIVE or Classroom LIVE.

All major brands start their full-length programmes in June and in some cases, even by the January of the previous year, taking the maximum duration to twenty-four months.

Your personality type also plays a big role in the type of programme you should choose

The biggest obstacles to a successful prep campaign lie in our own mind. We start with the best of intentions and join a programme but the intention never translates into effort. A big reason why many aspirants crack the exam only on their second attempt is that their first attempt was half-hearted or a mere formality.

If you know that you are someone who is not very self-motivated and are likely to do things only at the last minute when the pressure is unbearable, then you are better off choosing a programme that has more people in the mix than just you—a good mentor and a good peer group. This means that despite being someone who can crack the exam with a test series or self-learning programme you should join a LIVE programme, be it online or offline, but preferably offline if you have access to good classroom coaching and your schedule permits you to attend regularly.

If your schedule can be a bit erratic, then it makes senses to opt for LIVE online classes since you will get access to recordings of classes. Some brands also have hybrid programmes where you can get the best of both worlds, offline and online classes.

I love taking online sessions and take around ten a year. While I enjoy the high of sometime addressing 1000 to 2000 students at a single go, it is very different from addressing the same crowd in person. When I take online sessions, I give energy to my students but because it is not possible to see so many students, and thus I keep their videos turned off, I cannot get energy from my students. After one three-hour session, I ate two biryanis back to back! At the same time, after a marathon eight-hour all-day offline session, I give and get so much energy that I am flying in the air. After one such session, when I went to Hyderabad airport to fly back to Mumbai, the person at the check-in counter offered me any seat I wanted. Apparently, it was a horribly hectic day but my cheerful hello had brightened things up. I was beaming at eight at night after teaching non-stop from ten to six.

Why this story? Well, there is a lot to gain from the in-person presence and energy of both mentors and peers. So, if after analysing yourself well, you feel you need full-length prep, then take up a classroom programme.

My best friends, with whom I am in regular touch even today, are the ones I made in my CAT prep days. Their company was fun enough to ensure that even if I did not prepare much at home, I attended most classes and took every mock.

What material is best to prepare for CAT?

As far as the mocks go, the big three brands—IMS, TIME and CL—offer the best mocks since they have dedicated teams creating mocks for many years now. It is not a bad idea to purchase the mocks of two brands since each brand has a different sectional expertise when it comes to creating mocks. Also, the flavour of the mocks in terms of the type of logic tested might get a bit repetitive if you subscribe to the mocks of only one brand. So taking the mocks of two brands is always a great idea.

For those looking at additional prep beyond mocks, I would always suggest additional practice material from these brands itself. This is because I have only used these brands myself. There might be books by individual authors that are quite good for a particular section—feel free to get those.

Do not make the mistake of gathering everything, pecking randomly and completing nothing

I do not need to mention that aspirants find a way to lay their hands on all the material available in the market. There is nothing worse than doing this. It is not different from our music playlists, now that we can have the entire world's music in our phones.

I think no one would need material from more than two brands to cover two serious attempts. So, what is most important is to finish the material that you have purchased rather than gathering material from all over the Internet and doing nothing with it.

When I was preparing, I was lucky that a friend's brother had purchased IMS material and had not used it at all. I had joined TIME for classroom coaching, the only one in Visakhapatnam at the time. Over two attempts, I finished the material of both these brands. So, what is important is that you finish the entire material of one of the big three brands rather than gather everything under the sun and do bits and pieces of each.

2

Should I Quit My Job to Prepare for the CAT?

This is one of the questions that I am asked most often, if not the most asked question! The question is also most likely to come from aspirants whose first or past attempts did not go well and who are thus looking to mount a serious retake attempt. You might also have these questions in your mind:

- Is it wise to quit my job to prepare for the CAT?
- Will quitting my job have a negative impact on my profile?
- How can I prepare if I am working twelve hours a day, six days a week?

These are the questions that many aspirants ask themselves since there is a huge premium on acquiring a degree from a prestigious college and an MBA is for most the last big shot that they can take to get a big brand name on their resume. Some might have faced this situation before as well when they had set their eyes for the first time on getting two Is—the IITs.

There are other reasons as well, ranging from a mind-numbingly monotonous IT job to a horrible boss, to the existential dread: *What will become of me and my life if I am stuck in my current situation forever?*

For most of my colleagues, the answer to this question is a simple NO. Quitting your job is akin to committing professional hara-kiri. But I think, under certain circumstances, quitting your job might be the best option in front of you with the proviso that:

- You quit at the right time, and
- You do more than just prep for the CAT

How will quitting affect your profile in terms of getting into an IIM?

First, let us look at the *quantitative* effect of quitting your job on your chances of getting a shortlist.

There are colleges, such as IIM-B and others, that give a weightage to work experience in the shortlisting process. In such cases, you will lose out on valuable points and will hence have to score higher on the test to get the shortlist than if you had stuck on in your job. So yes, there is a clear quantitative effect.

If you have two or more years of work experience, as of July of the year you will take the CAT, and the rest of your profile—Class X, Class XII, grad marks—is good, you can, on average, score 0.5–0.75 percentile points lower than someone with no or low work experience. So, those with two years of work experience can get an IIM-B call at a 98.5 percentile whereas freshers have to score in excess of 99.4. But remember that this is only in the case of institutes that give a weightage to work experience.

Just like they have for academics, even for work experience points are awarded based on slabs—less than twelve months, twelve to twenty-four months, etc. IIM-B gives maximum points for work experience of thirty-six months and above. So, if you have more than thirty-six months you are not going to get any more marks than you will if you have exactly thirty-six months.

In effect, if you have thirty-six months' work experience, quitting your job will not have any mathematical impact on your profile rating.

Will quitting affect your prospects during summer and final placements?

IIMs and other top schools slot candidates into two categories for placements—*regular* and *lateral*. Lateral placements are for people with a certain amount of work experience for roles that are above entry-level management roles. What is that certain amount of work experience?

It differs from college to college. Some base it on the absolute number of months such as twenty-two—IIM-B, while others decide the exact number based on the average work experience in the batch—IIM-A. Either way, it usually falls into the twenty to twenty-four-month range. Also, it is important to note that for some domains and for some firms, work experience is a must-have and hence, recruiters look purely at lateral candidates. What are the domains where relevant work experience is a prerequisite?

Operations roles, for example, most definitely go to people who have experience in shop-floor, product design, logistics, supply chain management, etc. So, engineers working in operations will do well to finish working for two years before entertaining thoughts of quitting. The rationale is simple: an individual with an idea of any aspect of operations cannot be given a managerial role since the stakes are very high.

IT consulting roles, for example, again typically go to those with two-plus years of experience in software. Again, the rationale is the same—an individual who has not worked on large-scale IT projects cannot take up consulting roles in IT. There might be exceptions to this rule but by and large, the rule holds.

Recruiters from new sectors, such as **e-commerce** from firms such as Amazon, also tend to look at candidates with a certain amount of work experience, usually IT or analytics or technology.

General management firms such as Tata Administrative Services (TAS) and the Aditya Birla Group (ABG) prefer people with work experience but they also take in freshers.

Roles in **marketing** do not need work experience, with marketing recruiters having a very strong preference for freshers or only those with relevant experience in sales or marketing analytics. The same applies to HR as well—experience is not mandatory.

For **finance**, your graduation discipline—commerce, economics, BBA-finance—the brand of the college you graduated from, and professional certifications such as CA, ICWA, CS, CFA and FRM matter way more than work experience. So if you are a commerce grad from a top-tier graduation college looking to build a career in finance, work experience is not a must unless it is relevant.

For **consulting** roles, the brand names on your resume matter more than anything else. It is not whether you have work experience or not but the brand value of the organization you worked with that matters more. IITian and NITian freshers with a strong academic profile stand a very high chance of getting shortlisted. Those from other colleges of national repute with stellar resumes in terms of academic (90-90-90) and extracurricular achievements also get shortlisted. This does not mean that work experience will not help you. A job with a good consulting firm, leading analytics firms or any other big brand firms—design or operations roles with firms such as Caterpillar or Mahindra—can always be something that boosts your resume. In short, work experience from a big brand will be a good addition.

Overall, to put things in perspective, about 30–40 per cent of students in the top B-schools are freshers.

How many months of work experience makes it safe to quit?

By now, it will be clear that quitting will not affect your chances if you do it after finishing two years of working. I would say around twenty-four months is the ideal amount of work experience to have to go into an Indian B-school.

If you already have three years' experience and a relatively weak resume, it makes sense to quit your job, prepare for CAT and build your profile.

In what cases does quitting before twenty-four months make sense?

The only reason to quit before twenty-four months is if you are very clear that you want an industry and domain shift. So, if you are an engineer from one of the core departments working in IT and you want to do an MBA to get away from not just IT services but also technology, then it makes sense to quit your job before twenty-four months of experience.

The more work experience you accumulate in your industry, the more likely you are to get roles within that industry or domain. A domain shift is not impossible but not easy either, and it gets difficult the more work experience you accumulate.

To keep it simple, those looking at marketing or finance or HR roles after your MBA and with no time to prepare, can quit before twenty-four months. Just to add, there is no reason to quit if you can work and prepare for the CAT!

What is the best time to quit to prepare for CAT?

The simple answer is that if all you want to do is quit and prepare for eight to ten hours a day, you will not need more than three months. So working backwards, your break should not start before 1 August.

It might seem as if I am speaking about aspirants who are already at a particular level, say 85 percentile. Or, if you are someone who is very out of touch with maths, you will need more time. But these arguments assume that you will have done no prep till August, which is not the case.

Even if we consider these concerns legitimate and you know yourself better than I ever will, and given that I know the CAT better than you ever will, your break should not start earlier than 1June.

So, at most, your break will need to start six months before the CAT, not before that.

If you quit, be prepared to face the music in every single interview

The other way of looking at this question is from a *qualitative* perspective—in terms of how panellists will view you in the interview. Panelists who see candidates who have left what is on paper a promising professional opportunity, will expect them to justify the same.

So, before anything else, please understand that if you quit, in every single interview that you face you will have to answer the question: *Why did you quit your job?*

This question is bound to be followed by others such as:

- Surely you did it just to prepare for the CAT!
- So it means you are not good at multitasking?
- More than half of our students have work experience. Do you mean to say that all of them had jobs that allowed them to put their feet up?

Forget at the interview stage, some institutes such as IIM-A and SPJIMR ask this question in the form they send out to candidates they shortlist for the Written Assessment Test and Personal Interview (WAT-PI) round: Do you have any breaks in your professional career? If YES, then please explain.

Having said this, you can rest assured that these questions have been successfully tackled by aspirants in the past and in IIM interviews at that. What is important is that you quit at the right time, plan your break to take up activities that enhance your profile and achieve things that will help you make a great pitch in the interview.

What you should be doing if you quit before August

If you have made up your mind to start your break for CAT prep by June this year, then you should do more than just prepare for the CAT. Otherwise, as discussed above, interviewers will have a great time turning you over on both sides of a red-hot grill.

In all the cases where my students have successfully made it to a top B-school despite a break of eight to ten months by the time they faced their interviews, they had taken up things to improve their skills and profile.

What are the things they took up? They chose from the list of things I have outlined in the how to build your profile chapter.

Too much of anything, even CAT prep can be harmful

Apart from resume-building, these activities also ensure that you do not become obsessed with the CAT and pile up the pressure on yourself leading to test day. They offer a good break from CAT prep in terms of taking your mind off the test and also helping you peak at the right time.

Peaking at the right time is very important because if you are doing nothing but CAT prep for eight or more hours a day, you will peak in about three months' time and come test day, you will have exhausted yourself.

This is the reason why sometimes teams that do not start off well in a tournament such as the World Cups manage to get their act together over a period of time and peak in the final (the ultimate example being Australia in the 1999 Cricket World Cup), whereas teams that seem to be hot favourites crash out.

How do you defend your break for CAT prep?

A gap is bad only if it has been taken heedlessly; say, quitting because you did not like your job and then chilling for a long time. A gap that is taken with a view to take your career from point A to point B, and improve your profile as well, is the right strategy if you can present the same compellingly.

Your answer has to be straightforward—you need to show that continuing in your job was not aligned to your career goals. Even though your work was relevant to your long-term career plans, continuing in the same would have meant absolutely no time to prep for a B-school admit. I know many students who work in top-tier firms such as GS and ZS say that they were working nothing less than twelve hours a day. So, the incremental learning and benefits from one more year of working are offset by the risk of not meeting your long-term career goals. Please bear in mind that you cannot use the same words verbatim in your interview; you have to personalize your story.

A student of mine had quit his job after three years of gruelling sixteen-hour days work experience at Goldman Sachs. He had calls from the old IIMs as well as NMIMS and SIBM. Before every interview, he used to call me to rehearse his answer because he knew what they would ask. Now, I cannot do the same with everyone, but what you have to do is come out of the smaller-level stuff—break in resume, etc.—and focus on the big stuff—the career path you want to take. If you can show them that the career path you have chalked out is in line with your profile, then the gap and other smaller things will cease to matter.

By now, you will have understood that you will never use the sentence: I quit to prepare for CAT. Instead, you should say—'My aspiration is to do an MBA and get into X, Y, Z firms and I felt that I needed to work on my profile and learn a few things about the specialization as well before I start the programme. So I quit my job and did A, B and C things and hopefully I can get into a good B-school.'

There are no right and wrong answers; there are only convincing or unconvincing answers.

If you took a thought-out call to pursue the best course of action for your career and worked towards it, then no one can tell you or prove to you that your path was wrong.

Also, you will have that conviction only if you do things apart from CAT prep during the break. All my students who successfully navigated a break did so because they did other things ranging from working part-time with a start-up to improving their English to investing in stock markets. If you just prep for CAT and generally chill and turn up at the interview, you will face the music.

How should you utilize your day if you quit your job for CAT prep?

You should quit your job only after you have made a full plan for your break period and taken concrete steps towards executing the same. What do I mean by this?

You need to draw up the three things you will do to strengthen your profile after evaluating the gaps. If you have no NGO experience and you want to pick up the same, you should find out avenues for doing this, discuss the timing and frequency of your volunteering work with the NGO, and commit dates to them. If you want to take up certification courses or language courses or trekking or fitness courses, you need to pay up and register for the same. Basically, from the first day of quitting, you should have too many things on your hand to do and CAT prep is a slot that you will fill in.

If you have free time, you will waste it—there is no shortage of sports events—football leagues, cricket, grand slams—or a dearth of updates on social media platforms. You may not even decide to waste it; these things will occupy all the free time you have.

During the course of those six months, you can either work wonders for your career by taking up all these things or feel good by watching other people win stuff on a field or feel bad by watching other people doing stuff on social media.

It goes without saying that you should front-load the profile-building activities towards the beginning of your break and reduce them as the CAT approaches.

This chapter can only provide the best possible outline to quitting your job. Your first managerial problem to solve is to design a plan to manage your break. If you cannot do that, then maybe you lack what it takes to become a manager, since an MBA can only amplify your capabilities and provide career opportunities to maximize them; it cannot create non-existent capabilities.

What about internships and family businesses?

Internships do not count as work experience; you cannot add it to months of work experience, whether you are a fresher or not. Only full-time, paid, work experience, after your graduation counts as work experience.

Some of you might have planned quitting and joining your family business. You can do this provided you have an offer letter, salary slips, bank statements and a work experience certificate for the said period—in short, it should be like any other work experience. Most importantly, you should be able to describe your family business and what role you played.

If you think you can tell them that there was a crisis in the family, you had to quit and go back to help out in the family business, and now that it is sorted you want to do an MBA, they will not buy your poor man's Michael Corleone story. The panel's first instinct is to not trust you since they know that Indians always try to do what we do best—*jugaad* (there are two well-known books on the Indians and *jugaad*, just google it).

You can say that since you wanted to do an MBA, you thought you would be better off doing a core MBA role instead of working in IT and thus decided to work in your family business. And if you have all the supporting documents mentioned above and can make a strong case for what you achieved in your family business, it should not be a problem.

Basically, your work experience with the family business should not look like an excuse to sit at home and prepare for CAT!

Should I join my campus placement job or prepare for CAT?

This is a relatively new query that I am getting from students who have just graduated or are on the cusp on graduating. The first and most important question you need to ask yourself is: Is this job aligned to my career goals? Unless your job role now is linked to your plans once your MBA is done, there is no point taking up the same.

So, it is better to look at the various paths you have open to you after your MBA and work backwards, to figure out if the job you have is aligned to the same. We have earlier discussed the role work experience plays in different domains.

If the domain you are interested in needs work experience and you have a job in hand that is aligned and relates to it, then take it up. Also, jobs in analytics or e-commerce firms, despite the role not being directly aligned to your future plans, will always be good in terms of learning and also have resume-value for interviews. However, two years in an IT job, when you are not interested in IT, can kill whatever spark you have inside you.

If, as a fresher, you do not take up a job, everything that I mentioned with respect to quitting applies to you as well. You cannot just sit at home and do CAT prep.

By now, you should be well aware of the larger picture that surrounds your decision to do an MBA and also the kind of prep to choose. It is time to move into aspects of actual prep and it starts with Learning to Learn.

3

How to Manage Work and CAT Prep at the Same Time

When the mountain called the CAT starts getting closer, most working professionals will be wondering how to mount another challenge to get into the old IIMs.

The biggest obstacle in front of working professionals will be juggling a job and prepping for CAT at the same time. Some of you in this situation will have decided to quit your job, hopefully only after having read my views on the same and having understood the implications of quitting.

Those of you who have not contemplated quitting might be wondering what could be a foolproof plan to manage both. Most of you will be happy if I gave you a daily to-do list. But managing work and prep requires more than having a to-do list. Unless you manage your life, work and energy in totality, even the best to-do list will stay just that—a to-do list. There is the whole gamut of things that you will have to execute to ensure that you crack this year's CAT.

The most precious commodity is your energy

Most people focus on the fact that they get just a small window of prep time after work and commute. The bigger problem, I feel, is the limited amount of energy that you have left after a full day's work.

Since our brains constantly crave rewards for each and everything that we do, the first thing that our brains and bodies want to do after a hard day's work is—RELAX.

What does this word RELAX usually translate into?

- BAD posture: lying down or slouching in a way that seems to say 'I don't want do anything'
- BAD food: something that will make us feel good, heavy and sleepy
- BAD food for the mind: since the body has been satiated, the mind wants its fix of unending videos and memes and what not. With the stomach you know when it's full; with videos, can you even say when your mind is full?

After two to three hours of relaxing, I am sure time, speed and distance (TSD) will not really seem even distantly inviting. We all know what follows next—a strong decision to wake up early and practise TSD before going to work and set the alarm with a clenched jaw. I am sure there is no need to elaborate what happens in the morning.

Revving yourself up in the morning

The first thing to do then is to manage your energy better right throughout the day so that you don't really crave the RELAX in the evening. If you can prevent the craving, then you don't need to resist the temptation.

I am not sure if yoga and *pranayama* are the cure-alls they are proclaimed to be but they definitely boost your energy and alertness levels drastically. This is both from personal experience and more so from the experience of my mother, who took it up at my suggestion and now has insane amounts of energy. She doesn't miss a yoga class for anything (even if her children are visiting).

Given the limited amount of time at your disposal, you can't possibly enrol for a class but you surely can do some basic breathing exercises such as *kapalbhati* and *nadi shodana pranayama* just to rev up the lungs.

You should spend fifteen to twenty minutes every morning doing these breathing exercises, after freshening up.

At any time during the day, if you feel sleepy and sluggish, you can always rely on straightening your back and taking deep breaths, which is a sure-fire way to getting back to alertness.

Resetting your body and mind in the evening

As much as the morning revving up is required, what is even more important is the evening reset. Our first instinct when we get back to our home is to plonk ourselves and start yapping with whoever is at home. While one can do this, it is best if one focusses first on resetting the mind and body to become fresh again.

Take a bath whether you feel like it or not and do another ten-to-fifteen-minute round of breathing exercises. Do this every day and you will notice a subtle change in the way you feel physically over a period of time, apart from higher energy levels:

- reduced craving for food, caffeine, alcohol or cigarettes
- reduced anxiety levels leading to a calmer disposition
- reduced brain fog and higher alertness

Another really good cure for low alertness and brain fog are Brahmi capsules; whenever I have been short of sleep or feel groggy even after a coffee, a Brahmi capsule does the trick.

Save energy by talking less during the day

One of the main ways we expend a lot of energy without knowing it is by talking a lot. If you treat the energy you have within you to be of a finite amount, then you will start conserving it at various points of time during the day. You have to manage your salary to last the whole month; you have to manage your energy to last the whole day. So talk less and you will save and build up energy reserves leading up to the CAT.

Choose the right slots

It does not matter whether you are a morning person or an evening person, you have to choose the time slot to prep that is least likely to be disrupted due to work.

Whether it is before or after work, choose a time slot that will not be disrupted.

- If you have flexible office timings, then choose a slightly skewed office time slot, say 8 a.m. to 4 p.m. or 11 a.m. to 7 p.m., instead of the standard 9 a.m. to 5 p.m. or 10 a.m. to 6 p.m. This will give you a longer, undisrupted time slot.
- If you have to work within fixed timings, then ensure that you hit those timings, finish your work and get out.

I know that some of you might be working on projects in which there is no respite at all. You will be working on weekends as well. If I say I have an answer for a such case, I would be lying.

Plan for a break around the September–October period

No matter how diligently you prepare on a daily basis, it is necessary that, for a brief period, the only current passing through your nervous system is that of the CAT. You need to get magnetized in a particular direction. Therefore, you need leave to prepare for the CAT.

You have to ensure that you have enough leave and inform your boss in advance to be able to take this break.

What can prevent you from taking this break?

- Losing leave for family weddings that you have to attend. If it is not your direct sibling, it is something that can be and has to be avoided.
- Losing leave for trips planned by close friends. If a trip with friends is more important than getting into IIM-A, then reconsidering your priorities is in order.

Do not take the break in November as it will be too close to the test for you to see the results of your prep.

The ideal break should be about three weeks long; even two weeks can suffice (I won't be discussing the best stories to make your boss grant you leave).

You have limited time, so use it judiciously

Today, anyone who tries to learn, or do anything, first googles it. The avalanche of information available from blogs, forums such as Quora and PaGaLGuY to Facebook groups is insane.

I did this a while ago when I started off on a fitness trip. Very soon I was so deep down the rabbit hole that more than actually doing anything, I was just trying to make sense of this maze of information hitting me from so many quarters. What I forgot during this search was setting myself realistic, achievable and enjoyable goals.

Even for CAT prep, you can end up spending a lot of time on forums accumulating information that might or might not directly help you prepare. We live in an age where we can easily accumulate tons and tons of content and never really use or enjoy the same—music, for instance.

So, be very aware of the point after which there are diminishing marginal returns on time invested in information-gathering.

Regulate your phone usage time

A smartphone has to be the most addictive time-sink known to man. I had seen a graphic a few years ago that Facebook, Gmail and Twitter formed the Bermuda triangle of productivity.

I think they don't even compare to what Netflix, Amazon Prime and YouTube can do. It starts with just one episode and then it's almost dawn.

Do not try to limit your consumption, just remove the temptation—remove the apps from your phone.

But your brain will crave a fix, so decide on that one cheat day a month and watch whatever you want for a specified time.

Getting into monk mode

All great sportsmen speak about getting into the zone—Michael Jordan and Ayrton Senna (F1 fans or not, everyone should watch the documentary *Senna* by Asif Kapadia) to name a couple. What does it mean, this 'being in the zone' business?

It essentially means that there is only action; the actor (not to be confused with films) is not aware that they are acting—they lose 'I' consciousness.

This happens occasionally, but exceptional performers always get close to this zone, where the mind is no longer dragging them down with doubt, worry and thought; they are aware that they are acting but there is no drag.

It is not possible to reach these states all of a sudden. It starts with the practice of breathing exercises and meditation (Senna was fully into it) and reading texts that give you the perspective that keeps you grounded.

Of all the books that I have read, the format and style of *I Am That* and *Zen Mind, Beginner's Mind* by Suzuki Shunryu are the ones best suited to daily reading.

Each book can be read over and over and over again. Both of them will more than test your Critical Reasoning (CR) skills. (I am not to be held responsible if any of you start reading the books and decide that CAT and MBA are just illusions!)

Aligning dreams, goals and actions

Every year, I meet several students with great potential and lots of plans to crack the test. Sometimes, things beyond their control derail their dreams but most of the time, it is the huge chasm between the dream and the everyday choices they make that come in the way of their plans being realized. Every choice you make, every single day, has an implication.

As I have written previously as well, most of us do not align our short-term actions to our long-term goals. We wake up only when we can feel the deadline of our long-term goal breathing down our neck.

It is my job to make you aware of the many things that go into converting a dream into a reality, especially if you are away from home and working.

Learning to Learn

1

Natural Talent or Hard Work?

Most blunders in life can be traced to not really understanding what something or someone actually is. We look at the surface and think we know. The word 'aptitude' is no different.

What does the word *aptitude* mean? The common, or rather most prevalent, understanding of an *aptitude* test is that:

- it does not involve answering questions in the long-form
- the questions often, if not always, involve choosing one out of four or five pre-decided options
- time is always a constraint and hence, shortcuts are of paramount importance

The dictionary meaning of the word has nothing to do with any of this and it is a very simple word to understand. I will dive deep into this so that you really understand what aptitude testing means and can then approach your CAT prep with a fresh pair of eyes and an open mind.

These are the various ideas defining or surrounding the word 'aptitude':

- Natural ability or skill to learn something well and do it quickly
- May be physical or mental such as solving the Rubik's cube or making a chair
- It is inborn or involves one's innate potential to do certain kinds of work whether developed or undeveloped unlike skills and achievement, which is knowledge and ability that is gained through learning

In all of the above definitions of aptitude, the synonymous words used to describe a quality of aptitude are *natural*, *innate* and *inborn*.

What contributes to the area of a rectangle? The length or the breadth?

The SAT is possibly one of the first aptitude tests in the world and it was administered in 1928 to be used as a metric in admitting students into college in the US. Before that, colleges used things such as family background, the schools that applicants attended, their school marks, etc., to decide which students to admit.

The father of the modern test preparation industry, Stanley Kaplan, the founder of Kaplan Test Prep, was a public school student. He felt the SAT gave talented students from modest or impoverished backgrounds a chance to prove themselves against candidates from affluent backgrounds who attended private schools.

After graduating, he started coaching students for the SAT. This did not go down well with the College Board, which owns and administers the SAT. It was of the view that coaching *could not* improve test scores since it was a measure of natural ability.

Stanley Kaplan successfully challenged this claim and the Federal Trade Commission ruled in 1979 that test preparation *could, in fact,* improve students' scores.

We have come a long way since 1979 and now it is accepted that it is tough to attribute an outstanding performance either to talent or to extensive training. I personally feel that the question is no longer moot.

I feel that asking what contributes to great test scores or performances in sports or music—*natural talent* or *deliberate practice*—is like asking what contributes more to the area of a rectangle—the length or the breadth? It is length into breadth, a product of both. Both 10*10 and 1*100 give the same result—it varies from individual to individual.

But yet, people place great store on this thing called 'natural talent', forgetting that everything does not come naturally to everyone.

A CAT aspirant beginning his or her prep will be at least nineteen years old, long enough to start the test with sizeable psychological baggage—a mental make-up that stems from one's experiences, and successes or failures with tests throughout school and college.

- I am good at maths since I have got good marks throughout school
- I hate maths, I can never get my head around it
- My English should be pretty good, I can speak the language fairly well
- I am hardworking and sincere but I am not really sure if I am smart enough
- I come from a vernacular background, so English is always going to be an uphill battle
- I am talented but not really brilliant, the way my friend or my sibling is

The heaviest baggage is the one that people have about natural talent or rather, the importance that people attribute to it. All of us would have a cousin or a friend or a classmate who could always achieve the same or better results with seemingly no effort. In fact, my best friend, whom I met during my CAT prep, was one of this sort.

During my stint at the IIM and during the course of my professional life, I have met a few of those individuals whose abilities fall into the *outlier* category—people who are in a different category as far as pure aptitude goes.

But the key thing is this—*there are only a few of them!* The rest of the people at elite institutions and major corporations are people who are highly competitive, people who work really hard to make the most of what they have, and also constantly work to keep getting better or becoming more complete by adding things to their repertoire.

I have always found sport, especially cricket, given our national obsession for the game, a great metaphor to put many things into perspective.

One interesting story that I often recount is of going to watch India play England in a test match at the Wankhede in 2006. We went to watch just the last day's play; India needed 300 runs to win and had ten wickets in hand. On the way to the stadium, my friend and I scripted how we wanted the day's play to unfold—300 to win was tight but then all we needed was a good start from Sehwag and then for the rest, preferably Sachin, to take the team to victory. We had reached well before the start and thus got a chance to watch the players warm up and do some light practice.

Sehwag came out first to warm up—dressed in shorts and a T-shirt, he was practising his shots against a young kid throwing down a tennis ball from 11 yards; all in all, it seemed as if he was having a good time and fooling around.

Then came Rahul Dravid—dressed in a pair of shorts and T-shirt but also wearing a thigh guard, an arm guard and a helmet—everything he would have on when he is on the field. He was also practising shots against the same young kid throwing down a tennis ball from 11 yards!

This small episode possibly throws more light on the reason behind the longevity of Rahul Dravid's career, his ability to adapt to different formats and different roles in the team, and his stand-out successes on foreign soil.

Dravid was never called *gifted* or *talented* or all those adjectives that were used to describe those to whom things come easily; players like Sehwag or Rohit Sharma. Dravid was, I think, rightly called The Wall—built brick by brick with patience and effort.

If you look at the biggest achievers in cricket, the players who top the record books, not all of them were geniuses. It will usually be players who really maximized their ability—Dravid, Kallis, Sangakkara, Border, Gavaskar. And even the geniuses at the top were not just supremely talented but intensely competitive and put crazy hours into the game—Sachin, Lara and Warne.

The same thing applies to other sports as well. The word 'genius' is applied only to the incomparable Federer. Agassi once famously said that Sampras could play most shots better than everyone else, but Federer plays shots that nobody else can play! So, genius is essentially that—the inventor of the new.

The other two in the triumvirate, Nadal and Djokovic, are where they are through sheer hard work; the word 'genius' is never used for them. Nadal has made so many changes to his *natural* game, which suits the clay courts, to ensure that he has won all the other three slams as well.

This is what Nadal has to say about Federer in general: '. . . but he just seems to have been born to play the game. His physique—his DNA—seems perfectly adapted to tennis, rendering him immune to the injuries the rest of us are doomed to put up with.'

This is what Nadal has to say about playing Federer: 'When Federer has these patches of utter brilliance, the only thing you can do is try and stay calm, wait for the storm to pass. There is not much you can do when the best player in history is seeing the ball as big as a football and hitting it with power, confidence and laser accuracy.'

And yet, despite all of this, Nadal comfortably leads the head-to-head with Federer and despite all of his 'genius', Federer had a mental block against him until he beat him in the Australian Open Final in 2017. Djokovic, on the other hand, has shown that to play close to tennis perfection one need not be a genius. He is not afraid of Federer and Nadal and has better head-to-head records against both.

I have a colleague and good friend who is the God of CAT. He has, at the time of writing this book, fourteen 100-percentiles. In CAT 2016, he had a score of 287 out of 300 with 100-percentiles on all sections as well, a feat he has achieved many times.

Am I intimidated by his ability? Absolutely.

Does he come up with brilliant, elegant, unconventional solutions in under 30 seconds to seemingly routine problems, solutions that just leave you open-mouthed in wonder? Yes!

Instead of thinking that only he can do it or that it is a gift from the gods, I understood his mindset towards problem-solving in a very fundamental way. I have internalized it so much that solving problems using unconventional methods has now become my natural inclination. Maths has gone from being my Achilles heel to my favourite teaching area (more about this and lateral thinking solutions in the chapter titled 'The Elegant Solution').

2

Wipe the Slate Clean

The most interesting part of teaching for me is not finding the best way to demonstrate how to split open a knotty problem but rather to figure out the psychological hurdles that are inhibiting some of my students from grasping what is obvious to others.

The reason I call this psychological is because it is linked to your past academic performance. You need to forget your accomplishments or disappointments in school; neither of them matter at this point. If you have a great academic profile, it does not guarantee great scores on the CAT. School and college exams test your memory, your achievement orientation and your handwriting! There are many students with great marks in school or college who do not crack an aptitude test. And similarly, there are students who did not do well at school but take to aptitude tests like fish to water.

If you have not been good at maths throughout school, it does not mean that you do not understand maths or that you suck at it. It might very well mean that you have not really been taught maths the way it is supposed to be (as was the case with me). If you are from a vernacular background, it does not mean that you cannot crack CAT Verbal.

You might not be good at something because you hate it

The first thing that we have to acknowledge is that we might not like the things we are not naturally good at. For example, despite having pretty good logical reasoning skills, I have never ever touched programming or anything remotely related to software coding with a bargepole. Why? I simply do not like it!

The same applied to my dislike for certain topics during my CAT preparation—numbers, functions, graphs, modulus and some parts of algebra, like the number of solutions to equations. So high was my aversion to these areas that if I saw f(x), I would not even read the problem before moving on to the next.

The question is, what came first—my dislike for these concepts or the fact that I did not think I was naturally good at them?

I was always good at languages and logic, so I absolutely loved to solve the Verbal section. The Data Interpretation and Logical Reasoning (DI-LR) section and Arithmetic problems express logic in words and thus I loved to solve them as well. The moment it came to problems where the logic moved from words to symbols or numbers, I hated it. Why did I instinctively hate it? I still do not know.

When I took the CAT the first time around, the QA section used to have fifty questions and a sufficient number from arithmetic and geometry for me to comfortably clear the cut-off. I could easily solve enough questions in the other two sections to clear the overall cut-off.

Come D-Day, and there were barely any arithmetic problems. I only remember a tough TSD question. The majority of the questions in the QA section were from numbers, algebra and functions, which, when I look back, I think psyched me out. I knew then and there that my attempt had gone down the drain. I was consistently in the top five of my centre and everyone expected me to crack the test. People in my college as well, small town that it is, knew that along with a few others, I was expected to crack the test.

Thankfully, back in the day, they gave out only interview calls—no scores, no percentiles. When people came to know I didn't get one, they assumed that I had missed out narrowly and came up to commiserate with me—just miss *ho gaya hoga*.

I knew that I would have missed it by a mile, but I didn't bother to clarify their assumptions. But the setback really set me thinking: I can't be good at Verbal, DI and LR and bomb only at certain topics in maths. How can it be that I am selectively dumb?

So, I decided that if I am good at logic, then maths shouldn't be a problem. I told myself that different areas communicate logical information using different means—*arithmetic* uses words, *geometry* uses figures, whereas the rest use symbols and numbers and graphs.

All I needed to do was to parse the logic when it was not expressed in words—something akin to learning sign language or learning the rules of a new card game or board game. Once I made this shift in my head, learning became dramatically easy. I embraced f(x), albeit reluctantly.

You can become the *best* at something you are currently merely *good* at

Another thing about learning is that you need to want to get better at things that you are good at. A lot of times I have seen students not really pay attention to or not really adopt a different, more efficient method of solving a problem, if they have solved it correctly in the way they know.

When I was preparing and I saw the teacher solve the same arithmetic question using ratios instead of equations, I wanted to do it the way he did. I wanted to become as good as him. I straightaway jettisoned equations and adopted ratios.

In the case of test prep, the phrase 'If it is not broken, why fix it' does not apply. You will be better off employing the maxim 'If it is slower, upgrade or replace it'!

Good is not good enough.

Your brain is still very plastic

They say that the plasticity of the brain is highest when we are born and decreases gradually. This explains how we pick up our mother tongues (or whatever is spoken at home) without being taught, how we can absorb many things all at once, when we are quite young. As we age, the plasticity decreases; we move from having the capability to learn many things—*width*—to having the capability to really understand one field—*depth*.

This is why old people (parents above sixty) sometimes have trouble learning new things. Most of you are only in your twenties so your brain still has enough plasticity to absorb new things. So, you are far from fulfilling the potentialities that lie in your brain.

Overcoming the resistance from your brain

Whenever you learn something new, something that you do not enjoy, your brain will resist. I do not have a fascination for bikes and cars in that I was not the kid trying to somehow get a bike or car. It was a necessity, not something I liked.

So when I began to learn to drive a car at twenty-six, the first months were pure torture. It seemed like such a huge ordeal in terms of the amount of concentration it required. But once I had driven enough miles, I was driving on autopilot mode—I could do the task with very little concentration, thus expending very little energy.

The same thing will happen when you try to learn a topic that has not come naturally to you in the past or you think that you have a handicap in—maths with no prior background or Verbal without having done any reading ever.

You will feel absolutely horrible trying to get your head around geometry. Your brain will stage a revolt since it is being made to work doubly hard. Just like your body would balk at all plans to take a run in the afternoon sun, your brain will refuse to learn geometry when it is not your cup of tea.

Each session will leave you exhausted since the brain also works on glucose and it will be using up copious amounts of glucose since it is not functioning on autopilot mode. You need to stick through this torture period; it can last a few weeks before you slowly start feeling comfortable. You will gradually create new pathways in your brain and will eventually be able to solve geometry problems expending less energy and needing lesser concentration.

Knowing that you have to push your brain into the sun and that it will get comfortable with it in a few weeks is key to overcoming the resistance it will put up.

When you sit down to learn, sit down to get better

How many of you have actually learnt things at school and college in a way that is fundamental to you?

How many times have we looked at what we are learning not as a means to an end but as an end in itself? Learning not because the marks will lead you to a job, but learning because what you learn will actually teach you how something in the world works or adds to your skill sets? Those who have done this will have experienced a certain sense of happiness and fulfilment. For those few subjects, you will not have looked at studying as a burden, a chore to be done.

During my formal education, I experienced this when I learnt economics I and II over two trimesters at IIM-L. It was the first time that I did not wait for the exams to read the textbooks, the first time that I knew I would get good grades irrespective of all the studs and gods around. I felt that way because I really understood the concepts and it was not a function of memory. I had enjoyed subjects before, almost anything to do with problem-solving (barring engineering mathematics). But it was a pleasure that I did not connect with the real world; it was not very different from the pleasure derived from solving a sudoku puzzle.

You are not learning to crack the CAT but to do an MBA programme

A lot of the way you prep or your motivation for prep can change if you change the way you look at the CAT as a test. One way is to look at it as English, maths and reasoning. The other is to look at it as a test of skills needed for an MBA later.

On the face of it, the claim might seem ridiculous. How can any of the questions we solve on the CAT be related to an MBA, will I ever solve a geometry problem in my work-life? Did Dhirubhai Ambani know how to solve geometry problems?

Firstly, people such as Dhirubhai Ambani, Steve Jobs and Bill Gates are outliers. No school can produce such people. Secondly, they do not run their firms day in and day out. The people who help them run these firms; the people who head marketing, finance and ops functions in such firms will be people with an MBA degree or a really good technical education degree. By looking at outliers at the top of organizations, we tend to forget the many people under them in the pyramid who bring the skill sets that the leaders lack.

At the core, the CAT tests reasoning in three contexts—a language context, a numerical context and an analytical context.

If you are looking at one of the most sought-after sectors at premier B-schools worldwide—business consulting—you need all three in abundance.

Firstly, to advise on strategy you should be very conversant with macroeconomic, technological and geopolitical trends. You keep abreast of these things through reading publications such as *Economist*, *Wall Street Journal*, Bloomberg and others that look at trends. As consultants, you will also be preparing reports for your clients and it goes without saying that having top-notch language skills are a must.

Throughout your life as an MBA, you will be making pitches—you will be pitching small ideas to your boss, pitching big ideas to your CEO, pitching campaign ideas to your advertising agencies. How will you make these pitches? You will use numbers for sure, but you will be making the presentations using language. I am not talking about using flowery language but the ability to wield English cogently.

So, verbal ability does not remain a section whose cut-off you have to clear but a skill that you have to develop to understand what is happening around you and make yourself heard in the best way possible.

Data interpretation and number-crunching are skills you will use almost every day in your job. You are not going to flip out a calculator to figure out by how much per cent your business is up or down or how much of the target you have achieved. Even HR requires you to deal with numbers constantly since you are continually designing salary packages and adjusting numbers up and down.

You might still be thinking: But what about geometry? It is essential for architecture and design but for an MBA? Well, it tests your logical reasoning skills in a different context—the visual.

Managers keep mouthing the phrase 'don't bring me problems, bring me solutions'. And how do you come up with solutions to problems ranging from day-to-day issues, to firefighting, to event planning?

Using your raw logical reasoning skills. I like to approach my work as solving a set of problems. Isn't that what we are essentially doing at every level—finding solutions?

The CAT, and for that matter even the GMAT, does not test knowledge-intensive subjects such as physics or chemistry. They want to test the core abilities that you would have picked up in school.

The big thing that you need to keep in mind is that the CAT is a test to determine your *aptitude to do an MBA.*

The two-years of B-school will be as academic as it can get with subjects testing all of these skill sets. The quantitative subjects in your first year will have concepts tougher than what you will solve in the CAT. You will have to read fifty-page case studies across subjects to prepare for a class. In short, the CAT tests whether you can survive the academic rigour of an MBA. In my batch at IIM-L, only 220 students out of the 240 who began completed the course in two years.

A few years ago, a student had anonymously posted a query on Quora. She wanted to get into IIM-A but CAT prep bored her to death and she felt sleepy whenever she opened her books—what should she do?

Many of my peers in the industry who were in senior positions or had their own firms responded with long posts aimed at motivating the student. I was wondering if it was really the right advice.

From my own personal experience and from those of my students, one thing was crystal-clear— no one who had a serious shot at cracking the CAT disliked it fully or found it boring. Everyone found preparing or practising for one or the other areas interesting and challenging. It cannot be that you can crack the CAT even when your brain doesn't find any of the nine areas tested even remotely engaging. You need not enjoy it but at the very least, your brain finds the problems challenging enough to spend time on.

So I told the student who posted the query about how the CAT tests skills required to do an academically demanding course such as an MBA (it is not two years of listening to stories about Steve Jobs) and if she doesn't like CAT prep at all, she might not like an MBA as a course as well and maybe she would be better off considering other career options.

The phrase 'wipe the slate clean' is not just a phrase but rather a concept called *tabula rasa*, a Latin phrase that is often translated as *blank slate*. It originates from the word *tabula*, which refers to a slate used for note-taking. It was blanked by heating the wax and then smoothing it.

Proponents of tabula rasa, including Aristotle, disagree with 'innatism', which holds that people are born with certain skills or knowledge.

Even Daoism has a related and more practical concept called *pu*, meaning unworked wood, asking people to let go of all of their received notions (even innatism and tabula rasa are just that— notions) and become *like wood as it came from the tree before man had dressed it.*

So, dump all the notions you have about your ability at the next full stop and start afresh.

3

Seven Skills to Crack the CAT and Enter an IIM

Sportspersons across different sports do not just practise to get better at specifics of their sport. For example, cricketers do not just practise perfecting certain shots or deliveries. Everyone also trains in the gym and on the track to become a great athlete. The ability to run superfast between the wickets, the ability to twist and contort to convert defence to offence, the ability to leap above the tallest defenders are vital to Virat Kohli, Novak Djokovic and Cristiano Ronaldo executing their skills and strategies perfectly.

Similarly even for the sport that is the CAT, you need to develop mental skills apart from concepts and formulas to ace the exam. So, before we jump into the next section of the book, which will deal with strategies to tackle each of the areas on the CAT, let's look at this video to understand the seven skills to crack the CAT and enter the IIMs. **This video is available on the Bell the CAT YouTube Page. The QR code on page 332 will take you to the same.**

Part III

The Verbal Ability and Reading Comprehension (VA-RC) Section

1

How To Measure Your Effective Reading Speed

In the *Seven Skills* video, the first and most important skill that I list is reading speed. It is important not just for Reading Comprehension (RC) but for the entire exam. The faster you read and comprehend the text and the questions that follow, the more time you will have to solve the questions. Otherwise, you will end up solving only a few questions with a high degree of accuracy or rushing through the questions while making a lot of mistakes. In both cases, your scores will consistently keep falling short of your target.

So, the first task is to measure your effective reading speed and then, in a short span of time, work to improve it.

What is effective reading speed?

It is your reading speed multiplied by your comprehension percentage. Comprehension percentage is the percentage of questions you will get right if administered a simple test consisting solely of direct questions based on the information given in the text that you have read.

Thus, if you read a text at 400 words per minute (wpm) and you have a comprehension percentage of 75 per cent, you will have an effective reading speed of 300 wpm. Let us take up a small exercise to measure your effective reading speed.

Before you start reading the text below, start the stopwatch on your phone. Read the text and at the end of your reading, measure and note down the time you took.

Practically speaking, the artistic maturing of cinema was the single-handed achievement of David W. Griffith (1875–1948). Before Griffith, photography in dramatic films consisted of little more than placing the actors before a stationary camera and showing them in full length as they would have appeared on stage. From the beginning of his career as a director, however, Griffith, because of his love of Victorian painting, employed composition. He conceived of the camera image as having a foreground and a rear ground, as well as the middle distance preferred by most directors. By 1910, he was using close-ups to reveal significant details of the scene or of the acting and extreme long shots to achieve a sense of spectacle and distance. His appreciation of the camera's possibilities produced novel dramatic effects. By splitting an event into fragments and recording each from the most suitable camera position, he could significantly vary the emphasis from camera shot to camera shot.

Griffith also achieved dramatic effects by means of creative editing. By juxtaposing images and varying the speed and rhythm of their presentation, he could control the dramatic intensity of the events as the story progressed. Despite the reluctance of his producers, who feared that the public would not be able to follow a plot that was made up of such juxtaposed images, Griffith persisted, and experimented as well with other elements of cinematic syntax that have become standard ever since. These included the flashback, permitting broad psychological and emotional exploration as well as narrative that was not chronological, and the crosscut between two parallel actions to heighten suspense and excitement. In thus exploiting fully the possibilities of editing, Griffith transposed devices of the Victorian novel to film and gave film mastery of time as well as space.

Besides developing cinema's language, Griffith immensely broadened its range and treatment of subjects. His early output was remarkably eclectic: it included not only the standard comedies, melodramas, westerns and thrillers, but also such novelties as adaptations from Browning and Tennyson, and treatments of social issues. As his successes mounted, his ambitions grew, and with them the whole of American cinema. When he remade Enoch Arden *in 1911, he insisted that a subject of such importance could not be treated in the then conventional length of one reel. Griffith's introduction of the American-made multi-reel picture began an immense revolution. Two years later,* Judith of Bethulia, *an elaborate historico-philosophical spectacle, reached the unprecedented length of four reels, or one hour's running time. From our contemporary viewpoint, the pretensions of this film may seem a trifle ludicrous, but at the time, it provoked endless debate and discussion and gave a new intellectual respectability to cinema.*

Stop the stopwatch and note down the time you took.

Answer the questions that follow WITHOUT referring to the passage and note down your choice of answer options.

1. Griffith's film innovations had a direct effect on all of the following EXCEPT:

    (A) film editing
    (B) camera work
    (C) scene composing
    (D) sound editing
    (E) directing

2. Griffith introduced all of the following into American cinema EXCEPT:

   (A) consideration of social issues
   (B) adaptations from Tennyson
   (C) the flashback and other editing techniques
   (D) photographic approaches inspired by Victorian paintings
   (E) dramatic plots suggested by Victorian theatre

3. The main concern of Griffith's producers was that the public might not:

   (A) appreciate Griffith's innovation
   (B) be able to follow the plot
   (C) like to sit for a long duration
   (D) prefer close-ups
   (E) accept Victorian themes

4. The normal length of the film before 1910 was:

   (A) 15 minutes or less
   (B) 15 to 30 minutes
   (C) 30 to 45 minutes
   (D) 45 to 60 minutes
   (E) more than 1 hour

Calculating your effective reading speed

1. Calculate the time you took in minutes by dividing the time you took in seconds by 60, for example, 3 minutes 45 seconds, 3 + (45/60) or 3.75 minutes
2. Divide 450 (the number of words in the passage) by the time you took in minutes to get your reading speed—A
3. Calculate the number of answers you have got right using the following answer key—1-D, 2-E, 3-B, 4-A
4. Divide the number of answers you got right by 4 to get your comprehension quotient—B. For example, if you got three questions correct, 3/4, two questions correct 2/4 and so on.
5. Calculate your effective reading speed by multiplying A and B—A*B
6. For example, reading speed A = 200, comprehension quotient B = 3/4, effective reading speed = 200*.75 = 150 wpm

What is a good effective reading speed?

On the CAT and other exams, an effective reading speed of:

- less than 100 will be below par
- 100–125 wpm is a good speed to begin with
- 125–175 wpm will place you in the 90th to 95th percentile bracket
- 175–200 wpm will place you in the 95th to 98th percentile
- 200–250 wpm will place you in the 98th to 99th percentile
- above 250 wpm will place you in the 99th to 100 percentile category

My reading speed was great but effective reading speed was low

Imagine listening to a YouTube video at 2x speed, and retaining 50 per cent of what you listened to. Are you not better off listening at 1.5x speed and retaining 75 per cent or more of what you have listened to?

When someone talks to you, you are not just taking in some sounds but making sense of what has been said. Reading is no different! It does not make sense to break the whole process into reading and comprehension. This is the reason why effective reading speed is a better measure of your abilities.

2

How to Improve Reading Speed and Comprehension at the Same Time

The common advice given by all mentors is to read editorials from famous newspapers, articles from online magazines such as Aeon, and novels. Essentially, all that the mentors are trying to do is make you follow the same process that made them great readers.

The trouble, though, is that this process does not happen over the course of a few months but over the course of an entire childhood or adolescence. You do not have more than six months at the most since you have to work not just on your reading speed but also on learning the concepts, strategies and techniques. The second problem with this approach is that you do not know if your comprehension has improved since there are no questions following the text that you are reading.

It definitely will help with your text processing power—your ability to read and understand written material will improve. Reading editorials, novels and/or non-fiction books will help you develop a reading habit because of the focus on current affairs, interesting plotlines or insightful analyses. But the problem again is that the text you will encounter in these exams might or might not have content that you like!

Read and solve a crazy number of reading comprehension passages in a short span of time

All the RC passages that you will encounter in your prep material and on the CAT are taken from editorials, journals, magazines and books. What's more, they have questions based on the same. So, why not solve RC passages instead?

You need to make your brain comfortable with reading lots of text in a short span of time. You have to build RC muscles quickly. What is the best way to do it? Train a lot for a short span of time or train little by little over a long period?

Given the time constraint, I believe it should be the latter. Each one of you will have a different starting point. So, the quantum of reading to be done will be different. I suggest the following sets of passages of easy and medium levels of difficulty. You can pick and choose based on your starting level.

- 100 passages in 30 days
- 200 passages in 45 days
- 300 passages in 60 days

An easier schedule can be to solve three passages a day for three months without missing a single day. Easy and medium passages will more than suffice for two reasons. Since the text is dense, they will always slow you down, since there is no other way to process them. So, building speed and comprehension at the same time will not happen. Secondly, in the actual exam, difficult passages are supposed to be spotted and left alone since they will eat away all of your time.

How to go about this practice

- Any single practice session should involve you solving three passages along with questions back to back.
- Do not bother about the timer.
- Do not check answers until you finish all three passages.
- Check the meanings of all the words you do not know as you are reading the sentence.
- At the end of the session, make a note of the new words you learnt and the meanings of the same in a notebook.
- Before you begin your next session, go over the words written in your notebook.
- You can go back to the passage and check the content to answer the questions.

This type of practice will mean that you are conditioning your brain to feel the exact stress that you will face in the test. And do not forget you will be solving passages of easy and medium levels of difficulty as well as looking up meanings of words you do not understand!

You will find the task absolutely painful at first. One student who started this practice came back after one week and said that his head was ready to burst. I told him that if I had another solution, say an injection to increase reading speed, I would have given that to him. Over time, you will find that things will get easier, you will start feeling more comfortable.

The brain is no different from the body. Your first week in the gym would have felt like hell but slowly the same weights that seemed like torture started feeling comfortable. Reading comprehension as a skill is not different from any other skill. If you have never driven a bike or a car, the first week of training might seem like a nightmare—how do you manage so many things at the same time? Once you have driven enough, you will be singing songs and driving on autopilot. The student went back and stuck with it; eventually he cracked NMAT and got into NMIMS Mumbai.

From where do you get RC passages to solve?

The prep material that you subscribe to will have a good quantity of passages divided into easy and medium levels. If you run out of those or if you want to save them for later, you can get the GMAT Official Guide and/or the GMAT Verbal Review and solve passages from them. The style and content might differ from those of the Indian exams but they will be ideal practice to improve your reading and comprehension.

Once you see significant improvement over the course of three months, you will be reading and solving so much text as part of the entire preparation across all sections that separate practice for reading and comprehension speed itself will not be required.

Do not start solving any RC passage before you read the next chapter on 'The Five Pauses Technique'.

3

The Five Pauses Technique: How to Read and Solve an RC Passage

On the face of it, RC is the most straightforward of the question types—read passage, answer questions. But if there is a question type that every Indian test-taker (maybe even Asian test-takers of the GMAT, or rather every non-native speaker of the English language, or to make it comprehensive—anyone who does not think in English) would like to do away with, it would be RC.

To simplify the process, let us break up the whole task into two parts: reading the passage (well) and answering questions (with good accuracy).

What is a good first reading of an RC passage?

A lot of your success in RC will depend on a good first reading of the passage. What is a good first reading? At the end of reading a passage, a good reader should be able to:

1. **Answer any summary questions that follow the passage**—summary questions test your understanding of the passage as a whole, such as, what is the primary purpose of the author, what is the main idea of the passage, what can be a suitable title for the passage. This is crucial since you cannot go back and read the entire passage all over again. It should be a process that is built into your reading itself. If there is a summary question you cannot answer, move on to another question.

2. **Remember exactly where in the passage the answer to a specific question lies**—specific questions are questions that pertain to specific sections of the passage—a sentence, a paragraph, a group of paragraphs: The author cites the example of the 'earlier discoveries' in order to . . ., or Which of the following inferences about squatter cities is supported by the passage? This ability to know which portion of the passage contains the answer is critical since you cannot start searching the entire passage all over again.

What is preventing you from a good reading?

Those who do not read are not used to using logic while processing information from a text. Their primary association with long-format text has always been about *memorizing* not *reasoning*—memorizing large chunks to regurgitate in an exam. Reasoning and logic were required only in problem-solving subjects.

So, reading an absolutely new 600-word passage (not something related to what a teacher has taught or a part of a syllabus) and parsing the logic behind it, and then answering questions based on it is not something that many people enjoy.

One of the big reasons for the success of social media platforms is that the primary mode of information dissemination is an image, a video or a textual image (meme). Social media also highlights the aversion to reading through the popular acronym tl;dr, too long; didn't read.

The aversion to reading is something that content creators of magazines and websites are aware of and hence, from time immemorial they have been getting you to read by dumbing down the content: Seven ways to . . ., How to . . ., Want to . . .?, Are you . . .?, You won't believe what happened next . . .

Unfortunately, the passages on the CAT and the case studies in a B-school will not be written in such formats; the only images you will see are graphs and charts. Given all of this, you will realize that you just cannot read a passage as you normally would.

Critical Reading or Reading for Purpose

Every passage is written to serve a particular purpose, say:

- *explain* a concept, technology or phenomenon
- *evaluate* the pros and cons of a particular book, social change, phenomenon or technology
- *highlight* the implications of a particular finding or ruling
- *describe* the role of X in Y

Critical reading is the act of reading with the intent of decoding the purpose of the author and the main idea the author wants to convey. To do this, you need to consciously incorporate two PAUSES at different junctures of your reading of the passages.

PAUSE I: After every paragraph

The first habit you need to incorporate in your reading is to consciously pause at the end of every paragraph. In an RC passage, not all paragraphs are equal. The first paragraphs are always more important than others since most of the time, the *topic of the passage* and the *argument that the passage wants to explore* are revealed in the first paragraph.

What is the TOPIC of a passage?

The topic of the passage is just that—a phrase that answers the question: What is this passage about? It is very similar to what a person might ask you about a movie or a book. It is usually revealed in the first two sentences of the first paragraph of the passage or at least by the end of the first paragraph.

What is the ARGUMENT of a passage?

The argument of the passage is the specific thing about the topic that the passage wants to explore in the rest of the paragraphs.

For example, the topic could be *globalization* and the argument could be the *impact of globalization on income inequality*. Or the topic could be *multinationals* and the argument could be the *origin of multinationals*.

Let us take a passage to understand the topic and argument better.

In the 1980s, a Neanderthal cave dwelling was identified on the coast of Portugal, some 20 miles south of Lisbon. Ten years ago, a team of experts revisited the cave, and in one of its tiny nooks, they found a rich cache of remains from aquatic animals such as fish, mussels, crustaceans, sharks, dolphins and seals—signs of a seafood smorgasbord. The discovery was a remarkable one. Scientists had previously unearthed hints that Neanderthals exploited marine resources; the extinct hominids fashioned tools out of clam shells and used shells to make jewellery beads. But there had been no evidence that Neanderthals were hunting aquatic animals in a significant way. In fact, some experts had posited that the consumption of seafood helped give Homo sapiens an edge over Neanderthals; fish and other marine creatures are rich in omega–3 fatty acids, which promote the development of brain tissue.

Identifying the topic and the argument can happen on two levels of detail.

Level 1: The topic of the passage is *Neanderthals*, the argument that the passage is seeking to explore is *the diet of Neanderthals*.

Level 2: The topic of the passage is the *diet of Neanderthals*, the argument that the passage is going to explore is *the implications of the discovery that the Neanderthals might have been eating seafood*.

To begin with, identify the topic and argument at Level 1 (if your language processing skills are on the weaker side) but eventually you will have to move to Level 2.

Any detail beyond Level 2 will defeat the purpose since the idea is to get a top-level understanding as to what direction the passage will take.

Will the first paragraph always reveal the topic and argument of the passage without fail?

It depends on the source of the text of the passage. If the passage is taken from scholarly magazines or journals, then the writing will always have a scientific style and will be very similar to the abstract of a PhD. In such passages, the topic and idea will always be stated in the first paragraph without fail. The GMAT has passages only from such sources and thus this method is absolutely foolproof.

Whereas on the CAT, passages are taken not only from scholarly magazines or journals such as *Nature* and *Scientific American* but also from newspapers and magazines for general reading such as *Atlantic* or *New York Times*. Writers in regular newspapers and magazines are not obligated to follow a scientific style; they can choose their own style and hence, they might start with an anecdote in the first paragraph and introduce the topic and argument much later.

So, while you need to pause after the first paragraph to identify the topic and argument of the passage, do not be perturbed if you do not find it in some passages; you will have to wait until it is revealed. We will look at such a passage later.

After the first paragraph, you need to continue pausing after every paragraph to track how the argument is being developed since each paragraph is linked to the argument that is being explored in the passage. For example, the second paragraph might introduce the advantages of a new technology and the third the disadvantages of the same.

Let us take a passage and execute the first pause—pausing after every paragraph.

Passage I, Metric Fixation, 437 words

More and more companies, government agencies, educational institutions and philanthropic organizations are today in the grip of a new phenomenon: 'metric fixation'. The key components of metric fixation are the beliefs that it is possible—and desirable—to replace professional judgement (acquired through personal experience and talent) with numerical indicators of comparative performance based upon standardized data (metrics); and that the best way to motivate people within these organizations is by attaching rewards and penalties to their measured performance.

What is the TOPIC of the passage?

Metric Fixation

What is the ARGUMENT that the passage seeks to explore?

Many firms are embracing metric fixation—using numbers to measure and incentivize performance.

The rewards can be monetary, in the form of pay for performance, say, or reputational, in the form of college rankings, hospital ratings, surgical report cards and so on. But the most dramatic negative effect of metric fixation is its propensity to incentivize gaming: that is, encouraging professionals to maximize the metrics in ways that are at odds with the larger purpose of the organization. If the rate of major crimes in a district becomes the metric according to which police officers are promoted, then some officers will respond by simply not recording crimes or downgrading them from major offences to misdemeanours. Or take the case of surgeons. When the metrics of success and failure are made public—affecting their reputation and income—some surgeons will improve their metric scores by refusing to operate on patients with more complex problems, whose surgical outcomes are more likely to be negative. Who suffers? The patients who don't get operated upon.

How is the ARGUMENT being explored in this paragraph?

The biggest drawback of metric fixation is that it incentivizes gaming—maximizing numbers that are measured at the expense of larger goals of the organization or societal needs.

When reward is tied to measured performance, metric fixation invites just this sort of gaming. But metric fixation also leads to a variety of more subtle unintended negative consequences. These include goal displacement, which comes in many varieties: when performance is judged by a few measures, and the stakes are high (keeping one's job, getting a pay rise or raising the stock price at the time that stock options are vested), people focus on satisfying those measures – often at the expense of other, more important organizational goals that are not measured. The best-known example is 'teaching to the test', a widespread phenomenon that has distorted primary and secondary education in the United States since the adoption of the No Child Left Behind Act of 2001.

How is the ARGUMENT being explored in this paragraph?

The other drawback of metric fixation is goal displacement—metrics that are important but not measured get ignored.

Short-termism is another negative. Measured performance encourages what the US sociologist Robert K. Merton in 1936 called 'the imperious immediacy of interests . . . where the actor's paramount concern with the foreseen immediate consequences excludes consideration of further or other consequences'. In short, advancing short-term goals at the expense of long-range considerations . . . To the debit side of the ledger must also be added the transactional costs of metrics . . .

How is the **ARGUMENT** being explored in this paragraph?
The last drawback of metric fixation is short-term thinking and wastage of resources.

PAUSE II: At the end of the passage

The second habit you need to inculcate is to consciously pause at the end of reading the passage to identify the *main idea* of the passage. As I mentioned earlier, all passages are written with a *purpose*. It is at this pause that you identify that purpose.

How do you do it? By stringing together the main ideas of each paragraph to see how the argument has been explored.

PARA 1: Many firms are embracing metric fixation—using numbers to measure and incentivize performance.

PARA 2: The biggest drawback of metric fixation is that it incentivizes gaming—at the expense of larger goals.

PARA 3: The other drawback of metric fixation is goal displacement—metrics that are important but not measured get ignored.

PARA 4: The last drawback of metric fixation is short-term thinking and wastage of resources.

The author introduces the topic—*metric fixation*—in the first paragraph and goes on to highlight the drawbacks of metric fixation in each of the following paragraphs.

MAIN IDEA: *Metric fixation has a lot of negative consequences that are at cross purposes with the larger goals of the organization.*

PAUSE II is probably the most important pause since your understanding of the passage as a whole hinges on you taking this pause. It does not matter if there is not a single direct summary question that follows the passage:

- Which of the following best captures the main idea of the passage?
- Which of the following is the author primarily concerned with?
- Which of the following is a suitable title for the passage?

Your understanding of the main argument or the author's position can be tested indirectly as well. For instance, on this passage there can be a question such as this:

- Which of the following changes to performance evaluation methods is the author LEAST likely to disagree with?

Should you be taking notes after reading each paragraph and at the end of the passage?

From what we have discussed so far, you should have deduced that the core skill tested is this: the ability to read, comprehend and summarize the main idea presented in the passage, give a title that captures the essence of the passage, and identify the primary purpose of the passage.

What I have outlined so far through the two pauses is the method to do the same. Does it need to be written down?

A better question would be to ask, do you have enough time to write things down for three to four passages? I do not think so.

To start off with, if you have a lot of trouble sticking through the entire passage and threading the main idea, write things down. But eventually, you have to be able to pause, process and retain things in your head. This is the skill that is being tested. This is the skill that you have to develop. And the only way you can develop this skill is by practising the technique day in and day out till you feel you have mastered it.

While I am sure everyone teaches the first two pauses, very few people teach the next three.

PAUSE III: After reading the question

The next stage is the actual answering of a reading comprehension question and for me, this pause is the most important and also the least taught one. I have been teaching for a while now and have seen that most teachers focus a lot on the first part of how to read and understand. I am sure even they advocate pausing after each paragraph and pausing after reading the passage.

But the moment it comes to explaining the answer to a question, no one teaches a technique or a process to answer a question, irrespective of the content. Everyone jumps directly to the explanation: From the second sentence of the third paragraph it is clear that . . .

Test-takers also exhibit a certain kind of hastiness when it comes to answering RC questions. They read the question and are in a tearing hurry to quickly read all the options. They treat the RC question like a *swayamvar*, where they are the groom or the bride, and the *one* they will know, they feel it in their hearts.

What happens, though? Do they end up always knowing the *one*, the *right* option? No, the heart gets stuck on more than one! 'Sir, I am always caught between two options and end up choosing the wrong one—what should I do?' is the single most commonly asked query on RC. In fact, I do not think there is any other symptom with which students meet their instructors.

So, it goes without saying that this *pause* is something that anyone who wants high accuracy on RC questions, be it the CAT, GMAT or GRE, has to take.

What do you do with this pause after reading the question?

Frame the *shadow answer* or frame the *function that the right answer* has to perform for you.

If you do not take this pause, you will be led astray by the traps set for you by the test-setter.

'The most common trap is an option that makes perfect sense in context but does not answer the question.'

Most test-takers will mark this option since they have not precisely defined what they are looking for in the right answer. Let us take a question from the passage we discussed above and execute this pause.

Q. Of the following, which would have added the least depth to the author's argument?

A. More real-life illustrations of the consequences of employees and professionals gaming metrics-based performance measurement systems.
B. A comparative case study of metrics and non-metrics-based evaluation, and its impact on the main goals of an organization.
C. Assessment of the pros and cons of a professional judgement-based evaluation system.
D. An analysis of the reasons why metrics fixation is becoming popular despite its drawbacks.

Framing a shadow answer

To identify which option adds LEAST depth to the author's ARGUMENT, start with the author's argument. The author has argued using examples that metric fixation, which people are using instead of professional judgement, has a lot of negative consequences.

What will add depth to the author's argument?
Anything that brings in more insight that will enrich our understanding of the author's argument.

What will add LEAST depth to the author's argument?
Anything that does not add anything to the author's argument.

A. More real-life illustrations of the consequences of employees and professionals gaming metrics-based performance measurement systems—Will be more of the same and will not add any additional depth or enrich our understanding of the argument
B. A comparative case study of metrics and non-metrics-based evaluation, and its impact on the main goals of an organization—Will ADD DEPTH to the author's argument by showing how non-metrics-based evaluations work since they have not been discussed in the passage
C. Assessment of the pros and cons of a professional judgement-based evaluation system—Will ADD DEPTH to the author's argument by showing how the method cited but not described by the author will work
D. An analysis of the reasons why metrics fixation is becoming popular despite its drawbacks—Will ADD DEPTH by showing why metric fixation is still popular

Option (A) is the perfect trap since it is very relevant to the passage—we would like to read why it is so popular. So they keep (A) aside, revisit the rest of the options and choose option (A) since it might seem that more examples of the kind already presented in the passage might be redundant or will not add anything.

PAUSE IV: After reading each option

As discussed earlier, test-takers tend to look at options as if they were going through a swayamvar and are always keen to read out all the options at the earliest. In short, test-takers rely on the process of SELECTION—selecting the right answer—rather than the process of ELIMINATION—rejecting options that do not fit the shadow answer.

As questions get tougher, it might be very difficult to ascertain why the right answer is the right answer. It is thus always desirable to eliminate the incorrect answers and choose what is left, provided you do PAUSE III correctly.

'After reading you need to either REJECT an option or KEEP the option based on the shadow answer, DO NOT SELECT.'

On an easy question, you will reject all the incorrect options and the one you are left with is the right option. On a tougher question, you may be left with two options.

When faced with two options, most test-takers are confused since they are weighing options against each other. It is similar to having the two options in the two pans of a weighing scale and comparing them against each other. But how do you decide? It is no wonder they are confused.

What you should do is always keep the shadow answer in the left pan, put one option at a time into the right pan and compare which one better fits the bill.

In case you are left with two options, go back to your shadow answer, and eliminate one of the options based on the criteria.

PAUSE V: After reading all the options

The last step is to confirm your final choice. If you were unable to choose between the two options at the end of the last step, leave the question. Just because you have reached this far does not mean you have to do guesswork.

A CAT question has four options and if you are stuck with two options, it means that you still only have a 50 per cent chance of getting it right. And once you get into the bad habit of guessing when left with two options, you will find it tough to break the habit.

The Five Pauses

To summarize the Five Pauses:

PAUSE I—At the end of every paragraph, pause to summarize the main argument of the paragraph

PAUSE II—At the end of the passage, pause to summarize the main argument of the passage

PAUSE III—At the end of the question, pause to frame the shadow answer or the function of the right answer

PAUSE IV—At the end of every option, pause to reject or keep an option

PAUSE V—At the end of all options, pause to confirm the final answer

The Five Pauses are the five stages where you are *actively comprehending* and *reasoning* instead of passively going through the entire process. Contrast this with what most test-takers do:

- read the first paragraph with full interest,
- lose interest midway and somehow finish the passage,
- read the question and rush through the options, and
- then for the first time start to actively, consciously, reason

And we know what happens when we leave reasoning right to the end. Let us take another passage and execute the Five Pauses from start to end.

Passage II: Digital Colonization, 488 words

War, natural disasters and climate change are destroying some of the world's most precious cultural sites. Google is trying to help preserve these archaeological wonders by allowing users access to 3D images of these treasures through its site. But the project is raising questions about Google's motivations and about who should own the digital copyrights. Some critics call it a form of 'digital colonialism'. When it comes to archaeological treasures, the losses have been mounting. ISIS blew up parts of the ancient city of Palmyra in Syria and an earthquake hit Bagan, an ancient city in Myanmar, damaging dozens of temples, in 2016. In the past, all archaeologists and historians had for restoration and research were photos, drawings, remnants and intuition.

What is the TOPIC of the passage?

Digitization of archaeological wonders.

What is the ARGUMENT the passage is seeking to explore?

Who should own the copyrights of the digital archives of archaeological wonders?

But that's changing. Before the earthquake at Bagan, many of the temples on the site were scanned. These scans are on Google's Arts and Culture site. The digital renditions allow viewers to virtually wander the halls of the temple, look up-close at paintings and turn the building over, to look up at its chambers. Google Arts and Culture works with museums and other nonprofits to put high-quality images online.

The images of the temples in Bagan are part of a collaboration with CyArk, a nonprofit that creates the 3D scanning of historic sites. Google says it doesn't make money off this website, but it fits in with Google's mission to make the world's information available and useful.

What is the ARGUMENT the paragraphs are seeking to explore?

Google is working with nonprofits such as CyArk to make the digital archives available online and claims that it is not making any profits from the enterprise.

Critics say the collaboration could be an attempt by a large corporation to wrap itself in the sheen of culture. Ethan Watrall, an archaeologist, professor at Michigan State University and a member of the Society for American Archaeology, says he's not comfortable with the arrangement between CyArk and Google. Watrall says this project is just a way for Google to promote Google. 'They want to make this material accessible so people will browse it and be filled with wonder by it,' he says. 'But at its core, it's all about advertisements and driving traffic.' Watrall says these images belong on the site of a museum or educational institution, where there is serious scholarship and a very different mission.

What is the ARGUMENT the paragraph is seeking to explore?

Critics say that the project will indirectly end up benefiting Google and that the images should be on the sites of museums or educational institutions whose goals are different since ultimately Google is a commercial enterprise.

There's another issue for some archaeologists and art historians. CyArk owns the copyrights of the scans—not the countries where these sites are located. That means the countries need CyArk's permission to use these images for commercial purposes.

Erin Thompson, a professor of art crime at John Jay College of Criminal Justice in New York City, says it's the latest example of a Western nation appropriating a foreign culture, a centuries-long battle. CyArk says it copyrights the scans so no one can use them in an inappropriate way. The company says it works closely with authorities during the process, even training local people to help. But critics like Thompson are not persuaded. She would prefer the scans to be owned by the countries and people where these sites are located.

What is the ARGUMENT the paragraphs are seeking to explore?

Critics argue that the rights should be owned by the countries where these sites are present and not CyArk.

Passage Recap

- Who should own the copyrights of the digital archives of archaeological wonders?
- Google is working with nonprofits such as CyArk to make the digital archives available online and claims that it is not making any profits from the enterprise.
- Critics say that the project will indirectly end up benefiting Google and that the images should be on the sites of museums or educational institutions whose goals are different since ultimately, Google is a commercial enterprise.
- Critics argue that the rights should be owned by the countries where these sites are present and not CyArk.

MAIN IDEA: There is a debate over whether the copyrights of the digital archives of archaeological wonders should be owned by organizations such as Google and CyArk that are currently doing the process of digitization; critics feel the rights should be owned by the countries where these sites are present.

Solve questions by incorporating Pauses III, IV and V.

Question 1

By 'digital colonialism', critics of the CyArk–Google project are referring to the fact that:

A. CyArk and Google have not shared the details of digitization with the host countries
B. countries where the scanned sites are located do not own the scan copyrights
C. the scanning process can damage delicate frescos and statues at the sites
D. CyArk and Google have been scanning images without copyright permission from host countries

Question 2

Based on his views mentioned in the passage, one could best characterize Dr Watrall as being:

A. opposed to the use of digital technology in archaeological and cultural sites in developing countries
B. uneasy about the marketing of archaeological images for commercial use by firms such as Google and CyArk
C. dismissive of laypeople's access to specialist images of archaeological and cultural sites
D. critical about the links between a non-profit and a commercial tech platform for distributing archaeological images

Question 3

Which of the following, if true, would most strongly invalidate Dr Watrall's objections?

A. CyArk does not own the copyright on scanned images of archaeological sites
B. There is a ban on CyArk scanning archaeological sites located in other countries
C. CyArk uploads its scanned images of archaeological sites on to museum websites only
D. Google takes down advertisements on its website hosting CyArk's scanned images

Question 4

In Dr Thompson's view, CyArk owning the copyright of its digital scans of archaeological sites is akin to:

A. the illegal downloading of content from the Internet
B. the seizing of ancient Egyptian artefacts by a Western museum
C. tourists uploading photos of monuments on to social media
D. digital platforms capturing users' data for market research

Question 5

Of the following arguments, which one is LEAST likely to be used by the companies that digitally scan cultural sites?

A. It enables people who cannot physically visit these sites to experience them
B. It allows a large corporation to project itself as a protector of culture
C. It provides images free of cost to all users
D. It helps preserve precious images in case the sites are damaged or destroyed

Explanatory Answers

Question 1

By 'digital colonialism', critics of the CyArk–Google project are referring to the fact that:

SHADOW ANSWER: *The term 'digital colonialism' is introduced in the first paragraph—the rights of the digital archives of archaeological sites are not owned by the country where the sites are located but by organizations that are undertaking the digitization process.*

A. CyArk and Google have not shared the details of digitization with the host countries—REJECT, *it does not mention the ownership of rights.*
B. Countries where the scanned sites are located do not own the scan copyrights—KEEP, *captures the shadow answer in a concise format.*
C. The scanning process can damage delicate frescos and statues at the sites—REJECT, *unrelated to the shadow answer and the question.*
D. CyArk and Google have been scanning images without copyright permission from host countries—REJECT, *there is no information about whether CyArk and Google need to ask permission; the passage mentions the reverse—under the current copyright ownership, host countries need to ask CyArk permission to use the images.*

There are no close options so B can be confirmed.

Correct Answer: B

Question 2

Based on his views mentioned in the passage, one could best characterize Dr Watrall as being:

SHADOW ANSWER: *The reference to Ethan Watrall is in the third paragraph; he says he's not comfortable with the arrangement between CyArk and Google. Watrall says this project is just a way for Google to promote Google. 'They want to make this material accessible so people will browse it and be filled with wonder by it,' he says. 'But at its core, it's all about advertisements and driving traffic.'*

What's the shadow answer—He is opposed to the idea of Google being involved in the process, despite the presence of a nonprofit—CyArk—since Google is a commercial enterprise.

A. opposed to the use of digital technology in archaeological and cultural sites in developing countries—REJECT, *there is no mention of Watrall being against digitization itself.*

B. uneasy about the marketing of archaeological images for commercial use by firms such as Google and CyArk—REJECT, *Watrall only says that the project will promote Google, whose goals are ultimately advertising and traffic; there is no mention of Google and CyArk actually marketing the images for commercial use.*

C. dismissive of laypeople's access to specialist images of archaeological and cultural sites—REJECT, *there is no mention of Watrall's opposition to laypeople's access.*

D. critical about the links between a non-profit and a commercial tech platform for distributing archaeological images—KEEP, *paraphrases the shadow answer using different words.*

Correct Answer: D

Question 3

Which of the following, if true, would most strongly invalidate Dr Watrall's objections?

SHADOW ANSWER: *This question is directly linked to the previous one. To know what will invalidate Dr Watrall's objection we need to first revisit his objection, which is the shadow answer to the previous question. He is opposed to the idea of Google being involved in the process, despite the presence of a nonprofit— CyArk—since Google is a commercial enterprise. If this has to be invalidated, it has to be shown that there is no commercial use that the images are being put to or can be put to (the question can be re-interpreted as what will make Dr Watrall happy!).*

A. CyArk does not own the copyright on scanned images of archaeological sites—KEEP, *if CyArk does not own the copyright, it cannot use the images for commercial purposes, maybe not, not a direct reject, can be considered.*

B. There is a ban on CyArk scanning archaeological sites located in other countries—REJECT, *Watrall is primarily uncomfortable with the presence of commercial organizations such as Google, so even if CyArk is scanning sites in its own country, Watrall's argument will not be invalidated due to their relationship with Google.*

C. CyArk uploads its scanned images of archaeological sites on to museum websites only—KEEP, *Watrall's argument will be invalidated since Google cannot make any money off traffic or advertisements.*

D. Google takes down advertisements on its website hosting CyArk's scanned images—KEEP, *seems like it will invalidate the commercial option.*

We need to choose among three options: A, C and D. Option A does not address the issue of commercialization; it can be rejected. D is close since it shuts down advertising revenue but since traffic will still indirectly promote brand Google, D only partially counters Watrall and hence, can be rejected. C moves the whole hosting operations on to museum websites, which means both traffic and advertisements to Google will not hold *(the question can be re-interpreted as what will make Dr Watrall happy!)*.

Correct Answer: C

Question 4

In Dr Thompson's view, CyArk owning the copyright of its digital scans of archaeological sites is akin to:

SHADOW ANSWER: *Dr Thompson's views are mentioned in the last paragraph. She says that as long as the rights are with CyArk, it is similar to Western countries appropriating foreign cultures and claiming ownership.*

A. the illegal downloading of content from the Internet—REJECT, *not an example of Western appropriation*
B. the seizing of ancient Egyptian artefacts by a Western museum—KEEP, *in line with the shadow answer*
C. tourists uploading photos of monuments on to social media—REJECT, *not an example of Western appropriation*
D. digital platforms capturing users' data for market research—REJECT, *not an example of Western appropriation*

Correct Answer: B

Question 5

Of the following arguments, which one is LEAST likely to be used by the companies that digitally scan cultural sites?

SHADOW ANSWER: *The entire passage is about companies using digitization to promote themselves directly or indirectly for commercial gain. So any company should avoid arguing that they are gaining anything from it. The correct option will show that the company gains.*

A. It enables people who cannot physically visit these sites to experience them—REJECT, *benefits people.*
B. It allows a large corporation to project itself as a protector of culture—KEEP, *projects and promotes the company.*
C. It provides images free of cost to all users—REJECT, *benefits people.*
D. It helps preserve precious images in case the sites are damaged or destroyed—REJECT, *benefits culture.*

Correct Answer: B

4

Becoming an Expert Critical Reader

Executing the first two pauses is a way to become a critical reader but even in reading, like in every other field, there is a difference between those who merely execute the processes and those who take it to the next level—the experts.

The ability to distinguish between Main Ideas and Supporting Ideas

All sentences in a passage are not equally important. There are usually three kinds of sentences in order of importance.

Main Arguments

Sentences that deal with the main argument of the passage—these sentences clearly state a position held by the author or by someone else.

Supporting Ideas

Supporting ideas are important sentences that *strengthen* the main arguments by elaborating or providing additional information.

Context Providers

The least important sentences are the ones that provide the background information of context in which the main argument is made. For example, all the sentences about wars, natural disasters, ISIS, Palmyra, serve to provide context to the main argument.

I have colour-coded both the passages discussed so far—*Digital Colonization* and *Metric Fixation*—to indicate which sentences are the Main Arguments—*black*, which ones are the Supporting Ideas—*dark grey*, and which ones are the Context Providers—*light grey*.

Passage X-Ray—Digital Colonization

War, natural disasters and climate change are destroying some of the world's most precious cultural sites. Google is trying to help preserve these archaeological wonders by allowing users access to 3D images of these treasures through its site. But the project is raising questions about Google's motivations and about who should own the digital copyrights. Some critics call it a form of 'digital colonialism.' When it comes to archaeological treasures, the losses have been mounting. ISIS blew up parts of the ancient city of Palmyra in Syria and an earthquake hit Bagan, an ancient city in Myanmar, damaging dozens of temples, in 2016. In the past, all archaeologists and historians had for restoration and research were photos, drawings, remnants and intuition.

But that's changing. Before the earthquake at Bagan, many of the temples on the site were scanned. These scans are on Google's Arts and Culture site. The digital renditions allow viewers to virtually wander the halls of the temple, look up-close at paintings and turn the building over, to look up at its chambers. Google Arts and Culture works with museums and other nonprofits to put high-quality images online.

The images of the temples in Bagan are part of a collaboration with CyArk, a nonprofit that creates the 3D scanning of historic sites. Google says it doesn't make money off this website, but it fits in with Google's mission to make the world's information available and useful.

Critics say the collaboration could be an attempt by a large corporation to wrap itself in the sheen of culture. Ethan Watrall, an archaeologist, professor at Michigan State University and a member of the Society for American Archaeology, says he's not comfortable with the arrangement between CyArk and Google. Watrall says this project is just a way for Google to promote Google. 'They want to make this material accessible so people will browse it and be filled with wonder by it,' he says. 'But at its core, it's all about advertisements and driving traffic.' Watrall says these images belong on the site of a museum or educational institution, where there is serious scholarship and a very different mission.

There's another issue for some archaeologists and art historians. CyArk owns the copyrights of the scans—not the countries where these sites are located. That means the countries need CyArk's permission to use these images for commercial purposes.

Erin Thompson, a professor of art crime at John Jay College of Criminal Justice in New York City, says it's the latest example of a Western nation appropriating a foreign culture, a centuries-long battle. CyArk says it copyrights the scans so no one can use them in an inappropriate way. The company says it works closely with authorities during the process, even training local people to help. But critics like Thompson are not persuaded. She would prefer the scans to be owned by the countries and people where these sites are located.

Passage X-Ray—Metric Fixation

More and more companies, government agencies, educational institutions and philanthropic organizations are today in the grip of a new phenomenon: 'metric fixation'. The key components of metric fixation are the belief that it is possible – and desirable – to replace professional judgement (acquired through personal experience and talent) with numerical indicators of comparative performance based upon standardized data (metrics); and that the best way to motivate people within these organizations is by attaching rewards and penalties to their measured performance.

The rewards can be monetary, in the form of pay for performance, say, or reputational, in the form of college rankings, hospital ratings, surgical report cards and so on. **But the most dramatic negative effect of metric fixation is its propensity to incentivize gaming: that is, encouraging professionals to maximize the metrics in ways that are at odds with the larger purpose of the organization.** *If the rate of major crimes in a district becomes the metric according to which police officers are promoted, then some officers will respond by simply not recording crimes or downgrading them from major offences to misdemeanours. Or take the case of surgeons. When the metrics of success and failure are made public – affecting their reputation and income – some surgeons will improve their metric scores by refusing to operate on patients with more complex problems, whose surgical outcomes are more likely to be negative. Who suffers? The patients who don't get operated upon.*

When reward is tied to measured performance, metric fixation invites just this sort of gaming. But metric fixation also leads to a variety of more subtle unintended negative consequences. **These include goal displacement, which comes in many varieties: when performance is judged by a few measures, and the stakes are high (keeping one's job, getting a pay rise or raising the stock price at the time that stock options are vested), people focus on satisfying those measures – often at the expense of other, more important organizational goals that are not measured.** *The best-known example is 'teaching to the test', a widespread phenomenon that has distorted primary and secondary education in the United States since the adoption of the No Child Left Behind Act of 2001.*

Short-termism is another negative. *Measured performance encourages what the US sociologist Robert K. Merton in 1936 called 'the imperious immediacy of interests . . . where the actor's paramount concern with the foreseen immediate consequences excludes consideration of further or other consequences'. In short, advancing short-term goals at the expense of long-range considerations . . .* **To the debit side of the ledger must also be added the transactional costs of metrics . . .**

The ability to vary the pace of reading based on the text

An expert reader is always tracking the *main idea* of the passage and this varies his reading speed as per the importance of the sentence, deliberately reading *context providers* at a very fast pace, slowing down below normal (if required) at *main arguments* and reading *supporting ideas* at a normal pace (slightly faster, if possible).

The difference between Easy, Moderate and Tough passages

If a passage is EASY, then the number of main arguments will be few and a bulk of the sentences will be context providers that you can read at a fast pace—more than half the passage will be in *light grey*, which will end up being the dominant colour. Such passages can be read at a faster rate and will not require you to concentrate very hard.

If a passage is MODERATE, then the context providers will comprise around 25 to 40 per cent of the passage; the passage will have more supporting ideas. Such passages can be read at your normal or slightly above normal speed and will require your usual levels of concentration. The *Digital Colonization* passage belongs to this category.

If a passage is TOUGH, there will barely be any context providers; almost every sentence will be either a supporting idea or a main idea. Your reading speed will definitely slow down and you will be required to put in more concentration. The *Metric Fixation* passage is tough because there are no context providers—all sentences are *dark grey* or *black*. All the examples are not background but premises used to prove the argument.

So, an expert critical reader will not be going through the five passages with the same speed and concentration. The reading time per passage can vary from as low as two minutes to as high as five minutes based on the passage.

It is no different from cricket—a good length, medium-paced delivery pitching way outside the off stump and not doing much will require far less concentration than a length delivery bowled at pace, close to the off stump, and darting in or moving away.

The ability to pick up the direction of the passage very early

Just like great batsmen are characterized by their ability to pick up the length of the ball very early and thus move into position—back or forward—early (hence the usual comment—he has so much time to play his strokes), those with advanced reading skills can pick up the direction of the passage at an earlier stage. This stems from their understanding of the connotations of particular words and phrases.

The word *fixation,* for example, is used primarily with a negative connotation, being *fixated* on something means being unduly obsessed with something. It is used in contexts such as the one used in the *Metric Fixation* passage, the *fixation* with particular ideas or concepts.

So while reading the Metric Fixation passage, expert critical readers would, from the very first sentence itself, deduce that the author is going to highlight why this fixation is not healthy.

More and more companies, government agencies, educational institutions and philanthropic organizations are today in the grip of a new phenomenon: 'metric fixation'.

That the author thinks it is unhealthy is also revealed by the usage of the word *grip*, which means 'hold'; being in the *grip* of something is usually used in a negative context—fear *gripped* the population. This does not mean that *grip* is never used in a positive context; for example, a *gripping* movie means that the movie sustains your interest.

While varying reading speed by differentiating between context providers and other sentences is a skill that can be picked up in a moderate amount of time, picking up direction based on usage is something that is based on the cumulative reading one has done over a long period of time. This is not meant to be discouraging since even without this skill, it is possible to get high scores by following the processes outlined above with a good reading speed.

What I have done with this method is to try to break down the steps that those who are really good at Verbal Reasoning undertake subconsciously.

5

The RC Question Types

While the technique will be more than sufficient to tackle all question types, there are particular types of mistakes that test-takers are bound to make and are liable to make on particular question types.

Broadly, the questions that follow an RC passage fall into four types:

1. Main Idea and Primary Purpose Questions
2. Specific Detail Questions
3. Inference Questions
4. Logical Structure Questions

This chapter will deal with the specific errors that you can get lured into and how to avoid them.

Main Idea and Primary Purpose Questions

The biggest problem that most test-takers have is differentiating between the main idea and primary purpose. The easiest way to illustrate the difference between the two is through the analogy of PhD students.

If you ask PhD students what their PhD is about, they will tell you the topic and the argument they want to explore. For example, globalization and the effect of income inequality. This—the goal of their research—is the primary purpose.

After they are done with their thesis and presentation, if you ask them about their findings, they will tell you they concluded, for example, that globalization resulted in an increase in income inequality in urban areas more than in rural areas. This—the finding of their research—is the main idea.

The options of a primary purpose question thus follow a particular pattern:

- to *elaborate* the benefits of a new drug
- to *discuss* the implications of a new finding

- to *evaluate* the pros and cons of a new technology
- to *highlight* the negative consequences of metric fixation
- to *argue* that healthcare resources should be directed towards primary care and not tertiary care

Sometimes the main idea and the primary purpose can come together in an option question. This happens when the author of the passage is arguing for a particular position.

For example, the last one in the list above—*to argue that healthcare resources should be directed towards primary care and not tertiary care.* The main idea of the passage is that healthcare resources should be directed towards primary care and not tertiary care.

Main idea and primary purpose questions are not as frequently and as directly asked on the CAT as on the GMAT and the GRE, on which one question per passage is most likely to be either main idea or primary purpose.

The reason being, as I stated earlier, the fact that the passages on these tests are usually taken from scholarly journals and hence, they are written with a clear focus and purpose, which is not the case with the passages on the CAT.

How to differentiate between two really close main idea or primary purpose options

Let us take the Metric Fixation passage and look at two close options to the primary purpose question:

- To highlight the negative consequences of metric fixation to measure performance
- To argue for a change from using metrics to measure performance by listing the drawbacks of the same

Rule 1: Always choose the option that is clearly stated and not strongly implied.

The first rule is that the main idea or primary purpose should be something that is clearly stated in the passage and not implied. While the author lists all the negatives of metric fixation, making strong arguments in the process, he or she does not outrightly say that it is time we stop using metrics to measure performance.

The passage strongly implies that the author is most likely to support another form of performance measurement in place of metrics. But the author does not call for the same.

You can think of the author giving a talk to a group of business leaders as part of a management conference. It is up to the business leaders to decide whether they want to continue using metrics or explore other options.

Rule 2: How many paragraphs has the author spent on the idea.

The second way to differentiate between two close options on primary purpose and main idea questions is to see how many paragraphs the author has devoted to what is mentioned in each option. The right option always captures the idea and purpose that the whole passage is leading up to and not just one idea.

Rule 3: Check whether the topic of the passage is mentioned in the option.

The third way to detect an incorrect option is to check whether the topic of the passage is mentioned in the option. The right answer always has to have the topic of the passage.

Let us look at the main idea question of the Metric Fixation passage discussed in the previous chapter. If you need to, you can go back and read the whole passage once again before attempting the question.

What is the main idea that the author is trying to highlight in the passage?

A. Performance measurement needs to be precise and cost-effective to be useful for evaluating organizational performance.
B. Evaluating performance by using measurable performance metrics may misguide organizational goal achievement.
C. Long-term organizational goals should not be ignored for short-term measures of organizational success.
D. All kinds of organizations are now relying on metrics to measure performance and to give rewards and punishments.

Options (A) and (D) deal with only one part of the passage—(A) only with the last paragraph, (D) only with the first paragraph and can thus be eliminated.

Option (C) does not have the topic of the passage—metric fixation—and can thus be eliminated, making option (B) the right one.

Specific Detail Questions

These questions refer to direct questions based on specific parts of the passage.

- Which of the following statements about Neanderthals is true as per the passage?
- Based on the passage, all the following statements about zoning are true EXCEPT?
- According to the passage, the rise in the number of applications is because of?

Honestly, these are the easiest questions of the lot since the answer is clearly stated in the passage and does not involve drawing any inferences. So how do the test-setters go about setting a trap for you?

The biggest trap on specific detail questions is that the first half of the option will be exactly the same as that mentioned in the passage. It will also have the same words as those used in the passage, leading you to quickly choose the option only to find out later that you made a mistake since the second half is blatantly wrong and not mentioned in the passage.

In order to avoid making mistakes on specific detail questions, you should always read the question, check with the relevant portion of the passage, frame your shadow answer and then go to the options.

Also, when you are checking with the relevant portion, do not just read the sentence containing the word or phrase mentioned in the question, read the whole sentence and also the sentence preceding or succeeding it, if required.

Do not forget that *RC is not match the following*—matching words and phrases from the question with those in the passage.

Inference Questions

Inference questions on RCs end up posing the most problems for test-takers; it is on these questions that test-takers end up tripping up the most. There are two types of inference questions:

The **Specific Inference Question**: In such inference questions, the specific idea or part of the passage is clearly stated in the question stem itself:

- Based on the passage, which of the following can be inferred about unemployment rates?
- Which of the following statements about carbon credits is the author most likely to agree with?

The **Generic Inference Question**: In such questions, you have no idea which part of the passage the question belongs to:

- Which of the following can be inferred based on the passage?
- Which of the following inferences is best supported by the passage?

The best way to avoid making mistakes on *inference* questions is by using the following guidelines:

- For specific questions pertaining to a particular part of the passage, always go back to that part of the passage and frame a shadow answer before you go to the options.
- For generic questions, you cannot frame a shadow answer; you need to budget more time, go to the specific part of the passage for each option and then eliminate or keep the option.
- Once you frame a shadow answer or read the relevant portion of the passage, always ask yourself: Can this option be inferred based purely on the information given in the passage?

Every possibility based on the passage is not an inference—an inference is a valid deduction. So, always ask yourself: Is this a valid deduction or only a possibility?

Logical Structure Questions

Possibly the most underrated of question types, logical structure questions induce more errors than other question types. Test-takers place a lot of focus on inference questions and ignore the mistakes they make on this question type since they feel it is a question that is very specific to the passage and not a generic question type.

Logical structure questions are usually framed as follows:

- The author cites the example of the scavengers in order to?
- The Supreme Court verdict is used to highlight which of the following?

The reason why most test-takers make a mistake on these questions is that they do not understand that the question is not related to the scavengers or the Supreme Court verdict.

The question is related to the larger argument that the author intends to make. The example is used to drive home the larger point that has been made either before the example or after. The question is asking you to identify the larger argument.

To ensure that you do not make a mistake on this question type, **always read the preceding and succeeding sentence, when it comes to a logical structure question; that is how you see the structure.**

Otherwise you will always be tempted to choose the option that refers to the specific content of the example, option (A), instead of the right one, option (B) as shown in the example below.

The author cites the example of the scavengers in order to:

A. show that scavengers work in jobs that put their health at serious risk
B. show that in some professions, medical insurance should be mandatorily provided

Miscellaneous Question Types

The four question types mentioned are the ones that are asked without fail almost on every passage. There are some miscellaneous question types that turn up occasionally that test your understanding of the whole passage.

Style and Tone Questions

From the name itself, it is clear that this question is not about WHAT the author said but HOW the author has said things.

The questions are usually framed in the following ways:

*   Which of the following best captures the tone of the passage/author?
*   Which of the following best captures the attitude of the author?
*   What part of the passage best captures the way ideas are presented in the passage?

Style refers to the way the ideas have been expressed in terms of language used and organization of the content.

Tone refers to the attitude of the author towards the topic at hand or in the context of the passage.

There are two steps to correctly answering a style and tone question.

Step 1: Focus on the kind of language and arguments used in the passage

*   Has the author used formal language or flowery, literary language?
*   Has the author taken a very strong position and attacked what they are against or has the author calmly stated the drawbacks?
*   Has the author presented a balanced view by presenting both sides or has the author been unclear in explaining their position?

Step 2: Identify the answer option that best captures the author's style and tone

For this, you need to know the list of words that best captures various styles, tones and positions. With respect to a topic or an issue, an author can be in *agreement*, in *disagreement* or *neutral*. But within each of these three positions, the degree and way of expressing the same can vary.

What are the words that indicate support or a supportive tone or attitude?
Positive, affirmative, adulatory, approbatory, laudatory, panegyric, eulogistic.

What are the words that indicate a negative and critical tone?
Negative, disapproving, derogatory, trenchant, withering, critical, sarcastic, caustic, acerbic.

What are the words that indicate a neutral tone or stance?
Balanced, indifferent, disinterested, equivocal.

What are the words that indicate a style of writing?
Academic, scholarly, journalistic, literary, informal, formal, stylized, metaphorical, allegorical.

These are just a few words and all words have distinctive shades of meaning, so please refer to a dictionary and understand when each of these is used.

Style and tone questions have rarely appeared on the CAT in the last few years and even if they have, it has always been the one odd question. The reason for this is that unless the passages themselves are written in a particularly distinctive style, all passages more or less fall into the same category. It follows that there is no point mugging up words just for this one question type.

Source of the passage

This question type is closely related to style and tone but goes one step further. Instead of directly asking you for the style in which the passage is written, it asks you to go one step further and identify in what sort of a publication is such a passage likely to appear—a newspaper, a magazine, a journal, a PhD thesis, etc.

Based on the kind of the language used and the way the arguments are presented, one has to identify the source.

If the language is casual, expressive, literary, indirect and flowery, it is likely to be from a magazine or a newspaper. The more formal, direct and precise the language, the more likely it is to appear in a scholarly, academic or niche journal or be a PhD thesis.

Title Questions

Another extremely rare question type is the title question. These questions give you a set of four options and ask you to choose which will be the most suitable *title* for the passage.

Since a title question is a summary question, you have to go back to the main idea and primary purpose of the passage and then see which option is closest to them.

6

The Paragraph to Questions Approach:
An Alternative Reading Strategy

What I have outlined in the preceding chapters is the Passage to Questions method—read each paragraph, make a note of the main idea, at the end of the passage make a note of the main idea of the passage as a whole, and then proceed to the questions one by one.

The problem with reading the entire passage first is that it is a great strategy for those who are exceptionally good and comfortable with reading long texts. What does being exceptionally good and comfortable mean?

1. The ability to read through the whole passage without losing concentration and the thread of the passage
2. The ability to answer the primary purpose, the central idea or other summary questions (questions that test your understanding of the passage as a whole) without going back to the passage
3. The ability to remember the exact part of the passage to go back to find the answer to a specific question

With most Indian test-takers, the first ability itself is suspect. While they might start with the best of intentions, by the time they reach the middle of the passage they:

- start losing interest
- start sneaking a peek at the questions
- somehow manage to reach the end, or
- start going back and forth between the questions and the passage

So, it is not a surprise that many test-takers who have a problem with RCs, experiment with what seems to them the best way forward—the Questions to Passage method—read the questions and then search for the answers in the passage.

As a strategy, this is always problematic since this converts RC to Match the Following. The focus shifts from understanding the context in its entirety to understanding narrow parts of the passage. All in all, it is a strategy that should be dumped straightaway.

But this still does not solve the problem. I found that despite my best intentions and their best efforts, a lot of students were finding it very difficult to execute the Passage to Questions reading method for genuine reasons:

- slow reading speed resulting in a constant fear that the clock will run out
- inability to retain large chunks of information for extended periods

And since my goal is always to help students improve their scores, I came up with a new method—*the Paragraph to Questions method.*

The Paragraph to Questions Method

What I would recommend to most test-takers is a third way that addresses the problems of the first two.

1. Read one paragraph, go through the questions to check if there is any question related to it.
2. If there is a question related to the paragraph, then solve it immediately.
3. If there is no question related to it, then go ahead to the next paragraph and repeat the exercise.
4. Leave all summary questions or questions that require you to read the whole passage for the end.
5. If the paragraphs are short in length, say four lines or fewer, you can read two at a time and then go to the questions.

The biggest advantage of this method is increased accuracy due to better short-term retention.

Questions are not sequenced in the same sequence as the paragraphs—the first question will not be based on the first paragraph. Since the questions are jumbled for all test-takers, the question based on the first paragraph can very well be the last one in the sequence and by the time you reach it, you are likely to have forgotten the content and might need to read that paragraph again.

With this method, you will not need to re-read the paragraph and your accuracy on specific questions can increase significantly because you have just read it. The other advantage is that this method automatically breaks down the entire passage into smaller chunks, making it easier for test-takers who cannot retain large amounts of information.

Let us take an actual CAT passage and solve it using *the Paragraph to Questions method.*

Passage I, 544 words

Creativity is at once our most precious resource and our most inexhaustible one. As anyone who has ever spent any time with children knows, every single human being is born creative; every human being is innately endowed with the ability to combine and recombine data, perceptions, materials and ideas, and devise new ways of thinking and doing. What fosters creativity? More than anything else: the presence of other creative people. The big myth is that creativity is the province of great individual geniuses. In fact, creativity is a social process. Our biggest creative breakthroughs come when people learn from, compete with, and collaborate with other people.

Cities are the true fonts of creativity. With their diverse populations, dense social networks, and public spaces where people can meet spontaneously and serendipitously, they spark and catalyze new ideas. With their infrastructure for finance, organization and trade, they allow those ideas to be swiftly actualized.

As for what staunches creativity, that's easy, if ironic. It's the very institutions that we build to manage, exploit and perpetuate the fruits of creativity—our big bureaucracies, and sad to say, too many of our schools. Creativity is disruptive; schools and organizations are regimented, standardized and stultifying.

The education expert Sir Ken Robinson points to a 1968 study reporting on a group of 1600 children who were tested over time for their ability to think in out-of-the-box ways. When the children were between three and five years old, 98 per cent achieved positive scores. When they were eight to ten, only 32 per cent passed the same test, and only 10 per cent at thirteen to fifteen. When 2,80,000 twenty-five-year-olds took the test, just 2 per cent passed. By the time we are adults, our creativity has been wrung out of us.

I once asked the great urbanist Jane Jacobs what makes some places more creative than others. She said, essentially, that the question was an easy one. All cities, she said, were filled with creative people; that's our default state as people. But some cities had more than their shares of leaders, people and institutions that blocked out that creativity. She called them 'squelchers'.

Creativity (or the lack of it) follows the same general contours of the great socio-economic divide— our rising inequality—that plagues us. According to my own estimates, roughly a third of us across the United States, and perhaps as much as half of us in our most creative cities—are able to do work which engages our creative faculties to some extent, whether as artists, musicians, writers, techies, innovators, entrepreneurs, doctors, lawyers, journalists or educators—those of us who work with our minds. That leaves a group that I term 'the other 66 per cent', who toil in low-wage rote and rotten jobs—if they have jobs at all—in which their creativity is subjugated, ignored or wasted.

Creativity itself is not in danger. It's flourishing all around us—in science and technology, arts and culture, in our rapidly revitalizing cities. But we still have a long way to go if we want to build a truly creative society that supports and rewards the creativity of each and every one of us.

1. In the author's view, cities promote human creativity for all the following reasons EXCEPT that they contain spaces that:

    A) enable people to meet and share new ideas
    B) expose people to different and novel ideas, because they are home to varied groups of people
    C) provide the financial and institutional networks that enable ideas to become reality
    D) provide access to cultural activities that promote new and creative ways of thinking

2. The author uses 'ironic' in the third paragraph to point out that:

   A) people need social contact rather than isolation to nurture their creativity
   B) institutions created to promote creativity eventually stifle it
   C) the larger the creative population in a city, the more likely it is to be stifled
   D) large bureaucracies and institutions are the inevitable outcome of successful cities

3. The central idea of this passage is that:

   A) social interaction is necessary to nurture creativity
   B) creativity and ideas are gradually declining in all societies
   C) the creativity divide is widening in societies in line with socio-economic trends
   D) more people should work in jobs that engage their creative faculties

4. Jane Jacobs believed that cities that are more creative:

   A) have to struggle to retain their creativity
   B) have to 'squelch' unproductive people and promote creative ones
   C) have leaders and institutions that do not block creativity
   D) typically do not start off as creative hubs

5. The 1968 study is used here to show that:

   A) as they get older, children usually learn to be more creative
   B) schooling today does not encourage creative thinking in children
   C) the more children learn, the less creative they become
   D) technology today prevents children from being creative

6. The author's conclusions about the most 'creative cities' in the US (paragraph 6) are based on his assumption that:

   A) people who work with their hands are not doing creative work
   B) more than half the population works in non-creative jobs
   C) only artists, musicians, writers and so on should be valued in a society
   D) most cities ignore or waste the creativity of low-wage workers

Paragraph 1

A quick scan through the questions shows that there is no question based on the first paragraph. So you can move to the second one without answering any question. Do not try to remember questions; if you do so, then you will again be doing method 2—match the following instead of RC.

Paragraph 2

The first question is a specific question based on paragraph 2. It is an EXCEPT question that is asking you to identify the reason that is NOT stated to make the claim that cities promote creativity.

This has to be the easiest RC question of all time—A, B and C are clearly stated in the passage, D is not mentioned anywhere. In effect, you have 3 marks in the bag in under 4 minutes.

Paragraph 3

As you start reading the first sentence of the third paragraph itself you should know that there will be a question on this; the first sentence itself says—*it's ironic*. It goes without saying that they will test your understanding of what *ironic* means. The paragraph itself explains it. You go to the questions to find the question based on it and pocket 3 more marks.

It is again pretty direct and you should have no trouble confirming option B as the right option. By now you should have 6 marks in 6 minutes.

If you find this question tough, then I am afraid there is a fundamental comprehension problem that no amount of strategies or shortcuts can solve. It might sound harsh but you might have to really take another shot at the CAT and spend a lot of time improving your ability in reading and comprehending text written in English.

If you have taken 10 minutes to score these 6 marks from three paragraphs, then reading speed is a major issue. The only way out is to practise RCs alone non-stop for a week so that you put so much stress on your reading muscle that it has to grow.

Paragraph 4

After reading this paragraph, you should again scan the questions and you will find that question 5 is related to it. This is where you will first encounter a mild case of 'I am caught between two options'. Options B and C might seem to be vying for your vote. So how do you break this deadlock?

The first step is to identify the superficial difference between the options. When caught between two options:

1. Phrase the difference between the two options.
2. See which one is relevant to the question and eliminate if possible.
3. If not, go the specific part of the passage.
4. If you are still unable to break the deadlock, go the previous paragraph.

Option B—Schooling smothers creativity
Option C—Learning smothers creativity

Even without going back to the paragraph, you can see that C has to be wrong! Between learning and schooling, the latter is definitely the culprit. If you go to the paragraph, it will be clear that Ken Robinson is an education expert and he is referring to schools. If it is still not clear, then go to the previous paragraph; the last sentence screams the answer out loud. How are we doing so far? 9 marks in 8 minutes.

Paragraph 5

There is a question on this paragraph as well—question 4—and as mildly indirect as a question can get. If you are keeping count, 12 marks in 10 minutes.

Paragraph 6

The last question is based on this. It is an assumption question that is pretty direct.

The author says—in most of our cities one-third, and in some half, of our people work in creative jobs or jobs of the mind, while the other two-thirds have no jobs or do rotten jobs. The assumption is captured only by option A.

Initially, I only wrote this much about the last question of this passage. But then I realized that the test-takers with weak VA scores have a basic problem with a few fundamentals. They do not clearly look at what the question is asking but only look at the content that the question refers to.

What do I mean by this?

The last question is an assumption question. What is an assumption?

Something that is not stated but is central to drawing a conclusion. Unlike the real world in which anything that is stated but not proven is not an assumption, on aptitude tests, it is an incorrect premise. Which is why an assumption is also called the missing premise.

Premise 1 + Missing Premise (Assumption) = Conclusion

The paragraph is asking you to identify the assumption behind the conclusion drawn in paragraph 6. So, before you go to the options, go back and paraphrase the conclusion—Creativity divide mirrors the socio-economic divide.

Premise 1—Cities that are more creative have half of the population doing work of the mind. Cities that are less creative have one-third doing work of the mind.

Premise 2—The rest of the population is doing rotten jobs or is unemployed.

The conclusion has the term—creativity. The two premises have the terms work of the mind and rotten work. So, the missing premise has to connect creativity and work of the mind or rotten work. Only the first option does that.

So, when it comes to assumption questions, please follow this process. Otherwise, you will always end up being caught between the option that is relevant to the content but is not the actual assumption.

End of the passage

At the end of the exercise, you are left with one unanswered summary question. This is one of those typical CAT RC questions on which the options frustrate me since I don't find any of them to be precisely correct.

So, the best option on CAT RC questions: **reject don't select**. Your heart won't leap and dance when you see the correct option; you have to reject and be happy with whatever is left.

The central idea of this passage is that:

A)   social interaction is necessary to nurture creativity
B)   creativity and ideas are gradually declining in all societies
C)   the creativity divide is widening in societies in line with socio-economic trends
D)   more people should work in jobs that engage their creative faculties

If we go by rejection then:

- A can be kept
- B can be rejected since the last paragraph categorically says that creativity is flourishing
- C can be rejected since the passage only says that the creative divide follows the socio-economic divide; it does not say that the divide has increased
- D can be kept

Now we boil down to two options again and this is a summary question. Assuming you are not able to do the deadlock at this stage, what do you do?

You can defend and not score instead of getting out.

Should you always mark an answer for every RC question you encounter?

The summary question above is a poorly made one since neither option exactly captures the central idea. Now, if I look at my time spent so far, I have 15 marks in about 16 minutes, which is great from a marks per minute (MPM) perspective.

So, do I need to break my head and waste my time over this silly question? No, I will be better off moving on without collecting a negative.

Test-takers refuse to consider letting a question go an option. If they have spent so much time reading the passage, they think they might as well answer the question.

The odds of getting it right when stuck between two options are still 50 per cent, provided you haven't eliminated the correct option!

So, do yourself a favour—defend and not score instead of getting out.

Just to close things on this passage, between the options A and D, I would choose A since it covers a larger portion of the passage and the author is not directly making a claim that more people should be doing creative jobs. The author only says that more people can be in creative jobs.

I know that one passage isn't enough to prove my point. So let's take up all the passages from a recent CAT exam and analyse them through this lens.

Passage II, 536 words

During the frigid season it's often necessary to nestle under a blanket to try to stay warm. The temperature difference between the blanket and the air outside is so palpable that we often have trouble leaving our warm refuge. Many plants and animals similarly hunker down, relying on snow cover for safety from winter's harsh conditions. The small area between the snowpack and the ground, called the subnivium, might be the most important ecosystem that you have never heard of.

The subnivium is so well-insulated and stable that its temperature holds steady at around 32 degrees Fahrenheit. Although that might still sound cold, a constant temperature of 32 degrees Fahrenheit can often be 30 to 40 degrees warmer than the air temperature during the peak of winter. Because of this large temperature difference, a wide variety of species depend on the subnivium for winter protection.

For many organisms living in temperate and Arctic regions, the difference between being under the snow or outside it is a matter of life and death. Consequently, disruptions to the subnivium brought about by climate change will affect everything from population dynamics to nutrient cycling through the ecosystem.

The formation and stability of the subnivium requires more than a few flurries. Winter ecologists have suggested that eight inches of snow is necessary to develop a stable layer of insulation. Depth is not the only factor, however. More accurately, the stability of the subnivium depends on the interaction between snow depth and snow density. Imagine being under a stack of blankets that are all flattened and pressed together. When compressed, the blankets essentially form one compacted layer. In contrast, when they are lightly placed on top of one another, their insulative capacity increases because the air pockets between them trap heat. Greater depths of low-density snow are therefore better at insulating the ground.

Both depth and density of snow are sensitive to temperature. Scientists are now beginning to explore how climate change will affect the subnivium, as well as the species that depend on it. At first glance, warmer winters seem beneficial for species have difficulty surviving subzero temperatures; however, as with most ecological phenomena, the consequences are not so straightforward. Research has shown that the snow season (the period when snow is more likely than rain) has become shorter since 1970. When rain falls on snow, it increases the density of the snow and reduces its insulative capacity. Therefore, even though winters are expected to become warmer overall from future climate change, the subnivium will tend to become colder and more variable with less protection from the above-ground temperatures.

The effects of a colder subnivium are complex. For example, shrubs such as crowberry and alpine azalea that grow along the forest floor tend to block the wind and so retain higher depths of snow around them. This captured snow helps to keep soils insulated and in turn increases plant decomposition and nutrient release. In field experiments, researchers removed a portion of the snow cover to investigate the importance of the subnivium's insulation. They found that soil frost in the snow-free area resulted in damage to plant roots and sometimes even the death of the plant.

1. The purpose of this passage is to:

    A) introduce readers to a relatively unknown ecosystem: the subnivium.
    B) explain how the subnivium works to provide shelter and food to several species.
    C) outline the effects of climate change on the subnivium.
    D) draw an analogy between the effect of blankets on humans and of snow cover on species living in the subnivium.

2. All of the following statements are true EXCEPT:

    A) Snow depth and snow density both influence the stability of the subnivium.
    B) Climate change has some positive effects on the subnivium.
    C) The subnivium maintains a steady temperature that can be 30 to 40 degrees warmer than the winter air temperature.
    D) Researchers have established the adverse effects of dwindling snow cover on the subnivium.

3. Based on this extract, the author would support which one of the following actions?

    A) The use of snow machines in winter to ensure snow cover of at least eight inches.
    B) Government action to curb climate change.
    C) Adding nutrients to the soil in winter.
    D) Planting more shrubs in areas of the short snow season.

4. In paragraph 6, the author provides examples of crowberry and alpine azalea to demonstrate that:

    A) despite frigid temperatures, several species survive in temperate and Arctic regions.
    B) due to frigid temperatures in the temperate and Arctic regions, plant species that survive tend to be shrubs rather than trees.
    C) the crowberry and alpine azalea are abundant in temperate and Arctic regions.
    D) the stability of the subnivium depends on several interrelated factors, including shrubs on the forest floor.

5. Which one of the following statements can be inferred from the passage?

    A) In an ecosystem, altering any one element has a ripple effect on all others.
    B) Climate change affects temperate and Arctic regions more than equatorial or arid ones.
    C) A compact layer of wool is warmer than a similarly compact layer of goose down.
    D) The loss of the subnivium, while tragic, will affect only temperate and Arctic regions.

6. In paragraph 1, the author uses blankets as a device to:

    A) evoke the bitter cold of winter in the minds of readers.
    B) explain how blankets work to keep us warm.
    C) draw an analogy between blankets and the snowpack.
    D) alert readers to the fatal effects of excessive exposure to the cold.

Paragraph 1

The question on the first paragraph is way towards the end, the last one. Why does the author give the example of blankets? To show that the snowpack does for animals what blankets do for human beings. The only option that has both subnivium and snowpack is option C!

Going through the questions, you would have seen that the only other specific question is related to para 6; all the rest are based on the whole passage. So you can drop going from para to question until you reach para 6, which anyway is the last paragraph.

Since there are no questions pertaining to a single paragraph, you are left with no option but to read the whole passage before moving to the questions. It does make sense to write short one-liners for each para—para content outline—as you move ahead just to keep track.

- What is the subnivium?
- What does the subnivium do?
- Why is the subnivium important?
- How is the subnivium formed?
- How will climate change negatively affect the subnivium?
- Effects of a colder subnivium due to climate change

Question 1

To answer primary purpose questions, it is always useful to look at the para content outline we made above and analyse the same—four paras about the subnivium and two about climate change and the subnivium. So the two protagonists of this passage are the subnivium and climate change. The primary purpose thus must have both of these protagonists.

Options A, B and D are ruled out, leaving us with only C.

Question 2

This is a detail question and it makes sense to check the relevant para to verify the information. Everything EXCEPT B is stated. Another way to eliminate: Can climate change ever have any positive effect in general? Hence, B!

Question 3

Since the author is talking about the importance of the subnivium and the large-scale impacts of climate change on the same, he or she would support steps to prevent climate change—all the rest of the options cure the symptoms but not the disease—making option B the right answer.

Question 4

The beginning of the paragraph itself says that the effects of the colder subnivium are complex and then talks about the role played by shrubs and how the decomposition of shrubs releases nutrients.

The example of shrubs is used to support the argument that the effects of the colder subnivium are complex.

Only one option has both the words 'subnivium' and 'shrubs' in it, option D! The word 'complex' has been paraphrased as several unrelated factors.

Question 5

An inference question that is based on the whole passage. In case you forgot, always choose rejection over selection.

Option A cannot be rejected since it says everything is interrelated, which is what the passage is saying—climate change to the subnivium to shrubs to nutrients. So, keep option A.

- Option B is incorrect since we do not have any information about other regions.
- Option C will be a rocket since you might be coming across the term 'goose down' for the first time! Move to the next option.
- Option D cannot be inferred since there is no information about the effect on other regions.

You have two options, A and C. Since you do not understand C and cannot reject A, you can either mark A or leave the question.

Remember you have already scored 15 marks in quick time. So, do you want to break your head or waste time over 'goose down'? No.

The question-maker should have given some thought to the fact that the alternate meaning of the word 'down' itself is something that many test-takers would have absolutely no clue about. Knowing the meaning of the word *down*, when used a noun, should have no bearing on determining reasoning skills for a career in management!

Down as a noun refers to the soft, fine, fluffy feathers that form the first covering of a young bird or an insulating layer below the contour feathers of an adult bird.

The fourth paragraph says that low-density snow is warmer. So, which one is less dense—wool or goose down? Goose down, and hence it will be warmer, making C incorrect and A correct.

Passage III, 531 words

The end of the age of the internal combustion engine is in sight. There are small signs everywhere: the shift to hybrid vehicles is already underway among manufacturers. Volvo has announced it will make no purely petrol-engine cars after 2019 and Tesla has just started selling its first electric car aimed squarely at the middle classes: the Tesla 3 sells for $35,000 in the US, and 400,000 people have put down a small, refundable deposit towards one. Several thousand have already taken delivery, and the company hopes to sell half a million more next year. This is a remarkable figure for a machine with a fairly short-range and a very limited number of specialized charging stations.

Some of it reflects the remarkable abilities of Elon Musk, the company's founder, as a salesman, engineer, and a man able to get the most out his factory workers and the governments he deals with. Mr Musk is selling a dream that the world wants to believe in.

This last may be the most important factor in the story. The private car is a device of immense practical help and economic significance but at the same time a theatre for myths of unattainable self-fulfilment. The one thing you will never see in a car advertisement is traffic, even though that is the element in which drivers spend their lives. Every single driver in a traffic jam is trying to escape from it, yet it is the inevitable consequence of mass car ownership.

The sleek and swift electric car is at one level merely the most contemporary fantasy of autonomy and power. But it might also disrupt our exterior landscapes nearly as much as the fossil fuel-engine car did in the last century. Electrical cars would, of course, pollute far less than fossil fuel-driven ones; instead of oil reserves, the rarest materials for batteries would make undeserving despots and their dynasties fantastically rich. Petrol stations would disappear. The air in cities would once more be breathable and their streets as quiet as those of Venice. This isn't an unmixed good. Cars that were as silent as bicycles would still be as dangerous as they are now to anyone they hit without audible warning.

The dream goes further than that. The electric cars of the future will be so thoroughly equipped with sensors and reaction mechanisms that they will never hit anyone. Just as brakes don't let you skid today, the steering wheel of tomorrow will swerve you away from danger before you have even noticed it.

This is where the fantasy of autonomy comes full circle. The logical outcome of cars which need no driver is that they will become cars which need no owner either. Instead, they will work as taxis do, summoned at will but only for the journeys we actually need. This is the future towards which Uber is working. The ultimate development of the private car will be to reinvent public transport. Traffic jams will be abolished only when the private car becomes a public utility. What then will happen to our fantasies of independence? We'll all have to take to electrically powered bicycles.

1. Which of the following statements best reflects the author's argument?

   A) Hybrid and electric vehicles signal the end of the age of internal combustion engines.
   B) Elon Musk is a remarkably gifted salesman.
   C) The private car represents an unattainable myth of independence.
   D) The future Uber car will be environmentally friendlier than even the Tesla.

2. The author points out all of the following about electric cars EXCEPT:

   A) Their reliance on rare materials for batteries will support despotic rule.
   B) They will reduce air and noise pollution.
   C) They will not decrease the number of traffic jams.
   D) They will ultimately undermine rather than further driver autonomy.

3. According to the author, the main reason for Tesla's remarkable sales is that:

   A) in the long run, the Tesla is more cost-effective than fossil fuel-driven cars.
   B) the US government has announced a tax subsidy for Tesla buyers.
   C) the company is rapidly upscaling the number of specialized charging stations for customer convenience.
   D) people believe in the autonomy represented by private cars.

4. The author comes to the conclusion that:

   A) car drivers will no longer own cars but will have to use public transport.
   B) cars will be controlled by technology that is more efficient than car drivers.
   C) car drivers dream of autonomy but the future may be public transport.
   D) electrically powered bicycles are the only way to achieve autonomy in transportation.

5. In paragraphs 5 and 6, the author provides the example of Uber to argue that:

   A) in the future, electric cars will be equipped with mechanisms that prevent collisions.
   B) in the future, traffic jams will not exist.
   C) in the future, the private car will be transformed into a form of public transport.
   D) in the future, Uber rides will outstrip Tesla sales.

6. In paragraph 6, the author mentions electrically powered bicycles to argue that:

   A) if Musk were a true visionary, he would invest funds in developing electric bicycles.
   B) our fantasies of autonomy might unexpectedly require us to consider electric bicycles.
   C) in terms of environmental friendliness and safety, electric bicycles rather than electric cars are the future.
   D) electric buses are the best form of public transport.

What if the answer is spread out across paragraphs?

What if the answer to a question is spread out over two or three paragraphs and not a single one? And this is not the 'all of the following are stated EXCEPT' type of question but a question specific to one argument. The first paragraph and the question related to it is exactly this type. So let's dive in.

Paragraph 1

As soon as you read the first paragraph and go to the questions, you will come across the question that is related to it, question three, but will you find the answer in it?

The last sentence of this paragraph says: This is a remarkable figure for a machine with a fairly short-range and a very limited number of specialized charging stations.

The question—*According to the author, the main reason for Tesla's remarkable sales is that . . .*

The sentence says why the sales figure is remarkable. The question is asking you for the reason behind this remarkable sales figure and not why the figure is remarkable.

To suggest an analogy, if the passage is saying it is remarkable that such a young kid scored a century on debut, the question is asking how did he manage to score the century?

So, will you find the answer in paragraph 1? No.

Paragraph 2

You know that paragraph 2 will take this forward and give you reasons for this remarkable figure. The first sentence itself states that the partial reason is this. The next sentence gives another reason. At this juncture, since the reason is not yet clear, it makes sense to read the next paragraph. Even if you go to the question and read the options, you will find that none of the options have been mentioned in the first two paras.

Paragraph 3

This states that the most important factor for the sales has been that Mr Musk is selling a dream. What is the dream? The private car is a theatre for myths of unattainable self-fulfilment.

If you go back to question 3 after reading this paragraph, you should be able to answer the question by elimination.

Options A, B and C have nothing to do with a dream that Musk is selling! They can be eliminated. You can mark option D and change the answer if the subsequent paras counter it.

Paragraph 4

The first line of this para will validate your choice of option D: The sleek and swift electric car is at one level merely the most contemporary fantasy of autonomy and power.

Para 1 introduces the question, para 2 hints at the answer, para 3 gives you the answer through rejection and para 4 finally states the answer unequivocally.

This is what is meant by getting a big stride in to get right to the pitch of the ball. Commentators use this phrase most in case of batsmen playing spinners bowling into the rough. It is not a ball to go back to; if you do, you will be rapped on the pads or be bowled by the sharp turn. If you go half forward, it will sneak through the bat-pad gap or take an edge.

The only option is to get a big stride and smother the turn from the rough. You will have to take that big stride, read three paras, and answer the one question.

These are the kind of questions that really test your faith in the process and require you to make minor adjustments. Based on one odd question, test-takers tend to question the whole process and go back to their old methods, which never did them any good in the first place.

By now, you will have seen that the remaining questions are based on paras 5 and 6 and the passage as a whole. So, there's no point going through the questions again. Also, it makes sense to read 5 and 6 together since the questions refer to both 5 and 6, and 6 only.

Paragraphs 5 and 6

Question 5 asks you the reason the author uses the Uber example. The answer is fairly direct—the private car will become public transport as stated in option C.

Question 6 is also fairly easy—we have to buy bicycles to fulfil our fantasies of autonomy.

So you already have 9 marks by going para to questions. This will happen all the time when there are 6 questions; there will be at least 3 questions that refer to specific parts.

If you read the whole passage and then went to the questions, you would have answered questions in a different sequence and that might not be a pleasant experience as you will discover.

In what sequence should you answer the leftover questions?

What is really important when going back to the leftover questions is to pick out the detail questions first and not get stuck on summary questions such as central idea, primary purpose and main argument, which nine out of ten times will end up being tricky, especially if the options are going to use only five or six words! You are better off solving questions such as 'the passage states all the following EXCEPT'.

Question 2

This is again a question that is to be done using the method of rejection.

- Options A and B are clearly stated. It is handling options C and D that gets tricky.
- Option C is stated since the author says, in the last paragraph, that electric cars will not reduce traffic jams. It will result in fewer jams only when people shift from private transport to public transport. So, option C is also true as per the passage. Once you have rejected three options, you are left with the right option.
- Some of you might still feel that option D is implied. Option D, like option C, is not a direct consequence of electric cars, it is an outcome that is possible only when there is a larger shift that happens, of cars from private to public transport.

Now, you have to approach the two summary questions 3 and 6. At this point, you can take a call whether to further invest time to answer potentially tricky summary questions or collect 12 marks and exit.

Question 1

The best way to answer this question is to take each option and see if it best reflects the passage as a whole. What is the passage about if we want to do a para content outline?

- The remarkable sales of electric cars, especially Tesla
- The reason behind the sales of electric cars
- The reason behind the sales of electric cars
- The future imagined with implications of a switch to electric cars
- The future imagined with implications of a switch to electric cars
- The future imagined with implications of a switch to electric cars

The passage is about the reason behind the sales of the electric car and the future imagined with implications of a switch to electric cars.

- Option A refers only to the death of the internal combustion engine and is hence incorrect.
- Option B is limited to Elon Musk.

- Option C talks about the reason behind the sales of electric cars—the dream or myth of independence.
- Option D is not stated anywhere in the passage.

Even if option C is limited, by rejection it is still the best option you are left with.

Question 4

This talks about a conclusion that the author has reached. Whenever it is a conclusion or inference, one has to pay close attention to the wording—terms like *will happen, should happen*, etc.

Now, this is not the simplistic advice that is usually doled out: avoid extreme options. This assumes that authors will never advocate extreme options, which like all assumptions is just that—an assumption.

What I am asking you to do is to verify whether the author has made this specific claim or can it be inferred with certainty—this will happen or this should happen.

Coming to question 4:

- Option A says car drivers will have to use public transport. The passage says that private cars might become redundant; this does not mean that people have to use public transport, they might no longer feel the need to use cars.
- Option B says that technology will be more efficient than drivers, the passage only says that technology can do things that are currently done by drivers, not that it can do it better.
- Option C is mentioned in the last paragraph and also see that the option says 'may be the future', which is exactly what the passage does—imagine a possible future.
- Option D can be eliminated since the passage does not say that bicycles are the only way to autonomy.

From both these passages, you would have seen that going from para to questions can definitely increase your accuracy. Another learning is that rejection is always the best option on CAT RCs when faced with a tough question. And most importantly, you have the option to leave a few questions, having scored enough marks at a quick pace rather than get greedy and waste a lot of time with a few remaining tough ones.

What if there is only one paragraph?

The GMAT has over the years consistently had two long and two short passages—one para passages—in its Verbal Reasoning section.

The single paragraph RC has never appeared in the Verbal Ability section of the CAT—barring the sole passage in a recent year. Even Slot 1 did not have one. Suffice to say that it seems to be by accident rather than by design.

Passage IV, 258 words

Typewriters are the epitome of a technology that has been comprehensively rendered obsolete by the digital age. The ink comes off the ribbon, they weigh a ton, and second thoughts are a disaster. But they are also personal, portable and, above all, private. Type a document and lock it away and more or less the only way anyone else can get it is if you give it to them. That is why the Russians have decided to go back to typewriters in some government offices, and why in the US, some departments have never abandoned them. Yet it is not just their resistance to algorithms and secret surveillance that keeps typewriter production lines—well one, at least—in business (the last British one closed a year ago). Nor is it only the nostalgic appeal of the metal body and the stout well-defined keys that make them popular on eBay. A typewriter demands something particular: attentiveness. By the time the paper is loaded, the ribbon tightened, the carriage returned, the spacing and the margins set, there's a big premium on hitting the right key. That means sorting out ideas, pulling together a kind of order and organizing details before actually striking off. There can be no thinking on screen with a typewriter. Nor are there any easy distractions. No online shopping. No urgent emails. No Twitter. No need even for electricity—perfect for writing in a remote hideaway. The thinking process is accompanied by the encouraging clang of keys, and the ratchet of the carriage return. Ping!

1. Which one of the following best describes what the passage is trying to do?

    A) It describes why people continue to use typewriters even in the digital age.
    B) It argues that typewriters will continue to be used even though they are an obsolete technology.
    C) It highlights the personal benefits of using typewriters.
    D) It shows that computers offer fewer options than typewriters.

2. According to the passage, some governments still use typewriters because:

    A) they do not want to abandon old technologies that may be useful in the future.
    B) they want to ensure that typewriter production lines remain in business.
    C) they like the nostalgic appeal of a typewriter.
    D) they can control who reads the document.

3. The writer praises typewriters for all the following reasons EXCEPT:

    A) Unlike computers, they can only be used for typing.
    B) You cannot revise what you have typed on a typewriter.
    C) Typewriters are noisier than computers.
    D) Typewriters are messier to use than computers.

Now that there is only one paragraph to read, we know there is only one way to go—from the passage to the questions. Once you go to the questions, it becomes important to look at the sequence in which you have to attempt the questions. It is always advisable to finish off the specific detail questions first and then proceed to the summary questions.

The first question is a summary question and hence needs to be left for later.

Question 2

This is a specific detail question that is very direct and I don't need to solve it for you to arrive at the answer as option D.

Did you notice the paraphrasing? The passage says 'the only way anyone can get a typewritten document is if you hand it over', which is why some governments have reverted to them. This has been paraphrased to: 'they can control who reads the document'.

Very often, test-takers are subconsciously looking for the same wording to be used in the options, as in the passage. This expectation tends to have two negative fallouts.

- Falling for trap options that use *the same phrasing as the passage* but *tweak the logic*.
- Tending to quickly reject the correct option since it uses different words.

So, ensure that you are reading for logic and not for phrasing.

Question 3

This takes paraphrasing to a new level and hence, can become tricky. But any tricky question can become easy if you go by rejection.

- The author clearly says that when typing, there are no distractions and lists them out. This has been paraphrased to: 'they can't be used for anything other than typing'. So, this can be rejected since it is an EXCEPT question.
- Option B clearly states that since you can't revise, you have to be attentive to what you type. So this can be rejected since it is an EXCEPT question.
- Option C is tricky. Does the author praise the noisiness of typewriters? The word/phrase that is used is 'encouraging clang'. Clang does mean noise and the author finds the clang encouraging. The author lists this as one of the things to like about typewriters. So this can be rejected since it is an EXCEPT question.
- The author does not mention the messiness of typewriters as one of the reasons for liking it. So this has to be your answer.

Question 1

Now we can go to the summary question, which is the primary purpose question.

- Option A cannot be rejected since the passage talks about how some governments are using it for security reasons and then lists all the other positive things about typewriters.
- Option B is incorrect since the author makes no claim that typewriters will continue to be used.
- Option C is close but it talks only about the personal benefits and not the security benefits.
- Option D is incorrect since the passage is not about computers versus typewriters.

So by rejection, you are again left with the right option, in this case, A.

If you read this passage in under 3 minutes and answered the other two questions in about 4 minutes, you will have 6 marks in about 7 minutes. If you found yourself even remotely struggling with this question, then you should have asked yourself whether you want to waste time over this.

Passage V, 330 words

Despite their fierce reputation, Vikings may not have always been the plunderers and pillagers popular culture imagines them to be. In fact, they got their start trading in northern European markets, researchers suggest.

Combs carved from animal antlers, as well as comb manufacturing waste and raw antler material has turned up at three archaeological sites in Denmark, including a medieval marketplace in the city of Ribe. A team of researchers from Denmark and the U.K. hoped to identify the species of animal to which the antlers once belonged by analyzing collagen proteins in the samples and comparing them across the animal kingdom, Laura Geggel reports for LiveScience. Somewhat surprisingly, molecular analysis of the artifacts revealed that some combs and other material had been carved from reindeer antlers. Given that reindeer (*Rangifer tarandus*) don't live in Denmark, the researchers posit that it arrived on Viking ships from Norway. Antler craftsmanship, in the form of decorative combs, was part of Viking culture. Such combs served as symbols of good health, Geggel writes. The fact that the animals shed their antlers also made them easy to collect from the large herds that inhabited Norway.

Since the artifacts were found in marketplace areas at each site it's more likely that the Norsemen came to trade rather than pillage. Most of the artifacts also date to the 780s, but some are as old as 725. That predates the beginning of Viking raids on Great Britain by about 70 years. (Traditionally, the so-called 'Viking Age' began with these raids in 793 and ended with the Norman conquest of Great Britain in 1066.) Archaeologists had suspected that the Vikings had experience with long maritime voyages [that] might have preceded their raiding days.

Beyond Norway, these combs would have been a popular industry in Scandinavia as well. It's possible that the antler combs represent a larger trade network, where the Norsemen supplied raw material to craftsmen in Denmark and elsewhere.

1. The primary purpose of the passage is:

    A) to explain the presence of reindeer antler combs in Denmark.
    B) to contradict the widely-accepted beginning date for the Viking Age in Britain, and propose an alternate one.
    C) to challenge the popular perception of Vikings as raiders by using evidence that suggests their early trade relations with Europe.
    D) to argue that besides being violent pillagers, Vikings were also skilled craftsmen and efficient traders.

2. The evidence: 'Most of the artifacts also date to the 780s, but some are as old as 725' has been used in the passage to argue that:

    A) the beginning date of the Viking Age should be changed from 793 to 725.
    B) the Viking raids started as early as 725.

C) some of the antler artifacts found in Denmark and Great Britain could have come from Scandinavia.

D) the Vikings' trade relations with Europe pre-dates the Viking raids.

3. All of the following hold true for Vikings EXCEPT:

A) Vikings brought reindeer from Norway to Denmark for trade purposes.

B) Before becoming the raiders of northern Europe, Vikings had trade relations with European nations.

C) Antler combs, regarded by the Vikings as a symbol of good health, were part of the Viking culture.

D) Vikings, once upon a time, had trade relations with Denmark and Scandinavia.

Paragraphs 1, 2 and 3

Once you read the first two paragraphs, you will see there are no questions on both of them. The first specific question you will encounter will be question 2, which is based on the third paragraph.

This question is like a CR question and the answer to this is option D. The presence of artifacts seventy years before the raids is used to highlight the argument that trade relations began before the raids.

We are now left with questions 1 and question 3. As discussed, always move from detail to summary questions and so you should approach the last question.

Question 3

Option A is not mentioned and hence is the answer since this is an EXCEPT question. The passage says that Vikings might have brought raw material to make combs from Norway to Denmark. The question-maker cleverly slips in the reindeer instead of raw material.

Question 1

The summary question again is best solved by elimination. The passage is about the image of Vikings—they are not the fierce pillagers that they are considered to be.

- Based on this, you can eliminate options A and B since they do not mention or refer to the popular perception, image or view of Vikings.
- Between C and D, the latter says 'besides being violent pillagers'. This means that the author supports or acknowledges the fact that Vikings were violent pillagers. The author nowhere states this. Hence, C.

Whenever you are caught between two options, always look for ways to reject.

7

Notes on the Paragraph to Questions Approach

Over the years, I have got the same set of queries with respect to this approach and I am sure all of you will end up having the same set of issues when you try to execute the method.

Doesn't this method take longer?

You are not going to read all questions each and every time you finish a para or two by the end of the first question. By the time you do it twice, you will remember most of the questions.

If anything, you will save the time going back to the passage to answer specific questions and reading the paragraph all over again since you have completely forgotten para 3 of a six-para passage by the time you read question 5, which is based on the third paragraph!

So, no, it just feels longer in the beginning because you have not perfected it yet.

With this method, I find it tough to retain the overall thought flow of the passage.

Some test-takers have said that they find it difficult to retain the flow of the passage when they break off after every paragraph and go to the questions. They either feel disoriented or they feel that they lose track of the overall flow.

This is absolutely expected in the beginning; it is purely a question of getting used to the method. Once you solve about thirty passages, you will feel comfortable.

I feel that answering questions with respect to a paragraph makes your understanding of the paragraph stronger!

Also, if the passage to questions approach is working well for you and you are getting your desired accuracy on RCs, then there is no need for you to change!

There are passages that have very few specific questions.

Some readers have said that there are passages that have barely any specific questions. There can be a three-question passage with no question from a particular paragraph and all questions are summary questions. But on average, there will be at least two to three questions based on specific paragraphs.

And even if you encounter such a passage, it does not hurt you in any way since you know at the end of the first paragraph, when you read all the questions, that all of them are summary questions and there is no point going back to the questions after every paragraph!

Nothing can compensate for great *critical reading* skills.

The paragraph to questions approach will increase your accuracy on detail questions and improve your ability to navigate through the passage. But it still does not cover the big skill required to master RC.

One of the skills you need to master is to never lose track of what the passage is primarily about. This you should be able to spot in the first two paragraphs.

The really good readers:

- subconsciously follow the thread of the argument as it builds up to, supports or elaborates the main argument

  o they do not need to take notes to do the same

- know that all sentences are not equal and vary their reading speed accordingly

  o they do not read all passages and parts of the passages at the same speed and vary it according to the content

Writing and making notes can make the whole process of solving an RC way longer than it should be. What is a better way?

Pause after each paragraph and ask yourself what the main idea is, which this passage is obsessed with and plant that into your head using the fewest words possible.

If you can master this skill and execute the paragraphs to question strategy, then you will see your RC scores shoot up.

8

Notes on Reading Comprehension

Let us quickly summarize what we have covered so far:

The RC Commandments

I. Identify the right reading strategy for you

Based on what was outlined in the early parts of the chapter and your skill level based on your analysis, choose the right reading strategy for you: **Passage to Questions** or **Paragraph to Questions**

II. Execute the Five Pauses Method

The only way to do well on RC is to not go through the process passively but to **Read for Purpose** and the five pauses technique is the only way you can ensure that you have high accuracy levels.

III. Rejection over selection

Always reject options based on the shadow answer and choose the option that is left, instead trying to select the perfect answer.

IV. Decode the paraphrase and match the logic, not words

On tough questions, correct options *do not use* the same words as the ones in the passage; they paraphrase—*use different words to express the same idea.* The trap options use the same words with faulty logic. Ensure that you decode the paraphrase and the logic and do go by matching the words.

V. Leave the tough questions

Just because you have read a passage does not mean that you have to waste time answering all questions. It is better to leave tough questions and maintain a good MPM.

Now that we are done with all the things that I have to say about handling RC, let us discuss the problems that you are likely to face and the various reasons why your scores might be stuck.

Are you a passive reader?

This can be the single biggest roadblock to performing well on RCs and you might not even know it.

Passive reading is reading without actively engaging with the text. Passive readers just go from sentence to sentence and unless the author makes a big statement or argument, the passive reader does not notice the build-up to the argument or the hints lying in the text.

The key to overcoming this is to treat RC like extended critical reasoning. The same passive reader when it comes to critical reasoning will wear a logical reasoning hat and actively follow the development of the argument. But when it comes to RC, the attitude is that this is just text. Just because they have not put the word reasoning does not mean they are not testing reasoning!

And reasoning does not start when you read the options. It starts when you read the text so that you can weigh the logic in the passage against the logic mentioned in the option. So, you cannot just turn your reasoning hat on right at the climax and expect that everything will turn out fine.

To sum up, read RC paragraphs like CR paragraphs.

The graver form of passive reading is reading without registering anything. Passive readers suddenly realize that they have read the last three sentences but did not retain anything from it. This issue primarily arises from an inability to concentrate on written text.

This inability to concentrate can stem from two reasons. An inability to concentrate in general. Not just RC but even in QA, you need to read a question twice to understand it—the first time is just a passive read. The second is an inability to do this only with RC since the text is with a huge build-up.

In both cases, a good way can be to start subvocalizing, which means reading aloud mentally—you hear the sentence in your head loud and clear (but not even a whisper outside). Active hearing is a way to register what is being said and implanting it in your head.

This might seem counterintuitive since subvocalizing is often made out to be a major cause of low speed. I began subvocalizing many years ago, and I distinctly remember that I didn't do it earlier. But I did not beat myself up about it and it did not reduce my speed in any way. You always waste more time reading a piece of text twice passively than by reading the same text actively once.

As far as passive reading goes, any advice will eventually hit a brick wall, since it is finally about altering your mental processes while reading a text. Every single piece of information that appears as part of the questions on the test expresses logic, so your task is to keep decoding every piece of information.

Is your accuracy not going up?

The way to improve between tests is to identify the process mistakes you are making. You see that even after reading all of these chapters, your accuracy is wayward or 80 per cent. What should you do?

The biggest thing to do after the test is to analyse it and tie every mistake to a process deviation. This was incorrect due to:

1. Did not execute either *Reading Strategy—passage to questions* or *para to questions* properly
2. Did not execute *Pause I*, leading to errors on questions pertaining to a para
3. Did not execute *Pause II*, so got summary questions wrong
4. Did not execute *Pause III*, so did not have a shadow answer to eliminate options correctly

5. Did not execute *Pause IV*, so ended up *selecting* instead of *eliminating*
6. Did not execute *Pause V*, should have left this questions alone

The reason you need to do this is that despite reading all the chapters, you might not be executing all the steps every single time. It is like it is in cricket. The batsman always gets out because he made a technical mistake—foot was not to the pitch of the ball, played away from the body, took the eyes off the ball—it is only very rarely that the bowler delivers an absolute *jaffa* or *corker*—an unplayable delivery. The bowler keeps plugging away in the corridor of uncertainty to test your technique.

How important is vocabulary in the whole scheme of things?

Vocabulary is important but not by itself, the way it is in the case of the GRE, where half the test is purely vocabulary-based questions. The CAT that way has zero vocabulary-based questions.

But still a lot of students feel that their vocabulary is poor and that is the major impediment to their understanding. Even if this is partially true, it does not make sense to mug up words. It always makes sense to check the meanings of words in the passages that you solve and whatever else you read. So, make it a habit to ensure that whenever you encounter a word in your practice or general reading that you do not know, check the meaning. Do not think 'but in the actual exam I will not be able to use the dictionary app'! Use a dictionary app in all practice except section tests and full-length tests; you will end up learning many words and also remember them since you are learning them in context.

If you still want to mug up words then the two books that anyone will tell you are the best are: *Word Power Made Easy* by Norman Lewis and *All About Words* by Maxwell Nurnberg and Morris Rosenblum.

How important is reading newspapers and magazines?

Let me rephrase the question: If I am running every day, will I start scoring more goals in the match soon?

Reading newspapers and articles only help you get comfortable with reading in general. Over a period of time, it helps make reading a comfortable activity and not a drudgery. Over a longer period of time it can help increase your reading speed, and if you are in the habit of checking for the meanings of unfamiliar words in the articles that you read, then it will obviously boost your vocabulary.

But the key thing is this—just like your goal-scoring ability will not directly increase with running, it will not directly improve your accuracy since it has nothing to do with the technique involved to solve a question.

So between reading 100 articles from magazines and solving 100 passages in the same time slot, I would always suggest solving passages since the passages themselves have been made from articles, cover a wide variety of topics that you might not encounter in your general reading, and also test your comprehension through questions.

This does not mean that reading has no place. It plays a bigger role in your WAT-GD-PI performance and so you should make reading magazines and newspapers a habit.

9

Verbal Ability: The Summary Question

The Verbal Ability (VA) questions of the CAT are, according to me, the most illogical questions that have ever been invented. The reason being that they are not based on any rules of formal logic and have no counterpart in any other test anywhere in the world.

I can still agree with the utility of a summary question. One might argue that it tests comprehension but then the RC part with twenty-four questions tests the same skill through summary, detail and inference questions. There is no point wasting three more questions to test the same skill!

The other two question types—jumbled paragraphs and incorrect sentence—in context are honestly a joke. In any test across the world, one is expected to answer a question that has been designed by a question-maker based on standard logical constructs. On both of these question types, you are being asked to work with a text that was written by somebody with no intent to make a CAT question; the text, not its writer, knew that it was going to grow up and become a CAT question!

So, when the author himself has not written it with this purpose in mind, it does not make sense there should always be only one logical order in which the sentences can be arranged. Sure, there are many questions on which there is only one order possible but then I have never been able to figure out what special skill this actually tests.

All of the other most premier international exams—GMAT, GRE, LSAT—test critical reasoning skills in a major way.

The only logic I can see is that since there is no logic to these question types, this is the only way to eliminate a large number of students, given the number of test-takers!

So now that I have gotten my frustration with these question types out of the way, let me go ahead to the technique to deal with them.

The Summary Question

The only way to reach higher accuracy levels on VA is to move from solving questions based on gut feel to using a process to arrive at the answer. Leave your gut to what it does best—digestion!

What is the usual process?

Read the passage, read the options and then if it is an easy question, the answer will become obvious; if it is a tough question, you will get caught between two options.

Where is the space for reasoning in all of this or when does the reasoning happen?

So, the first step is to stop after reading the paragraph and formulate what you are looking for.

Every paragraph will be about three big ideas (at most)—X, Y and Z—all the rest of the sentences will be supporting arguments.

Imagine it this way. You have just read this passage and your CEO who is a super busy person asks you what it's about, what sentences or phrases from the passage will you use to describe the core idea.

The Summary Question Technique

1. Read only the paragraph
2. Split it into three big ideas—X-Y-Z—using the minimum number of phrases
3. Check each option to see whether it has the X, the Y and the Z
4. Eliminate options that are missing the most important ones among X, Y or Z
5. The correct options will have all three or the two most important ones.

Let us take a few questions from recent CAT papers to see how to execute this process and any changes you might need to make as the questions get tougher.

Question 1, EASY

Artificial embryo twinning is a relatively low-tech way to make clones. As the name suggests, this technique mimics the natural process that creates identical twins. In nature, twins form very early in development when the embryo splits in two. Twinning happens in the first days after egg and sperm join, while the embryo is made of just a small number of unspecialized cells. Each half of the embryo continues dividing on its own, ultimately developing into separate, complete individuals. Since they developed from the same fertilized egg, the resulting individuals are genetically identical.

X—Artificial embryo twinning is a relatively low-tech way to make clones.

This is usually in the first or second sentence of the passage and it introduces the main terms or topic of the passage. In this case, it is the first sentence of the passage and the main idea here is that it is a *low-tech way to make clones*. So X is usually the Title or the Introducer.

Y—As the name suggests, this technique mimics the natural process that creates identical twins.

This is the first supporting idea, that forms the bedrock of the passage, around which secondary ideas are built. In this case, it outlines *the principle of embryo twinning* in one line.

Z—Since they developed from the same fertilized egg, the resulting individuals are genetically identical.

This is the second supporting idea that either elaborates on the first idea or adds some additional element to it—and reiterates the fact that the process creates *genetically identical twins*.

A. Artificial embryo twinning is just like the natural development of twins, where during fertilization, twins are formed.
B. Artificial embryo twinning is low-tech and is close to the natural development of twins where the embryo splits into two identical twins.
C. Artificial embryo twinning is low-tech unlike the natural development of identical twins from the embryo after fertilization.
D. Artificial embryo twinning is low-tech and mimetic of the natural development of genetically identical twins from the embryo after fertilization.

Eliminate Options

A. Incorrect. Does not mention X and Z, and only indirectly mentions Y. This can be eliminated straightaway when you find there is no X.
B. Incorrect. Mentions X, mentions Y incorrectly—*close to* not *mimic*.
C. Incorrect. Does not mention Y and Z.
D. **Correct**. Mentions all three.

Question 2, EASY

For each of the past three years, temperatures have hit peaks not seen since the birth of meteorology, and probably not for more than 110,000 years. The amount of carbon dioxide in the air is at its highest level in 4 million years. This does not cause storms like Harvey—there have always been storms and hurricanes along the Gulf of Mexico—but it makes them wetter and more powerful. As the seas warm, they evaporate more easily and provide energy to storm fronts. As the air above them warms, it holds more water vapour. For every half a degree Celsius in warming, there is about a 3 per cent increase in atmospheric moisture content. Scientists call this the Clausius-Clapeyron equation. This means the skies fill more quickly and have more to dump. The storm surge was greater because sea levels have risen 20 cm as a result of more than 100 years of human-related global warming which has melted glaciers and thermally expanded the volume of seawater.

X—High temperatures like never before.

Sometimes, like it is in this passage, the ideas are not expressed crisply but are developed over longer sentences and packed with information: *For each . . . temperatures have hit peaks . . . 110,000 years.* Your task is to condense sentences into short phrases. This will enable you to hold it in your head when you are eliminating options.

Y—This makes storms like Harvey wetter and more powerful.

The big idea, high-temperatures do not cause storms; they make them bigger and wetter.

Z—Man-made warming melts glaciers, causing increase in sea volume.

First supporting idea that tells us how rising temperatures result in bigger and wetter storms and is the cause of rising temperatures.

A. The storm Harvey is one of the regular, annual ones from the Gulf of Mexico; global warming and Harvey are unrelated phenomena.
B. Global warming does not breed storms but makes them more destructive; the Clausius-Clapeyron equation, though it predicts a potential increase in atmospheric moisture content, cannot predict the scale of damage storms might wreak.
C. Global warming melts glaciers, resulting in seawater volume expansion; this enables more water vapour to fill the air above faster. Thus, modern storms contain more destructive energy.
D. It is naive to think that rising sea levels and the force of tropical storms are unrelated; Harvey was destructive as global warming had armed it with more moisture content, but this may not be true of all storms.

Eliminate Options

A. Incorrect. Does not mention X, Y or Z.
B. Incorrect. Only mentions Y.
C. **Correct**. Mentions X, Y, and Z. Paraphrases *more destructive* to *more powerful.*
D. Incorrect. Mentions all three but adds ideas that are not present—*it is naive, this may not be true of all storms.*

Question 3, EASY

North American walnut sphinx moth caterpillars (*Amorpha juglandis*) look like easy meals for birds, but they have a trick up their sleeves—they produce whistles that sound like bird alarm calls, scaring potential predators away. At first, scientists suspected birds were simply startled by the loud noise. But a new study suggests a more sophisticated mechanism: the caterpillar's whistle appears to mimic a bird alarm call, sending avian predators scrambling for cover. When pecked by a bird, the caterpillars whistle by compressing their bodies like an accordion and forcing air out through specialised holes in their sides. The whistles are impressively loud—they have been measured at over 50 dB from 5 cm away from the caterpillar—considering they are made by a two-inch-long insect.

X—North American walnut sphinx caterpillars look like easy meals but they are not.

This introduces the idea that this breed of caterpillar looks to be an easy prey for birds but it is not.

Y—They have a trick—they produce whistles that sound like bird alarm calls, scaring potential predators away.

The big idea is mentioned with as few words as possible so you do not need to paraphrase.

Z—The whistles are impressively loud (for their small size).

The supporting idea that gives an additional piece (not necessarily crucial) of information.

A. North American walnut sphinx moth caterpillars will whistle periodically to ward off predator birds; they have a specialized vocal tract that helps them whistle.
B. North American walnut sphinx moth caterpillars can whistle very loudly; the loudness of their whistles is shocking as they are very small insects.
C. North American walnut sphinx moth caterpillars, in a case of acoustic deception, produce whistles that mimic bird alarm calls to defend themselves.
D. North American walnut sphinx moth caterpillars, in a case of deception and camouflage, produce whistles that mimic bird alarm calls to defend themselves.

Eliminate Options

A. Incorrect. Does not mention X, Y or Z—an easy prey, alarm call, loudness.
B. Incorrect. Only mentions Z.
C. **Correct**. Mentions X and Y. Paraphrases *trick* to *acoustic deception*.
D. Incorrect. Mentions X and Y but adds an idea that is not present—*camouflage*, which means changing colour to blend in with surroundings to avoid detection, the passage only mentions vocal deception.

Question 4, EASY

A Japanese government panel announced that it recommends regulating only genetically modified organisms that have had foreign genes permanently introduced into their genomes and not those whose endogenous genes have been edited. The only stipulation is that researchers and businesses will have to register their modifications to plants or animals with the government, with the exception of microbes cultured in contained environments. Reactions to the decision are mixed. While lauding the potential benefits of genome editing, an editorial opposes across-the-board permission. Unforeseen risks in gene editing cannot be ruled out. All genetically modified products must go through the same safety and labeling processes regardless of method.

X—The Japanese government announced new regulations for GMO.

This introduces the topic that there is a new law on genetically modified organisms.

Y—Only genetic modifications with new foreign genes introduced will be regulated; endogenous gene modification will not be regulated.

This describes what the regulation is.

Z—While people have lauded the move, many have cited risks and say all types of modification should be subject to the same regulatory processes.

This is the big idea, the reaction to the law.

A. Exempting from regulations the editing of endogenous genes is not desirable as this procedure might be risk-prone.
B. Excepting microbes cultured in contained environments from the regulations of genome editing is premature.
C. A government panel in Japan says transgenic modification and genome editing are not the same.
D. Creating categories within genetically modified products in terms of transgenic modification and genome editing advances science but defies laws.

Eliminate Options

A. **Correct**. Mentions Y and Z by condensing them into one small sentence, X is not separately stated—exemption is risky.
B. Incorrect. Does not mention Y correctly, Z is missing, says *premature* instead of *risky*.
C. Incorrect. Does not mention Y or Z, introduces new term—*transgenic modification*.
D. Incorrect. Does not mention Y or Z, introduces new term—*transgenic modification*.

Question 5, MEDIUM

Should the moral obligation to rescue and aid persons in grave peril, felt by a few, be enforced by the criminal law? Should we follow the lead of a number of European countries and enact bad Samaritan laws? Proponents of bad Samaritan laws must overcome at least three different sorts of obstacles. First, they must show the laws are morally legitimate in principle, that is, that the duty to aid others is a proper candidate for legal enforcement. Second, they must show that this duty to aid can be defined in a way that can be fairly enforced by the courts. Third, they must show that the benefits of the laws are worth their problems, risks and costs.

X—The bad Samaritan law, do we need to enact one?

This introduces the idea of a bad Samaritan law, laws that will punish people for not fulfilling the moral obligation to rescue and aid persons in grave peril and asks whether there should be such a law. (The phrase *bad Samaritan* comes from the story of the *good Samaritan* in the Bible; the Samaritans being a community of people in ancient Israel.)

Y—Those who want such a law should overcome three legal obstacles.

The author is not taking a stand on whether such laws should be enacted or not but states that those who want such laws should overcome three legal obstacles.

Z—The three legal proofs needed are listed one by one.

All three obstacles or legal requirements are stated and all three have equal importance.

A. If bad Samaritan laws are found to be legally sound and enforceable, they must be enacted.
B. Bad Samaritan laws may be desirable but they need to be tested for legal soundness.
C. A number of European countries have successfully enacted bad Samaritan laws, which may serve as model statutes.
D. Everyone agrees that people ought to aid others; the only debate is whether to have a law on it.

Eliminate Options

A. Incorrect. Mentions X and Y but makes the author in favour of them. The author poses the question about their desirability and states the legal requirements.
B. **Correct**. Mentions X and Y and leaves the author's stance ambiguous—may be desirable.
C. Incorrect. Does not mention Y.
D. Incorrect. Does not mention Y.

Since Z has all three legal requirements and all three are equally important, it does not make sense for the summary to mention all three—it will become as big as the original paragraph—hence, all options exclude Z.

Question 6, MEDIUM

A translator of literary works needs a secure hold upon the two languages involved, supported by a good measure of familiarity with the two cultures. For an Indian translating works in an Indian language into English, finding satisfactory equivalents in a generalized western culture of practices and symbols in the original would be less difficult than gaining fluent control of contemporary English. When a westerner works on texts in Indian languages the interpretation of cultural elements will be the major challenge, rather than control over the grammar and essential vocabulary of the language concerned. It is much easier to remedy lapses in language in a text translated into English, than flaws of content. Since it is easier for an Indian to learn the English language than it is for a Briton or American to comprehend Indian culture, translations of Indian texts is better left to Indians.

X—A translator of literary works needs a secure hold upon the two languages involved, supported by a good measure of familiarity with the two cultures.

This introduces the topic, translation and skills required for the same.

Y—In translating Indian works into English, Indian translators will have problems with language and grammar but not with cultural understanding, while the reverse is true for a British or American translator.

The topic then moves to the specific case of translating works in Indian languages into English and the skills and challenges faced by two groups of translators.

Z—Since lack of language skills is easier to remedy than lack of cultural understanding, the job of such translation is better left to Indians.

The main idea of the passage is stated—the translation of works in Indian languages into English is better left to Indians.

A. While translating, the Indian and the westerner face the same challenges but they have different skill profiles and the former has the advantage.
B. As preserving cultural meanings is the essence of literary translation, Indians' knowledge of the local culture outweighs the initial disadvantage of lower fluency in English.
C. Indian translators should translate Indian texts into English as their work is less likely to pose cultural problems that are harder to address than the quality of language.
D. Westerners might be good at gaining reasonable fluency in new languages, but as understanding the culture reflected in literature is crucial, Indians remain better placed.

Eliminate Options

A. Incorrect. Mentions Y and Z but only at a general level without referring to the specific case of translating Indian texts into English and cultural understanding.
B. Incorrect. Mentions Y and Z but changes the reason—passage says language deficiency is easier to remedy as the reason and not that cultural understanding is more important than language skills. Both are equally important; one is easier to pick up than the other.
C. **Correct**. Clearly captures Y and Z, mentions the context—translating Indian texts into English—and the right reason.
D. Incorrect. Mentions Y and Z but makes the mistakes of A and B; does not specify the context and provides the wrong reason.

In this case, X is not explicitly stated in any option but is absorbed into Y and Z in all of them so that the summary does not become long.

Question 7, DIFFICULT

A fundamental property of language is that it is slippery and messy and more liquid than solid, a gelatinous mass that changes shape to fit. As Wittgenstein would remind us, 'usage has no sharp boundary.' Oftentimes, the only way to determine the meaning of a word is to examine how it is used. This insight is often described as the 'meaning is use' doctrine. There are differences between the 'meaning is use' doctrine and a dictionary-first theory of meaning. 'The dictionary's careful fixing of words to definitions, like butterflies pinned under glass, can suggest that this is how language works. The definitions can seem to ensure and fix the meaning of words, just as the gold standard can back a country's currency.' What Wittgenstein found in the circulation of ordinary language, however, was a free-floating currency of meaning. The value of each word arises out of the exchange. The lexicographer abstracts a meaning from that exchange, which is then set within the conventions of the dictionary definition.

X—Language and meanings of words are not fixed but changing.

This is a longer and more dense passage. You need to condense the first two sentences: 'A fundamental property of language is that it is slippery and messy and more liquid than solid, a gelatinous mass that changes shape to fit. As Wittgenstein would remind us, 'usage has no sharp boundary'—to arrive at the simple way to capture the topic.

Y—There are two ways to understand meanings of words—meaning in use and dictionary meanings.

The big idea is introduced here, the two ways of arriving at meanings of words.

Z—Dictionary definitions fix words into set meanings whereas in reality, the meanings are more fluid and change according to the context in which they are used.

The main idea of the passage is stated—meanings in use capture meanings as they are used in exchange and lexicographers then put these into dictionaries.

A. Dictionary definitions are like 'gold standards'—artificial, theoretical and dogmatic. Actual meaning of words is their free-exchange value.
B. Language is already slippery; given this, accounting for 'meaning in use' will only exasperate the problem. That is why lexicographers 'fix' meanings.
C. Meaning is dynamic; definitions are static. The 'meaning in use' theory helps us understand that definitions of words are culled from their meaning in exchange and use and not vice versa.
D. The meaning of words in dictionaries is clear, fixed and less dangerous and ambiguous than the meaning that arises when words are exchanged between people.

Eliminate Options

A. Incorrect. Mentions Y and Z but introduces ideas not mentioned—artificial, theoretical and dogmatic—dictionary meanings are only called static not artificial or theoretical since the passage states that the lexicographer extracts meaning from actual exchange and enters it into the dictionary.
B. Incorrect. Mentions X, Y and Z but adds a perspective that is not there in the passage—dictionary definitions are better.
C. **Correct**. Clearly captures X, Y and Z.
D. Incorrect. Mentions Y and Z but adds a perspective that is not there in the passage—meanings of words when used between people are dangerous.

Question 8, DIFFICULT

Production and legitimation of scientific knowledge can be approached from a number of perspectives. To study knowledge production from the sociology of professions perspective would mean a focus on the institutionalization of a body of knowledge. The professions-approach informed earlier research on managerial occupation, business schools and management knowledge. It however tends to reify institutional power structures in its understanding of the links between knowledge and authority. Knowledge production is restricted to the perspective of the selected members of the professional community, most notably to the university faculties and professional colleges. Power is understood as a negative mechanism, which prevents the non-professional actors from offering their ideas and information as legitimate knowledge.

X—Studying knowledge production through sociology of professions would mean institutionalization of a body of knowledge.

The topic is introduced.

Y—Knowledge production is restricted to the perspective of the selected members of the professional community.

The big idea is introduced here, the professions approach is restrictive.

Z—It prevents the non-professional actors from offering their ideas and information as legitimate knowledge.

The big idea is stated fully.

A. The study of knowledge production can be done through many perspectives.
B. The professions-approach has been one of the most-relied-upon perspectives in the study of management knowledge production.
C. The professions-approach focuses on the creation of institutions of higher education and disciplines to promote knowledge production.
D. The professions-approach aims at the institutionalization of knowledge but restricts knowledge production as a function of a select few.

Eliminate Options

A. Incorrect. Mentions neither X nor Y nor Z.
B. Incorrect. Mentions X but not Y and Z.
C. Incorrect. Mentions X, modifies Y, but does not mention Z.
D. **Correct**. Condenses X, Y and Z.

Question 9, DIFFICULT

The conceptualization of landscape as a geometric object first occurred in Europe and is historically related to the European conceptualization of the organism, particularly the human body, as a geometric object with parts having a rational, three-dimensional organization and integration. The European idea of landscape appeared before the science of landscape emerged, and it is no coincidence that Renaissance artists such as Leonardo da Vinci, who studied the structure of the human body, also facilitated an understanding of the structure of landscape. Landscape which had been a subordinate background to religious or historical narratives, became an independent genre or subject of art by the end of sixteenth century or the beginning of the seventeenth century.

X—The idea of landscape as a geometric object first occurred in Europe in relation to the idea of the organism as a geometric object.

An idea is introduced whose development will lead to an argument being made.

Y—An understanding of the structure of landscape was developed by artists such as da Vinci who also studied the human body.

The progression of the concept of landscape is discussed.

Z—By the seventeenth century, landscape was no longer just a background but an independent subject of art.

The big idea, what the whole passage is about, is how landscape developed into an independent subject.

A. The study of landscape as an independent genre was aided by the Renaissance artists.
B. The three-dimensional understanding of the organism in Europe led to a similar approach towards the understanding of landscape.
C. The Renaissance artists were responsible for the study of landscape as a subject of art.
D. Landscape became a major subject of art at the turn of the sixteenth century.

Eliminate Options

A. **Correct.** Mentions Z and Y and condenses the whole passage, ignores X but that is okay since X is only introducing the argument through a premise.
B. Incorrect. Mentions only Y and ignores the big idea Z.
C. Incorrect. Mentions Z and Y but makes two mistakes—instead of saying *influenced* or *aided*, it says Renaissance artists were *responsible* and misses mentioning *independent* subject of art. Landscape was always a subject; the novelty was it becoming an independent subject.
D. Incorrect. Mentions only Z, ignoring Y, and also extrapolates landscape becoming a major subject of art, whereas all we know is that it became an independent subject, the major subjects could still have been religious or historical.

Question 10, DIFFICULT

To me, a 'classic' means precisely the opposite of what my predecessors understood: a work is classical by reason of its resistance to contemporaneity and supposed universality, by reason of its capacity to indicate human particularity and difference in that past epoch. The classic is not what tells me about shared humanity—or, more truthfully put, what lets me recognize myself as already present in the past, what nourishes in me the illusion that everything has been like me and has existed only to prepare the way for me. Instead, the classic is what gives access to radically different forms of human consciousness for any given generation of readers, and thereby expands for them the range of possibilities of what it means to be a human being.

X—A classic means the opposite of what it meant previously.

An idea is introduced, the specifics will be discussed.

Y—A classic is not something universal, relevant today, or makes me feel continuous with the past.

Since almost five lines are spent describing what a classic it is not, this idea must be compressed into one line. The big idea to come will be what the classic actually is.

Z—A classic offers a view of a radically different way of being human, opening up more possibilities.

The big idea that the passage is all about, what the author thinks a classic is; this should be the focus of the summary, not Y.

A. A classic is able to focus on the contemporary human condition and a unified experience of human consciousness.
B. A classical work seeks to resist particularity and temporal difference even as it focuses on a common humanity.
C. A classic is a work exploring the new, going beyond the universal, the contemporary, and the notion of a unified human consciousness.
D. A classic is a work that provides access to a universal experience of the human race as opposed to radically different forms of human consciousness.

Eliminate Options

A. Incorrect. Incorrectly captures Z; classic does not offer a unified experience but a different experience of human consciousness.
B. Incorrect. Incorrectly captures Z; it does not focus on common humanity.
C. **Correct**. Captures Z correctly; going beyond—universal, contemporary and unified human consciousness.
D. Incorrect. Captures the exact opposite of Z.

Question 11, DIFFICULT

The early optimism about sport's deterrent effects on delinquency was premature as researchers failed to find any consistent relationships between sports participation and deviance. As the initial studies were based upon cross-sectional data and the effects captured were short-term, it was problematic to test and verify the temporal sequencing of events suggested by the deterrence theory. The correlation between sport and delinquency could not be disentangled from class and cultural variables known. Choosing individuals to play sports in the first place was problematic, which became more acute in the subsequent decades as researchers began to document just how closely sports participation was linked to social class indicators.

X—The early optimism about sport's deterrent effects on delinquency was premature as researchers failed to find any consistent relationships between sports participation and deviance.

An idea is introduced in full; this is the main argument. The rest of the sentences will explain why.

Y—The initial test results could not be validated over the long term.

The first premise is stated—the early tests could not be validated over the longer term.

Z—Over the years, as more data came, it was tough to separate other variables such as class and culture from the two variables between which a link was being explored.

The second premise is stated—it was tough to separate the many variables that were involved and isolate these two—*sports participation* and *delinquency*.

A. Contradicting the previous optimism, latter researchers have proved that there is no consistent relationship between sports participation and deviance.
B. Statistical and empirical weaknesses stand in the way of inferring any relationship between sports participation and deviance.
C. There is a direct relationship between sport participation and delinquency but it needs more empirical evidence.
D. Sports participation is linked to class and cultural variables such as education, income and social capital.

Eliminate Options

A. Incorrect. Incorrectly captures X—the relationship was not *disproved*; they were *not able to find any consistent relationships*, but this does not mean that they disproved it.
B. **Correct.** Captures Z correctly by saying that no relationship can be inferred—*not able to find any consistent relationships*; statistical and empirical weaknesses are used to condense—*it was problematic to test and verify the temporal sequencing of events, the correlation between sport and delinquency could not be disentangled from class and cultural variables known; choosing individuals to play sports in the first place was problematic.*
C. Incorrect. States the exact opposite of X—the relationship was not proved.
D. Incorrect. Does not state X; brings in a new relationship between sports participation and the other variables.

Question 12, DIFFICULT

Both Socrates and Bacon were very good at asking useful questions. In fact, Socrates is largely credited with coming up with a way of asking questions, 'the Socratic method', which itself is at the core of the 'scientific method', popularised by Bacon. The Socratic method disproves arguments by finding exceptions to them, and can therefore lead your opponent to a point where they admit something that contradicts their original position. In common with Socrates, Bacon stressed it was as important to disprove a theory as it was to prove one—and real-world observation and experimentation were key to achieving both aims. Bacon also saw science as a collaborative affair, with scientists working together, challenging each other.

X—Socrates introduced and Bacon popularized the scientific method and asking questions.

An idea is introduced, in three lines—it has to be condensed.

Y—Socrates and Bacon both tested theories by asking to determine exceptions and testing them against real-world observation and experimentation.

The idea is extended—the scientific method to test theories.

Z—In common with Socrates, Bacon stressed it was as important to disprove a theory as it was to prove one—and real-world observation and experimentation were key to achieving both aims.

The main idea is summarized—*proving and disproving are two sides of the same coin and are equally important to the goal of testing theories.* The additional idea about how Bacon saw science can be skipped since it is a minor idea and the main idea has already been stated.

A. Both Socrates and Bacon advocated clever questioning of the opponents to disprove their arguments and theories.
B. Both Socrates and Bacon advocated challenging arguments and theories by observation and experimentation.
C. Both Socrates and Bacon advocated confirming arguments and theories by finding exceptions.
D. Both Socrates and Bacon advocated examining arguments and theories from both sides to prove them.

Eliminate Options

A. Incorrect. Z is incorrectly captured—they did not advocate only disproving theories by asking questions but stressed the importance of both.
B. Incorrect. Z is incorrectly captured—they did not advocate only challenging arguments by asking questions but stressed the importance of both.

C. Incorrect. Z is incorrectly captured—they did not want to confirm arguments but to test them through questioning and finding exceptions.

D. **Correct**. Z is correctly encapsulated—examining arguments from both sides to prove them is nothing but a paraphrase of proving and disproving to test an argument.

Notes on the Summary Question

As you can see from the twelve questions above, there is a huge variation in the kind of passage and the kind of summary options that are given.

This wide variety is due to the fact that every year a different set of people make the paper and thus we owe the topic to their areas of interest.

Having said that, it is clear that every year they try to maintain a mix within the set. One has always been science and two have been from the humanities—literature, philosophy, history, art, etc.

On the easier questions, which are usually the science ones:

- the topics are from the sciences and the language is easy to decipher
- you can make your X, Y, Z using sentences from the passage itself
- the options are not close, you can eliminate incorrect ones based on the presence or absence of one of the three.

Whereas on the tough questions:

- the topics are from the humanities and the language is dense, so
- the first challenge is to understand the language and then condense the sentences from the passage into simpler language to be used as X, Y and Z, and
- identify the main idea(s) among X, Y and Z and the premises used to build up to it; correct options end up having only the main idea
- the structure can be either—premises building up to the conclusion or the conclusion backed up by premises
- the options are super short with many elements being condensed using different words
- the options cannot be eliminated on the presence or absence of X, Y, Z but on the incorrect logic with which they have been stated
- you have to actively reason to differentiate between two close options
- you might be trapped since it can be super-tough to separate options in a test situation; it is better to enter an answer and move on since there is no negative marking—you might as well save time!

Once you are aware of these elements and know what the question setter is doing, you can side-step the incorrect options.

10

Verbal Ability: The Jumbled Paragraph

I would have expressed my displeasure at the existence of a question type called the Jumbled Paragraph at the beginning of the previous chapter but, be that as it may, we still have to deal with it in a test situation.

The key to successfully solve jumbled paragraphs is to not always keep a track of two things—the overall idea as it is developing across the passage and the specific clues hidden in each sentence.

This is easier said than done because the readers want to end *ambiguity*. Everyone feels that if they read the whole thing, the paragraph will come together in their head, but the only thing it leads to is more confusion and loss of time.

So the task is thus twofold: resist the temptation to read all the sentences, and live with uncertainty and ambiguity.

The three-step process to solve jumbled paragraphs is the **Sort-Link-Sequence** method.

Step 1: Sort the sentence into one of two categories—Starter or Follower

When you read the first sentence, you need to figure out one of two things—is it a *starter* or a *follower*?

A starter is, as it will be obvious, a sentence that begins the paragraph. So, what qualities will a starter have? A starter will usually:

- introduce an idea, term, topic, concept, issue or a theme
- will thus be at a macro level and not a micro level
- will have no pronouns—*his, her, this, that*, etc.—or references to another sentence or idea—or logical continuations at the beginning of the sentence such as *but, thus, hence*—or time continuations at the beginning of the sentence—such as *after that, then*

Any sentence that has any of the things listed in the previous point is a follower and not a starter.

Step 2: Look for links

If you sort the sentence to be a *follower*, you will always get clues as to how it is linked to another sentence. Your task as you move to the next sentence is to identify links between sentences using these clues. The common links are:

- **Noun Link**—A sentence is a follower since it has pronouns such as *his/her/this/that*. So it means that this sentence is linked to another sentence that reveals the name of *his/her/this/that*. So, when you encounter a follower with a pronoun, look for a noun link.
- **Temporal Link**—Temporal means a series of events that have a chronological sequence—first X happened, then Y was discovered, etc. The words that hold clues to a temporal sequence are *after, before, then*, etc.
- **List Link**—A paragraph might be listing out things such as there are two kinds of X, three reasons for something, etc. The clues to the existence of such a list are words such as *first, firstly, secondly*, etc.
- **Logical**—When there is no other link, only logic is left. A few clues are words sentences with words such as *then*; this can mean a time sequence and it can also mean an *if-then* possibility—some precondition has to be fulfilled and only *then* something happens. Other logical links are revealed through words sentences that start with *but, since, hence, thus*, etc.

Step 3: Sequence the sentences for coherence

At the end of Step 2, you should (will) always know the starter sentence and a couple of links. The easier the question, the more the links. For example, 3 is the starter, and there are two links, 3-1 and 4-2. Then you know the sequence has to be 3142.

On a tougher question, you need to do the sequence using a starter and one link, which you should always be able to find. Let us take a dozen questions of varying levels and both four and five sentences and execute the strategy.

Question 1, EASY

1. It was his taxpayers who had to shell out as much as $1.6bn over 10 years to employees of failed companies.
2. Companies in many countries routinely engage in such activities which means that the employees are left with unpaid entitlements.
3. Deliberate and systematic liquidation of a company to avoid liabilities and then restarting the business is called phoenixing.
4. The Australian Minister for Revenue and Services discovered in an audit that phoenixing had cost the Australian economy between $2.9bn and $5.1bn last year.

ANALYSIS

Sentence 1—Not a starter due to *his*; it is linked to a person.

Sentence 2—Not a starter due to the word *such*; it is linked to some activities.

Sentence 3—Defines the *such* activities mentioned in 2 by the name *phoenixing*, has to precede 2—**3-2.**

Sentence 4—The reference to the word *his* is revealed in 4, so 4 precedes 1—**4-1.**

Sequence—We have two pairs, 3-2 and 4-1 and 4 refers to the concept of phoenixing introduced in 3, so 4 has to follow 3. The sequence has to be 3241.

CORRECT Sequence: 3241

Question 2, EASY

1. The eventual diagnosis was skin cancer and after treatment all seemed well.
2. The viola player didn't know what it was; nor did her GP.
3. Then a routine scan showed it had come back and spread to her lungs.
4. It started with a lump on Cathy Perkins' index finger.

ANALYSIS

Sentence 1—Not a starter since it has the word *eventual* so it seems like a sequence of events one after the other; this has to follow more than one sentence due to the word *eventual* and since it says *all seemed well*, this sentence can be the *closer*.

Sentence 2—Possibly not a starter due to *what it was*; *it* has to refer to a mysterious illness.

Sentence 3—Not a starter since it has the word *then*; this has to come after something; it has to precede 1 not necessarily immediately.

Sentence 4—This has to be the starter since it introduces the symptom which all the sentences are talking about.

Sequence—4 is the starter and it has to be followed by 2 since it says the doctor did not know what it was; 3 has to follow 2 since it talks about a scan that revealed, and 1 has to be the closer since the *eventual* diagnosis revealed what it is.

CORRECT Sequence: 4231

Question 3, EASY

1. Self-management is thus defined as the 'individual's ability to manage the symptoms, treatment, physical and psychosocial consequences and lifestyle changes inherent in living with a chronic condition'.

2. Most people with progressive diseases like dementia prefer to have control over their own lives and health care for as long as possible.
3. Having control means, among other things, that patients themselves perform self-management activities.
4. Supporting people in decisions and actions that promote self-management is called self-management support requiring a cooperative relationship between the patient, the family, and the professionals.

ANALYSIS

Sentence 1—Not a starter; has to follow something.

Sentence 2—Possible starter since it introduces an idea.

Sentence 3—Follows 2 immediately since it defines having control, introduces self-management and hence 1 has to follow 3 not necessarily immediately—**2-3.**

Sentence 4—Has to follow 1 which defines self-management and this defines self-management support—**1-4.**

Sequence—2 is the only possible starter, and we have two links 2-3 and 1-4, so the only possible sequence is **2314.**

CORRECT Sequence: 2314

Question 4, MEDIUM

1. But now we have another group: the unwitting enablers.
2. Democracy and high levels of inequality of the kind that have come to characterize the United States are simply incompatible.
3. Believing these people are working for a better world, they are, actually, at most, chipping away at the margins, making slight course corrections, ensuring the system goes on as it is, uninterrupted.
4. Very rich people will always use money to maintain their political and economic power.

ANALYSIS

Sentence 1—Not a starter since it has the word *but* and refers to another group, so there has to be a link with a first group mentioned later.

Sentence 2—Possible starter since it introduces a general idea.

Sentence 3—Has to be a follower since it says *these* people, this has to refer to either people in the first group or the second group.

Sentence 4—This has to be the first group and refers to sentence 2 with respect to inequality and 'these' in the sentence refers to rich people, so this has to follow 2, and 1 has to follow this—**2-4-1**.

Sequence—2-4-1 is a sequence and *these people* in 3 refers to the *enablers* in 1 since the passage is about the enablers.

CORRECT Sequence: 2413

Question 5, MEDIUM

1. The process of handing down implies not a passive transfer, but some contestation in defining what exactly is to be handed down.
2. Wherever Western scholars have worked on the Indian past, the selection is even more apparent and the inventing of a tradition much more recognisable.
3. Every generation selects what it requires from the past and makes its innovations, some more than others.
4. It is now a truism to say that traditions are not handed down unchanged, but are invented.
5. Just as life has death as its opposite, so is tradition by default the opposite of innovation.

ANALYSIS

Sentence 1—Does not seem to be a starter since it refers to a process of handing down and there has to be a reference to what is handed down.

Sentence 2—Not a starter due to the phrase *even more apparent*, it is linked to some selection.

Sentence 3—Can be a starter and has to precede 2 since it refers to selection—**3-2.**

Sentence 4—Can be a starter as it introduces the idea of traditions being handed down, so this has to precede 1 which talks about the process of handing down—**4-1.**

Sentence 5—Has to be the starter as it introduces the idea of tradition, continued in 4—**5-4-1.**

Sequence—5-4-1 with 5 as the starter and 3-2 is a link, 5-4-1-3-2.

CORRECT Sequence: 54132

Question 6, MEDIUM

1. The implications of retelling of Indian stories, hence, takes on new meaning in a modern India.
2. The stories we tell reflect the world around us.
3. We cannot help but retell the stories that we value—after all, they are never quite right for us—in our time.

4. And even if we manage to get them quite right, they are only right for us—other people living around us will have different reasons for telling similar stories.

5. As soon as we capture a story, the world we were trying to capture has changed.

Sentence 1—Not a starter since it uses the words *hence*; this means that it is logically following something else.

Sentence 2—Definitely seems like a starter since it is a statement that sounds like a quotation or a title.

Sentence 3—From stories it directly jumps to retelling stories so it might not follow 2 immediately.

Sentence 4—This has to follow 3 since it takes off where 3 ends—'and even if we manage to get them quite right'—**3-4.**

Sentence 5—This has to follow 2 since it continues the idea and takes it one step further, the beginning of the story—**1-2.**

Sequence—We have a starter in 2, and two pairs, 2-5 and 3-4, and all of them are related to the importance and implications of telling a story in general; 1 moves from stories in general to the implications of retelling Indian stories in a modern India and thus has to follow all the other sentences—**2-5-3-4-1.**

CORRECT Sequence: 25341

Question 7, MEDIUM

1. Scientists have for the first time managed to edit genes in a human embryo to repair a genetic mutation, fuelling hopes that such procedures may one day be available outside laboratory conditions.
2. The cardiac disease causes sudden death in otherwise healthy young athletes and affects about one in 500 people overall.
3. Correcting the mutation in the gene would not only ensure that the child is healthy but also prevents transmission of the mutation to future generations.
4. It is caused by a mutation in a particular gene and a child will suffer from the condition even if it inherits only one copy of the mutated gene.
5. In results announced in *Nature* this week, scientists fixed a mutation that thickens the heart muscle, a condition called hypertrophic cardiomyopathy.

Sentence 1—Definitely seems to be a starter since it introduces a new discovery—editing genetic mutation—and possible implications.

Sentence 2—Not a starter since it refers to *the* cardiac disease so this has to be type of a specific cardiac disease that will be mentioned later. If it was not a specific type of cardiac disease then the sentence would have been—*Cardiac disease causes . . . in 500 people overall.*

Sentence 3—Not a starter since it refers to *the* mutation, so it is linked to some mutation that will be mentioned later.

Sentence 4—Not a starter since it says *it* is caused; it refers to a disease and since 2 talks about a cardiac disease that causes sudden death and this talks about the causes of the same, 4 has to follow 2—**2-4.**

Sentence 5—Has to follow the starter, elaborates on the discovery mentioned in 1 and introduces the specific disease, hypertrophic cardiomyopathy, referred to in 2—**1-5-2-4.**

Sequence—1-5-2-4 has to be followed by 3, which talks about how correcting the mutation, an outcome of the discovery, can help future generations.

CORRECT Sequence: 15243

Question 8, MEDIUM

1. This has huge implications for the health care system as it operates today, where depleted resources and time lead to patients rotating in and out of doctors' offices, oftentimes receiving minimal care or concern (what is commonly referred to as 'bedside manner') from doctors.
2. The placebo effect is when an individual's medical condition or pain shows signs of improvement based on a fake intervention that has been presented to them as a real one and used to be regularly dismissed by researchers as a psychological effect.
3. The placebo effect is not solely based on believing in treatment, however, as the clinical setting in which treatments are administered is also paramount.
4. That the mind has the power to trigger biochemical changes because the individual believes that a given drug or intervention will be effective could empower chronic patients through the notion of our bodies' capacity for self-healing.
5. Placebo effects are now studied not just as foils for 'real' interventions but as a potential portal into the self-healing powers of the body.

Sentence 1—Not a starter since it says *this has huge implications.*

Sentence 2—Can be a starter since it defines and introduces a topic—the placebo effect.

Sentence 3—This has to follow 2 but we do not know in what position.

Sentence 4—This abruptly starts an idea for which so far there is no reference.

Sentence 5—This has to follow 2, since it is related to the idea introduced in the starter about *placebo effects used to be regularly dismissed*—**2-5.**

Sequence—2-5 is the starter and the context for 4 becomes clear after reading 5; 4 is elaborating on the self-healing powers of the body—2-5-4. We have two sentences left, 3 and 1; 1 refers to clinics and 3 talks about clinics while introducing a new idea about the placebo effect—it is not only a psychological belief in the power of the treatment but also a function of the surroundings in which the treatment is administered, which is what 1 is referring to—2-5-4-3-1.

CORRECT Sequence: 25431

Question 9, DIFFICULT

1. The study suggests that the disease did not spread with such intensity, but that it may have driven human migrations across Europe and Asia.
2. The oldest sample came from an individual who lived in southeast Russia about 5,000 years ago.
3. The ages of the skeletons correspond to a time of mass exodus from today's Russia and Ukraine into western Europe and central Asia, suggesting that a pandemic could have driven these migrations.
4. In the analysis of fragments of DNA from 101 Bronze Age skeletons for sequences from Yersinia pestis, the bacterium that causes the disease, seven tested positive.
5. DNA from Bronze Age human skeletons indicate that the black plague could have emerged as early as 3,000 BCE, long before the epidemic that swept through Europe in the mid-1300s.

Sentence 1—Not a starter since it says, *the study* and *the disease*; this sentence can only follow after the study and the disease are introduced.

Sentence 2—Not a starter since there is no reference to what sample is being discussed.

Sentence 3—Not a starter since we do not know what skeletons are being referred to here but this has to follow, not immediately, 1 since it gives evidence for the migrations introduced in sentence 1.

Sentence 4—Has to precede 1, 2 and 3 since it introduces both the study in the analysis of fragments; not a starter since it refers to *the disease*, we do not know what disease yet.

Sentence 5—Has to be the starter since it introduces the disease, the black plague.

Sequence—5 has to start and 4 has to precede 1, 2 and 3; 1 has to immediately follow 4 since it talks about 'the study' introduced in 4, so the order so far is 541 followed by 2 and 3. We need to determine whether it is 5-4-1-2-3 or 5-4-1-3-2.

2 cannot be a closer since it is a stand-alone piece of information; 3 can be a closer since it refers to the migration mentioned in 1 as a possible finding from the study and identifies the source of the pandemic to Russia referred to in 2. 3 can thus follow 1 and 2; 5-4-1-2-3.

CORRECT Sequence: 54123

Question 10, DIFFICULT

1. In the era of smart world, however, 'Universal Basic Income' is an ineffective instrument which cannot address the potential breakdown of the social contract when large swathes of the population would effectively be unemployed.
2. In the era of industrial revolution, the abolition of child labour, poor laws and the growth of trade unions helped families cope with the pressures of mechanised work.
3. Growing inequality could be matched by a creeping authoritarianism that is bolstered by technology that is increasingly able to peer into the deepest vestiges of our lives.
4. New institutions emerge which recognise ways in which workers could contribute to and benefit by economic growth when, rather than if, their jobs are automated.

ANALYSIS

Sentence 1—Not a starter due to the word, *however*, is linked to another sentence.

Sentence 2—Possible starter and has to precede 1, the *however* link—**2-1.**

Sentence 3—Describes a possible future scenario—*could be matched by*—future scenario outlined in 1 as well—*potential breakdown . . . when large swathes . . . would effectively be unemployed.* This continues the idea of *smart world* introduced in 1—*technology that is increasingly able to peer*—3 has to follow 1—**2-1-3.**

Sentence 4—Possible introductory sentence that speaks about institutional changes related to automation.

Sequence—2-1-3 is a sequence, 4 has to be the introductory sentence since 2 and 1 outline different kinds of institutional changes, one in the past and one suggested for the future.

CORRECT Sequence: 4213

Question 11, DIFFICULT

1. The woodland's canopy receives most of the sunlight that falls on the trees.
2. Swifts do not confine themselves to woodlands, but hunt wherever there are insects in the air.
3. With their streamlined bodies, swifts are agile flyers, ideally adapted to twisting and turning through the air as they chase flying insects—the creatures that form their staple diet.
4. Hundreds of thousands of insects fly in the sunshine up above the canopy, some falling prey to swifts and swallows

ANALYSIS

Sentence 1—Can be a starter since it introduces what a *woodland's canopy* is.

Sentence 2—Can be a starter but probably has to follow, not necessarily immediately, what defines a woodland's canopy.

Sentence 3—Might seem to follow 2 because of the word *their* but the reference to *their* is immediately given after the comma, *swifts*. It talks about swifts as hunters of insects; tough to figure out any order at this stage.

Sentence 4—Has to follow 1 since it adds to the idea of the woodlands' canopy—there are many insects there that fall prey to swifts and swallows; 3 which talks about how swifts are perfect to hunt insects has to follow 4—**1-4-3.**

Sequence—1-4-3 is a link and 2, which talks about hunting places other than woodlands, should end rather than begin the paragraph.

CORRECT Sequence: 1432

Question 12, DIFFICULT

1. Before plants can take life from atmosphere, nitrogen must undergo transformations similar to ones that food undergoes in our digestive machinery.
2. In its aerial form nitrogen is insoluble, unusable and is in need of transformation.
3. Lightning starts the series of chemical reactions that need to happen to nitrogen, ultimately helping it nourish our earth.
4. Nitrogen—an essential food for plants—is an abundant resource, with about 22 million tons of it floating over each square mile of earth.
5. One of the most dramatic examples in nature of ill wind that blows goodness is lightning.

Sentence 1—Does not seem like a starter but that still cannot be ruled out since the passage can be about the transformation that nitrogen has to undergo.

Sentence 2—A statement about nitrogen that introduces the idea about the need for nitrogen to undergo transformation that is elaborated in 1, so there is a link—**2-1.**

Sentence 3—This introduces lightning as an agent of transformation and now it seems like there is a link—**2-1-3.**

Sentence 4—This seems like a starter since it makes the most generic introductory statement about nitrogen; this cannot follow 2-1-3.

Sentence 5—This seems like an even bigger starter since it is not just defining something but stating a proverb citing an example of lightning in the context.

Sequence—Between 4 and 5, 5 has to be the starter since it introduces a theme and not a *term* or an *element*. So between *lightning* and *nitrogen*, *lightning* is the subject since 5 is the starter.

So, 3 which talks about what lightning does has to follow 5. Since 3 mentions nitrogen, nitrogen has to be introduced since the *good* that *lightning* brings has to be based on the importance of nitrogen. This is what 4 does. 5-3-4. 2-1 has to follow 4 since it talks about why nitrogen needs transformation.

CORRECT Sequence: 53421

Notes on Jumbled Paragraphs

Please remember that in the rush to execute the process in the shortest span of time, do not forget the most important thing of all, **reading for meaning**. It might very well happen that you stop understanding the meaning of the sentence and only look for pronouns, phrases and links.

Everything that I have mentioned in this chapter—the four types of links—can only be called Common *Verbal* Sense, which is what solving jumbled paragraphs needs. I solved enough and more JPs back in the day with no 'strategy'. So ensure that you do not throw the most basic thing—reading and understanding a sentence—out of the window.

11

Verbal Ability: The Missing Sentence in Paragraph

Most of the innovation in CAT Verbal Ability question types seems to revolve around the paragraph. This question type, introduced in 2022, is another iteration of the jumbled paragraph. In this version, a sentence is given, followed by a paragraph with numbered blanks. Your task is to determine which blank the sentence fits into. Take a look at the sample CAT question below.

Sentence: Most were first-time users of a tablet and a digital app.

Paragraph: Aage Badhein's USP lies in the ethnographic research that constituted the foundation of its development process. Customizations based on learning directly from potential users were critical to making this self-paced app suitable for both aliterate and non-literate audience. ___(1)___ The user interface caters to a Hindi-speaking audience who have minimal to no experience with digital services and devices. ___(2)___ The content and functionality of the app are suitable for a wide audience. This includes youth preparing for an independent role in life or a student ready to create a strong foundation of financial management early in her life. ___(3)___ Household members desirous of improving their family's financial strength to reach their aspirations can also benefit. We piloted Aage Badhein in early 2021 with over 400 women from rural areas. ___(4)___ The digital solution generated a large amount of interest in the communities.

The missing sentence can fit in anywhere—at the beginning of the paragraph, the middle or the end. The good part about this question type is that you need not test for all three possibilities—beginning, middle or end—for each and every question. If there is a possibility that the sentence can be taken for a starter, then the numbered blank (1) will be at the beginning of the paragraph.

The best technique to solve this question type is the Before–After Method.

Step 1: Read the given sentence and identify what ideas and/or nouns have to precede this sentence and what have to succeed this sentence.

Before—Introductory Ideas: For example, if the sentence says, 'this finding', then you know that the sentence has to appear only after the 'finding' is listed.

Nouns: For example, if the sentence says 'they', you need the reference of 'they' to precede the missing sentence

After—Supporting Ideas: For example, if the sentence says, 'This discovery explains the many similarities . . .', then the missing sentence has to be followed by the similarities.

All questions might not give clues to both Before and After ideas, but clues to at least one of them will definitely be there.

Step 2: Read sentences in sequence, looking for the Before Idea.

Step 3: Eliminate options that do not have the Before Idea preceding them.

Step 4: Resolve the position of the Missing Sentence using the After Idea.

Let's execute the Before–After Method over a series of questions.

Question 1

Sentence: Easing the anxiety and pressure of having a 'big day' is part of the appeal for many couples who marry in secret.

Before: Trend of marrying in secret or introduction or context for marrying in secret.

After: Since the sentence says 'easing the anxiety and pressure is part of the appeal', this has to be followed by other reasons.

Paragraph: Wedding season is upon us and—after two years of Covid chaos that saw nuptials scaled back—you may think the temptation would be to go all out. ___(1)___ But instead of expanding the guest list, many couples are opting to have entirely secret ceremonies. With Covid case numbers remaining high and the cost of living crisis meaning that many couples are feeling the pinch, it's no wonder that some are less than eager to send out invites. ___(2)___ Plus, it can't hurt that in celebrity circles, getting married in secret is all the rage. ___(3)___ 'I would definitely say that secret weddings are becoming more common,' says Landis Bejar, the founder of a therapy practice, which specializes in helping brides and grooms manage wedding stress. 'People are looking for ways to get out of the spotlight and avoid the pomp and circumstance of weddings. ___(4)___ They just want to get to the part where they are married.'

Explanatory Answer: Option (1) is incorrect since the idea of marrying in secret is not introduced. Option (2) is perfect since the idea is introduced, and the sentence that follows has the After we are looking for—other reasons for people marrying in secret. This is the exact reason why option (3) is incorrect. You can follow up with a new reason after saying plus. . . Option (4) is incorrect since it breaks the sequence of what the person is saying in casual language. The missing sentence is not written in the same language. Hence, (2).

Question 2

Sentence: Most were first-time users of a tablet and a digital app.

Before: There has to be a clear reference to 'who' were the first-time users of the app.

After: The reaction of the users.

Paragraph: Aage Badhein's USP lies in the ethnographic research that constituted the foundation of its development process. Customizations based on learning directly from potential users were critical to making this self-paced app suitable for both aliterate and non-literate audience. ___(1)___ The user interface caters to a Hindi-speaking audience who have minimal to no experience with digital services and devices. ___(2)___ The content and functionality of the app are suitable for a wide audience. This includes youth preparing for an independent role in life or a student ready to create a strong foundation of financial management early in her life. ___(3)___ Household members desirous of improving their family's financial strength to reach their aspirations can also benefit. We piloted Aage Badhein in early 2021 with over 400 women from rural areas. ___(4)___ The digital solution generated a large amount of interest in the communities.

Explanatory Answer: Options (1), (2) and (3) are incorrect since, before that, we cannot learn who the users are. The users are only clearly defined in the sentence before option (4)—the 400 women with whom Aage Badhein was piloted. Hence, (4).

Question 3

Sentence: This was years in the making but fast-tracked during the pandemic, when 'people started being more mindful about their food', he explained.

Before: The reference to 'this', some food philosophy. The reference to 'he', who is 'he?

After: The impact of this fast-tracking or related developments.

Paragraph: For millennia, ghee has been a venerated staple of the subcontinental diet, but it fell out of favour a few decades ago when saturated fats were largely considered to be unhealthy. ___(1)___ But more recently, as the thinking around saturated fats is shifting globally, Indians are finding their own way back to this ingredient that is so integral to their cuisine. ___(2)___ For Karmakar, a renewed interest in ghee is emblematic of a return-to-basics movement in India. ___(3)___ This movement is also part of an overall trend towards 'slow food'. In keeping with the movement's philosophy, ghee can be produced locally (even at home) and has inextricable cultural ties. ___(4)___ At a basic level, ghee is a type of clarified butter believed to have originated in India as a way to preserve butter from going rancid in the hot climate.

Explanatory Answer: Options (1) and (2) are ruled out since we do learn who the 'he' refers to. Option (3) fits best since it gives us the reference to 'he' and also the food philosophy. Option (4) is incorrect since it breaks the new idea of how ghee is made. Hence, (3).

Question 4

Sentence: Having made citizens more and less knowledgeable than their predecessors, the Internet has proved to be both a blessing and a curse.

Before: We need to know how the Internet has made citizens both more and less knowledgeable. So there will be many ideas that precede this.

After: It seems like a summary sentence with no ideas to follow.

Paragraph: Never before has a population, nearly all of whom has enjoyed at least a secondary school education, been exposed to so much information, whether in newspapers and magazines or through YouTube, Google and Facebook. ___(1)___ Yet it is not clear that people today are more knowledgeable than their barely literate predecessors. Contemporary advances in technology offered more serious and inquisitive students access to realms of knowledge previously unimaginable and unavailable. ___(2)___ But such readily available knowledge leads many more students away from serious study, the reading of actual texts, and towards an inability to write effectively and grammatically. ___(3)___ It has let people choose sources that reinforce their opinions rather than encouraging them to question inherited beliefs. ___(4)___

Explanatory Answer: Option (1) is incorrect since we do not learn how the Internet has made us more knowledgeable. Option (2) is incorrect since we do not learn how it has made us less knowledgeable. Option (3) is incorrect since it is followed by yet another reason why it has made us less knowledgeable—all these ideas should precede the missing sentence. Hence, (4).

Question 5

Sentence: And probably much earlier, moving the documentation for kissing back 1,000 years compared to what was acknowledged in the scientific community.

Before: There has to be a reference to the earlier documentation and the new timeline since the sentence says 'and probably much earlier'. So, the sentence immediately before this has to mention the new date.

After: Reasons for why probably much earlier as well.

Paragraph: Research has hypothesized that the earliest evidence of human lip kissing originated in a very specific geographical location in South Asia 3,500 years ago. ___(1)___ From there it may have spread to other regions, simultaneously accelerating the spread of the herpes simplex virus 1. According to Dr Troels Pank Arbøll and Dr Sophie Lund Rasmussen, who in a new article in the journal *Science* draw on a range of written sources from the earliest Mesopotamian societies, kissing was already a well-established practice 4,500 years ago in the Middle East. ___(2)___ In ancient Mesopotamia, people wrote in cuneiform script on clay tablets. ___(3)___ Many thousands of these clay tablets have survived to this day, and they contain clear examples that kissing was considered a part of romantic intimacy in ancient times. ___(4)___ 'Kissing could also have been part of friendships and family members' relations,' says Dr Troels Pank Arbøll, an expert on the history of medicine in Mesopotamia.

Explanatory Answer: Option (1) is incorrect since before it we only learn of the first documentation. We need to know the new date. Option (2) mentions the new date. So this has to be our answer. Option (2) is followed by reasons for much earlier. Hence, (2).

Question 6

Sentence: Dualism was long held to be the defining feature of developing countries in contrast to developed countries, where frontier technologies and high productivity were assumed to prevail.

Before: No clues as to the ideas that should precede this.

After: Sentence says 'dualism was long held to be'. This should be followed by why this view is no longer held.

Paragraph: ___(1)___ At the core of development economics lies the idea of 'productive dualism': that poor countries' economies are split between a narrow 'modern' that uses advanced technologies and a larger 'traditional' sector characterized by very low productivity. ___(2)___ While this distinction between developing and advanced economies may have made some sense in the 1950s and 1960s, it no longer appears to be very relevant. A combination of forces have produced a widening gap between the winners and those left behind. ___(3)___ Convergence between poor and rich parts of the economy was arrested and regional disparities widened.___(4)___ As a result, policymakers in advanced economies are now grappling with the same questions that have long preoccupied developing economies: mainly how to close the gap with the more advanced parts of the economy.

Explanatory Answer: Option (1) is incorrect since it is not followed by why this dualism does not hold. Option (2) is the answer since it gives the reason why this dualism does not hold.

Notes on the Missing Sentence in Paragraph

Solving the above questions, most of you will have had a doubt. Isn't it better to do the exact reverse—read the given sentence first and look for the missing link instead of not reading and looking for an unbreakable link?

Think about it from the question-maker's perspective. They would have removed the sentence from such a place in the paragraph where it would be most likely to be not considered missing. Only in the last question was it so easy that we could clearly spot the missing link.

More importantly, since we know that the given order is correct and there is a coherence that is missing only in one case, it makes sense to have a strategy that validates the coherence—look for unbreakable links rather than the other way around.

Once you start looking for coherence, you are likely to notice the links such as *there* and *this*. Otherwise, you will give primacy to the missing sentence and read the paragraph without noticing the links.

Jumbled paragraphs test your ability to identify links when they are out of sequence. In this question type, we should use those skills to identify links in sequence.

There will always be a temptation to read the sentence and fit it—that will be the method of selection. I would always trust the method of elimination over selection.

12

Verbal Ability: The Incorrect Sentence in Context

Another question type based on a paragraph, the Incorrect Sentence in Context, was first introduced in 2015, if I am not wrong, and has had a consistent presence since. I for one feel that this can be a tricky question type where a potential +9 (in under three minutes) can easily become a -3, and you know what an increase of 9 marks to your VA score can mean. While test-takers use a semblance of a strategy when faced with other VA question types, I am not sure if they have a specific approach to tackle this question type.

Even if they do have a strategy, it is likely to be related to jumbled paragraphs since this question type is seen as an offshoot of the same. If I am not wrong, most test-takers try to sequence the five sentences and see which one does not fit into a sequence. In my book, that is the last thing you should do.

Why should you not start by sequencing?

- The sentence that does not fit into the paragraph is not picked from some other passage but from the very same passage.
- To make the correct answer not very obvious, it has to be as close as possible to the actual paragraph.
- Since it is usually chosen a few sentences away—before or after the paragraph—you will be able to fit it into a sequence if you start with that intention. You will think—this can be the *starter*—or this can be the *closer*.
- Your job is to get the odd one out of your way and not sequence the sentences. Sequencing first will mean a huge waste of time

So what is a better method?

The Method of Labelling

Step 1—Label the first sentence

Read the first sentence and label the sentence with a phrase that captures a broad summary of the topic of the sentence. You can use the phrases from the sentence, say—*advantages of echolocation*—or put a top-level label to it—*latest advances in neuroscience.*

Think of the label as a sort of a generic title to the sentence—something that refers to a theme. The task now is to check whether:

- the label you have given to the first sentence is applicable to all but one other sentence—the out of context sentence, or
- the label you have given to the first sentence is applicable only to itself, the first sentence is the odd one out, and the other four need a different label

Step 2—Proceed to label the other sentences

When you label the other sentence even if you are not able to use the exact same title as the first one, see if you can apply a close enough one.

Step 3—Identify the common theme binding four labels and the odd one out

You will find that there is a common, very narrow theme cutting across four sentences and the theme will be the common label itself. The sentence that does not fit the theme should be the odd one out.

Step 4—Sequence (optional)

During the course of the reading, you would have found some links between the sentences. If you are not sure about the answer and want to double-check, sequence the remaining sentences using the links. If you develop the capability to label well, you will not need to sequence.

Question 1, EASY

1. Much has been recently discovered about the development of songs in birds.
2. Some species are restricted to a single song learned by all individuals, others have a range of songs.
3. The most important auditory stimuli for the birds are the sounds of other birds.
4. For all bird species there is a prescribed path to development of the final song,
5. A bird begins with the subsong, passes through plastic song, until it achieves the species song.

Sentence 1—Development of songs in birds

Sentence 2—Development of songs in birds

Sentence 3—Stimuli for sounds of birds

Sentence 4—Development of songs in birds

Sentence 5—Development of songs in birds

Theme: Development of songs in birds

Sequence: Not required

Correct Answer: 3

Question 2, MEDIUM

1. Our smartphones can now track our diets, our biological cycles, even our digestive systems and sleep patterns.
2. Researchers have even coined a new term, 'orthosomnia', to describe the insomnia brought on by paying too much attention to smartphones and sleep-tracking apps.
3. Sleep, nature's soft nurse, is a blissful, untroubled state all too easily disturbed by earthly worries or a guilty conscience.
4. The existence of a market for such apps is unsurprising: shift work, a long-hours culture and blue light from screens have conspired to rob many of us of sufficient rest.
5. A new threat to a good night's rest has emerged—smartphones, with sleep-tracking apps.

Sentence 1—Smartphones and self-tracking apps

Sentence 2—Smartphones, sleep-tracking apps, and insomnia

Sentence 3—Sleep

Sentence 4—Market for sleep-tracking apps

Sentence 5—Smartphones, sleep-tracking apps, and insomnia

Theme: Logos, hidden meanings and stories

Sequence: 2534

Correct Answer: 4

Question 3, EASY

1. Although we are born with the gift of language, research shows that we are surprisingly unskilled when it comes to communicating with others.
2. We must carefully orchestrate our speech if we want to achieve our goals and bring our dreams to fruition.

3. We often choose our words without thought, oblivious of the emotional effects they can have on others.

4. We talk more than we need to, ignoring the effect we are having on those listening to us.

5. We listen poorly, without realizing it, and we often fail to pay attention to the subtle meanings conveyed by facial expressions, body gestures, and the tone and cadence of our voice.

Sentence 1—Human troubles in communicating with others

Sentence 2—Speech control and goal achievement

Sentence 3—Human troubles in communicating with others (choose words without thought)

Sentence 4—Human troubles in communicating with others (talk more than necessary)

Sentence 5—Human troubles in communicating with others (listen poorly)

Theme: Human troubles in communicating with others

Sequence: Not necessary

Correct Answer: 2

*If we do not continually exercise our brain's language centers, we cripple our neurological ability to deal with problems we encounter with each other. Language shapes our behaviour, and each word is imbued with multitudes of personal meaning. The right words spoken in the right way can bring us love, money, and respect and the wrong words—or even the right words spoken in the wrong way—can lead a country to war. **We must carefully orchestrate our speech if we want to achieve our goals and bring our dreams to fruition.***

Although we are born with the gift of language, research shows that we are surprisingly unskilled when it comes to communicating with others. We often choose our words without thought, oblivious of the emotional effects they can have on others. We talk more than we need to, ignoring the effect we are having on those listening to us. We listen poorly, without realizing it, and we often fail to pay attention to the subtle meanings conveyed by facial expressions, body gestures, and the tone and cadence of our voice.

The incorrect sentence, as you can see, is the last sentence of the preceding paragraph.

Question 4, EASY

1. Over the past fortnight, one of its finest champions managed to pull off a similar impression.

2. Wimbledon's greatest illusion is the sense of timelessness it evokes.

3. At 35 years and 342 days, Roger Federer became the oldest man to win the singles title in the Open Era—a full 14 years after he first claimed the title as a scruffy, pony-tailed upstart.

4. Once he had survived the opening week, the second week witnessed the range of a rested Federer's genius.

5. Given that his method isn't reliant on explosive athleticism or muscular ball-striking, both vulnerable to decay, there is cause to believe that Federer will continue to enchant for a while longer.

Sentence 1—As you read the first sentence, it is clear that this question is going to be tough—there are no nouns that tell you what the subjects are, but yet, can you come up with a phrase, a few words? How about—a *championship*, a *player* and an *impression*? Let us start with this and work our way forward by looking at the second sentence.

Sentence 2—From this it is clear that the championship is *Wimbledon*, the impression is *timelessness* and unless you have just landed from a different planet and have decided to take the CAT, you would have figured that the player is Roger Federer. So what is the label? ***Wimbledon, Roger Federer and Timelessness.***

Sentence 3—Wimbledon, Roger Federer and Timelessness (explaining his long career)

Sentence 4—Wimbledon, Federer, Second week performance

Sentence 5—Roger Federer and Timelessness (the reasons behind the longevity of his career)

Theme: Roger Federer's timelessness (just like Wimbledon)

Sequence: Not necessary

Correct Answer: 4

Question 5, MEDIUM

1. Displacement in Bengal is thus not very significant in view of its magnitude.
2. A factor of displacement in Bengal is the shifting course of the Ganges leading to erosion of river banks.
3. The nature of displacement in Bengal makes it an interesting case study.
4. Since displacement due to erosion is well spread over a long period of time, it remains invisible.
5. Rapid displacement would have helped sensitize the public to its human costs.

Sentence 1—Displacement in Bengal, its significance

Sentence 2—Displacement in Bengal due to erosion

Sentence 3—Displacement in Bengal

Sentence 4—Displacement in Bengal due to erosion

Sentence 5—Human cost of displacement

Theme: Displacement in Bengal

5 also deals with displacement in Bengal but it brings in a new idea—the human cost of displacement—thus making it the odd one out.

Sequence: Not required

Correct Answer: 5

Question 6, MEDIUM

1. People who study children's language spend a lot of time watching how babies react to the speech they hear around them.
2. They make films of adults and babies interacting, and examine them very carefully to see whether the babies show any signs of understanding what the adults say.
3. They believe that babies begin to react to language from the very moment they are born.
4. Sometimes the signs are very subtle—slight movements of the baby's eyes or the head or the hands.
5. You'd never notice them if you were just sitting with the child, but by watching a recording over and over, you can spot them.

Sentence 1—Babies, study of children's language, reactions to speech

Sentence 2—Babies' reactions to speech

Sentence 3—Babies' reactions to speech

Sentence 4—Babies' reactions to speech

Sentence 5—Babies' reactions to speech

Theme: Babies' reactions to speech

The theme seems to strongly resonate in all the sentences. So, the challenge is to see if it needs to be narrowed down.

Sequence: Required

There is a clear link—1-2-4-5. So the only odd one out is sentence 3. It might seem like 3 follows 1 but it does not, since 1 states what was studied and 2, 4, 5 the process of studying, the observations through this process and why this process works.

If 3 follows 1 then suddenly the finding is revealed and again followed by the process of the study.

If we do not try to force fit it into the paragraph, we can see that it touches a larger theme or expresses the finding of the whole study, maybe a sentence much late in the passage, but not related to the narrow theme—the study of babies' reactions to speech.

Correct Answer: 3

Question 7, MEDIUM

1. Neuroscientists have just begun studying exercise's impact within brain cells—on the genes themselves.
2. Even there, in the roots of our biology, they've found signs of the body's influence on the mind.
3. It turns out that moving our muscles produces proteins that travel through the bloodstream and into the brain, where they play pivotal roles in the mechanisms of our highest thought processes.
4. In today's technology-driven, plasma-screened-in world, it's easy to forget that we are born movers—animals, in fact—because we've engineered movement right out of our lives.
5. It's only in the past few years that neuroscientists have begun to describe these factors and how they work, and each new discovery adds awe-inspiring depth to the picture.

Sentence 1—Impact of exercise within brain cells and genes

Sentence 2—Body's influence on mind

Sentence 3—Impact of exercise within brain cells and genes

Sentence 4—We no longer exercise

Sentence 5—Impact of exercise within brain cells and genes

Theme: Impact of exercise within brain cells and genes

2 seems to be related to exercise and brain cells whereas 4 introduces a completely new idea.

Sequence: Not required

While sequencing is not required, if you are unsure about 2, then you can sequence all the sentences excluding 4 and see if the rest fit. 1 has to be the starter since it outlines the study. 3 and 5 are more specific about the findings of the study while 2 is more generic and thus has to precede them and follow 1. The *there* in 2 refers to *within the brain cells*. So the sequence is 1235.

Correct Answer: 4

Question 8, MEDIUM

1. Those geometric symbols and aerodynamic swooshes are more than just skin deep.
2. The Commonwealth Bank logo—a yellow diamond, with a black chunk sliced out in one corner—is so recognisable that the bank doesn't even use its full name in its advertising.
3. It's not just logos with hidden shapes; sometimes brands will have meanings or stories within them that are deliberately vague or lost in time, urging you to delve deeper to solve the riddle.

4. Graphic designers embed cryptic references because it adds a story to the brand; they want people to spend more time with a brand and have that idea that they are an insider if they can understand the hidden message.

5. But the CommBank logo has more to it than meets the eye, as squirrelled away in that diamond is the Southern Cross constellation.

Sentence 1—Deeper meaning of symbols (those who know that swoosh is the name for Nike's logo will know that the reference is to logos, the label is *deeper meaning of symbols*)

Sentence 2—Recognizability of Commonwealth Bank logo

Sentence 3—Logos, hidden meanings, riddles, stories

Sentence 4—Logos, hidden meanings, riddles, stories

Sentence 5—Hidden things of the Commonwealth Bank logo

Theme: Logos, hidden meanings and stories

Sequence: 2534

Since Commonwealth Bank is common to both 2 and 5 and refers to the same thing, there is a link and they serve to introduce the idea that logos have hidden shapes and deliberately introduced stories and riddles. 3-4 are linked by the idea of deliberately hidden meanings and stories behind logos. The only sentence that, while having a related label, cannot be linked to the others is 1.

Correct Answer: 1

Question 9, MEDIUM

1. As India looks to increase the number of cities, our urban planning must factor in potential natural disasters and work out contingencies in advance.
2. Authorities must revise data and upgrade infrastructure and mitigation plans even if their local area hasn't been visited by a natural calamity yet.
3. Extreme temperatures, droughts, and forest fires have more than doubled since 1980.
4. There is no denying the fact that our baseline normal weather is changing.
5. It is no longer a question of whether we will be hit by nature's fury but rather when.

Sentence 1—Cities, urban planning, and contingencies for natural disasters

Sentence 2—Contingencies for natural disasters

Sentence 3—Incidence of extreme weather conditions

Sentence 4—Climate change and weather conditions

Sentence 5—Natural disasters

Theme: Planning for natural disasters

1, 2 and 5 are linked to the common theme of planning for natural disasters. We have to choose the odd one out.

3 refers to extreme weather conditions and how they have doubled. It is not directly related to contingency planning for cities since extreme temperatures, droughts and forest fires have no implications for city planning for natural disasters, which are likely to be floods.

4 refers to climate change in general and a change is what is normal. While it is not directly related to natural disasters and contingency planning, it can be an introductory sentence.

Sequence: Useful but not required

4125, 4512—There is a clear link between 1 and 2. 4 and 5 can be placed around it. Sentence 3 still does not fit anywhere. It can seem like a good follower to 4, citing examples of change in baseline but that is the risk you run if you sequence first before labelling.

Correct Answer: 3

Question 10, DIFFICULT

1. In many cases, time inconsistency is what prevents our going from intention to action.
2. For people to continuously postpone getting their children immunized, they would need to be constantly fooled by themselves.
3. In the specific case of immunization, however, it is hard to believe that time inconsistency by itself would be sufficient to make people permanently postpone the decision if they were fully cognizant of its benefits.
4. In most cases, even a small cost of immunization was large enough to discourage most people.
5. Not only do they have to think that they prefer to spend time going to the camp next month rather than today, they also have to believe that they will indeed go next month.

Sentence 1—Time inconsistency and postponement (not going from intention to action)

Sentence 2—Postponement of immunization, self-deception

Sentence 3—Time inconsistency, postponement of immunization

Sentence 4—Cost of immunization a discouragement

Sentence 5—Postponement of immunization, self-deception (link to 2)

Theme: Time inconsistency, postponement of immunization

3 also deals with discouragement or possibly postponement of immunization but it brings in a new idea of cost and thus is the odd one out.

Sequence: Not required

If you want to confirm, you can see that the sequence is 1325.

Correct Answer: 4

Question 11, DIFFICULT

1. The water that made up ancient lakes and perhaps an ocean was lost.
2. Particles from the Sun collided with molecules in the atmosphere, knocking them into space or giving them an electric charge that caused them to be swept away by the solar wind.
3. Most of the planet's remaining water is now frozen or buried, but clues over the past decade suggested that some liquid water, a presumed necessity for life, might survive in underground aquifers.
4. Data from NASA's MAVEN orbiter shows that solar storms stripped away most of Mars's once-thick atmosphere.
5. A recent study reveals how Mars lost much of its early water, while another indicates that some liquid water remains.

Sentence 1—Water, ancient lakes, ocean

Sentence 2—Sun, space, solar wind

Sentence 3—Planet, water, life

Sentence 4—Data from MAVEN, Mars' solar storms

Sentence 5—Study, Mars water

Theme: Mars, Water

The broad theme seems to be Mars and the presence or absence of water on Mars.

Sequence: Required

5 has to be the starter since it outlines the two studies about water on Mars—one about water loss and one about water left. 4-2 is a clear link—*solar storms stripped away most of Mars's once-thick atmosphere*—and—*the Sun collided with molecules in the atmosphere . . . swept away by the solar wind.* 5 talks about two studies—one about water loss, 4-2 seems to be the process of water loss. 1 talks about

the water that was lost and 3 about water that is left. So, the sequence seems to be 54213. But we have to choose, so 1 seems stand-alone.

Given Answer: 1

Source Text

A recent study reveals how Mars lost much of its early water, while another indicates that some liquid water still remains. Data from NASA's MAVEN orbiter shows that solar storms stripped away most of Mars's once-thick atmosphere. Particles from the Sun collided with molecules in the atmosphere, knocking them into space or giving them an electric charge that caused them to be swept away by the solar wind. **As the air was lost, so was the water that made up ancient lakes and perhaps an ocean.** Most of the planet's remaining water is now frozen or buried, but clues over the past decade suggested that some liquid water, a presumed necessity for life, might survive in underground aquifers.

Question 12, DIFFICULT

1. Translators are like bumblebees.
2. Though long since scientifically disproved, this factoid is still routinely trotted out.
3. Similar pronouncements about the impossibility of translation have dogged practitioners since Leonardo Bruni's *De interpretatione recta*, published in 1424.
4. Bees, unaware of these deliberations, have continued to flit from flower to flower, and translators continue to translate.
5. In 1934, the French entomologist August Magnan pronounced the flight of the bumblebee to be aerodynamically impossible.

Sentence 1—Translators, bumblebees

Sentence 2—Factoid

Sentence 3—Translation, pronouncements

Sentence 4—Translators, bumblebees

Sentence 5—Pronouncement, bumblebees, factoid

Theme: translators, bumblebees, pronouncement

Sequence: Definitely Required

The start seems to be 5 since it introduces the topic and 3 has to follow 5 since it talks about similar pronouncements. 4 is linked to 3 since *these deliberations* refer to the *pronouncements* of 5 and 3. So 5-3-4. 1 summarizes the idea, so it can come at the beginning or at the end—1534 or 5341.

2 seems to refer to the pronouncement made in 1. If we have to choose an odd one out, it has to be 2.

Given Answer: 2

Source Text

Translators are like bumblebees. In 1934, the French entomologist August Magnan pronounced the flight of the bumblebee to be aerodynamically impossible, **and though long since scientifically disproved, this factoid is still routinely trotted out.** Similar pronouncements about the impossibility of translation have dogged practitioners since Leonardo Bruni's *De interpretatione recta,* published in 1424. Meanwhile, bees, unaware of these deliberations, have continued to flit from flower to flower, and translators continue to translate.

Notes on Incorrect Sentence in Context

The last two questions clearly illustrate the worst of CAT Verbal Ability. None of these question types exist in any international test and they are not based on any rule of formal logic (GMAT/GRE/LSAT CR is not based on common sense; every question is based on the rules of formal logic).

In the last two questions, a sentence or part of the sentence from the actual paragraph written by an author has been deemed to be out of context by the question-maker. On what rules of formal logic, we do not know (*feels* over *rules,* I guess)!

The outcome of this is that while the question-setter has deemed it out of context, the sentence will seem to fit into context if one tries to sequence.

In other cases, sentences have been edited to remove sequencing clues—*Given the trend, it is no longer a question of whether we will be hit by nature's fury but rather when. It is Kerala today.*

The phrase, *given this trend* was removed. If it was not removed, it would be easy to put this sentence at the end since the rest of the sentences refer to the trend.

Since all of this is left to the discretion of the question-maker, it is always best to not proceed with a sequencing-first approach.

And if you find yourself getting stuck, do not waste any more time—enter an option and leave, since the way the question was made is not something that you can crack as it belongs to the peculiar logic of the question-maker.

Part IV

The QA Section

1

How to Solve Any Maths Question

As far as I know, all throughout school and college, no one ever taught us how to solve a maths problem. We were only taught solutions. We were required to reproduce all the steps in the right sequence. There were marks for steps (as if it were a dance competition).

This realization did not come to me after the debacle that was my first CAT attempt, which was solely due my disastrous performance on the Quant section. It did not come to me when I was working in the content-making department of IMS Academics. It came to me in the first few months after I moved to Chennai and started teaching on a regular basis.

It all started from a simple observation—I know how to best solve the problem and I am teaching my students the same solutions to the problems but they are not able to find solutions whenever they are faced with a new problem. The observation led to a key question that has maybe formed the bedrock of my teaching philosophy: What is preventing students from finding solutions? What are the obstacles in their mind, in their outlook, in their process of solving that is preventing them from doing the same?

And as it usually happens, I found the answer in a childhood memory.

Maths was the one subject that was my Achilles heel since childhood. My first informal tuition for maths was in Class III! My mother sent me to her colleague to help me better my maths. Nothing great came out of it, but maths tuitions became a regular feature of my mornings. My day would always start or end with maths tuitions all the way until I began my engineering! Only the teachers and the timings changed.

On one such morning when I was in Class VI, I was sitting in front of Venkat Rao Sir, a kind, old teacher who had retired after teaching maths at my school. Along with me at the wide table that filled the entire length of his veranda were my classmates. He threw a geometry problem at us and asked us to solve it.

All of us were looking at our notebooks and twirling our pencils trying to think which formula to apply. Before any of us could even warm up to a possible solution, a voice younger than us came up with the answer. It was the voice of the younger brother of one of my classmates who was studying in Class IV. What was he doing with kids older than him solving problems way beyond his age? He had already finished the Class IV and V books and was doing our problems for fun!

Our old teacher's eyes always lit up when he saw the young kid respond—the excitement of seeing what this young, exceptional mind could do. He asked the kid how he arrived at the answer. The kid said—*we drop a perpendicular to the base . . .*

The moment I heard him say that, I thought to myself—how does he know that we have to drop a perpendicular? Why don't any of us know?

It is only years later when I was thinking about what was preventing my students from solving problems that the answer came to me—*he was the only one in the group who was actively trying to solve a problem!* All the rest of us were occupied with just one thought—*what formula, what formula, what formula . . .*

You are in front of a river and you need find a way to cross it. You are not going to wait for some miraculous boatman to appear. You will try to find the best way to improvise a solution. Where is the water the shallowest? Can you break off a tree branch and lay it on the river?

The kid was doing the same thing when he was faced with the geometry question.

All through school and college, we did not need such skills since the problems were never unique. We learnt solutions by rote (not by heart) and regurgitated them on to the answer paper. We never learnt how to solve maths problems.

The CAT has problems that follow a pattern but, more often than not, the questions have one small twist that makes them unique. There are no marks for steps. And you have around two minutes to read and solve a question. So, everything that worked until now will stop working.

If you take the same old approach to learning and solving problems that you used to in school, then you will run into one or more of the following problems:

- You are able to solve questions during practice but not the unique problems you are faced with in the mocks
- You know how to solve but your accuracy is poor; you always end up making mistakes that later seem to have been avoidable
- You know the concept and have good accuracy but are unable to solve more than a few questions in total, leading to low scores

How do you ensure that you do not face these problems?

It starts with the first step of realizing that you have to actively *find* solutions to problems and not regurgitate standard solutions.

Once you make this distinction in your head, there are some clear skills you need to become great at CAT Quant—*Technique, Conceptual Clarity, Speed, Improvisation.*

The first thing—*Technique: How to Solve a Maths Problem*—is nothing but a foolproof process by which you ensure that nine out of ten times you can read a problem once, find the most appropriate solution, solve it without making a silly mistake and in reasonable time.

A video that discusses this technique in full is available on the Bell the CAT YouTube Page. The QR code on page 332 will take you to the same.

2

Learning to Learn Maths

While many of us know a lot of maths formulas, only a few really know how the formulas came about and how to understand things at a purely conceptual level. Every formula is a representation of the particular logic that governs a concept.

If you know the representation but not the underlying logic, it is like knowing how to draw a face but not really knowing that the eyes are to see, the ears are to listen, the nose to smell, and the mouth to eat.

Let us take the most basic concept of interest.

You put money in your bank and the bank offers you a simple interest (SI) rate of 10 per cent per annum.

What does this mean?

Every year, you will get 10 per cent of the amount you initially deposited in the bank.

So, if you deposited Rs 1,00,000, you will get 10 per cent (or 1 decimal point in from right to left of 1,00,000), i.e. Rs 10,000 every year. If you keep this money for five years, you will get Rs 50,000 as interest.

This is the logic that is converted into $I = PNR/100$ where P = principal or amount deposited, N = number of years and R = interest rate.

What happens when the same bank offers you an interest rate that is compounded annually (CI). You get interest on the interest earned annually and not just the principal deposited at the beginning.

If you deposited Rs 1,00,000 at 10 per cent, at the end of one year it becomes 110 per cent or 110/100 1.1 times. At the end of the year, you have 1.1 times the amount—1,00,000*1.1.

In the second year, this amount becomes the principal and you get 1.1 times this amount—1,00,000*1.1*1.1

From here you know that in the case of CI, the amount at the end of five years will be—1,00,000*1.1*1.1*1.1*1.1*1.1—$(1,00,000)*(1.1)^5$

So, in the first year, there is no difference between SI and CI in terms of the amount you earn, but from the second year, you are earning more in terms of interest on interest.

175

If a question asks you the difference in earnings between the SI and CI at the end of two years, one way is to use both the formulas and find the difference.

$$P(1 + r/100)^n - P(1 + nr/100)$$

But if you know the concept with clarity, you will know that the extra earning is just the interest on the first year interest.

So, if the principal is Rs 2,50,000 and interest is 12 per cent, you know that the first interest is 30,000 (10 per cent–25,000, 1 per cent–2500, 2 per cent–5000, 12 per cent-30,000) and 12 per cent on 30,000 is 3600.

Arithmetic is the area from which the maximum number of problems have appeared on the CAT Quant over the years. If you ask me, the whole of arithmetic is just three concepts—*Ratios, Averages* and *Weighted Averages*. But we like to subdivide them into *TSD, Percentages, Profit and Loss*, etc.

In the video 'Learning to Learn Math—I and II', I shall demonstrate how to understand the concept of weighted averages and use ratios to solve questions across topics in a more efficient manner. **This video is available on the Bell the CAT YouTube Page. The QR code on page 332 will take you to the same.**

How to Increase Your Speed: The T20 Skills Required for CAT Quant

While all the non-aptitude exams you have taken so far are like playing test cricket, aptitude, especially the CAT, is like playing T20. You do not have ten minutes per question; if that were the case, it would become an easy job—you have two minutes per question. So, you need to add three skills similar to those required in T20 cricket to take your speed to five times your normal speed.

Muscle Power: Increase your number-crunching muscle

One of the reasons why some batsmen are able to play high-impact innings and lead their team to victory is that they have superior power. Even shots that hit the toe-end of the bat of players such as Kieron Pollard, Andre Russel or Jos Buttler (who barely seems to hit the ball) go over the rope. They also bat in the death overs with confidence, which guys with their huge reach and immense power have, to send potential dot balls sailing into the crowd.

I know that at any point in time in the QA section, even when it is towards the fag end of the exam, I can count on my number-crunching muscle to power my way through seemingly tough problems. For example, let us take this problem below to see what I mean.

Q. Find $(1^2 + 3^2 + 4^2 + 5^2 + 7^2 + 8^2 + 9^2 + 11^2 + 12^2 + 13^2 + 15^2 + 16^2 + \ldots \ldots 49^2) / 1249$ if it is an integer. (TITA)

This is a question from a SimCAT and most people would have let the question go. Upon reading the regular long solution, they would have become doubly sure that it was a good leave. I decided to take on the above problem using my number-crunching muscle.

Firstly, I knew that this numerator was the sum of the first 49 squares minus the even squares—we just need to substitute n = 49 in the formula, $n(n+1)(2n+1)/6$ and minus the sum of the missing squares.

49*50*99/6 can be reduced to 49*25*33 which can be approximated to 50*25*33 = 1250*33. 12*3 = 36 so 1250*33 has to be a value greater than 36,000. Also, this has to end in a 5 since it is 49*25*33.

If I ignore the values that need to be subtracted—the even squares—and look at the denominator 1249, I know the answer has to be 35 since the value is greater than 36,000 and has to end in a 5. 1249 has to be multiplied by a number ending in 5 to get a value ending in 5, so the number has to be 35.

But the catch is that some values are missing from the sum of squares, which I promptly listed:

$$2^2 + 6^2 + 10^2 + 14^2 + 18^2 + 22^2 + 26^2 + 30^2 + 34^2 + 38^2 + 42^2 + 46^2$$

We can quickly estimate the last digit of the sum of these terms—4,6,0,6,4,4,6,0,6,4,4,6—0, so even after subtracting, the value has to end in 5, and hence the answer has to end in 5. If, without subtracting, it is 35, then after subtracting it has to be 25, 15 or 5. Remember, the question says—the answer is an integer.

I know that 46^2 is around 2000. There are twelve terms in total. If all terms are 46, then 2000*12 will be 20,000. But the values are decreasing so the total will be drastically less than 20,000. What is the best guess—10,000.

If I wanted to be dead sure, I would approximate it mentally as follows:

- $42^2 + 46^2$ = two 40s, around 2000 each, so around 3500
- $30^2 + 34^2 + 38^2$ = three 30s = more than 1000, 1000, 1000 = around 3500
- $22^2 + 26^2$ = 400, 600 = more than 1000
- $2^2 + 6^2 + 10^2 + 14^2 + 18^2$ = less than 1000

So, from a value greater than 36,000, I need to subtract around 10,000, so it will be around 26,000. Hence, a value greater than 26,000 ending in 5 when divided by 1249, to give an integer, has to yield 25 since 12*2 = 24 and 12*3 = 36.

Thinking is always faster than writing, so the actual time that I took for this crunching process was under two minutes.

Given that the CAT is a test of speed, what matters is not knowing how to solve but how quickly you can reach from knowing how to solve to the final answer.

This can only happen if you have some serious number-crunching muscle—extensive conceptual clarity cannot compensate for this muscle. You need to ask yourself: When the clock is ticking and you are executing a solution, can you break the numbers down or will you buckle under their load?

If your answer is sometimes I can crack, sometimes I buckle or most often I buckle, then you are not yet in shape to take the CAT. But you have three months to build some serious muscle by memorizing all of these:

- all squares from 2 to 30
- all cubes from 2 to 12
- all powers of 2 from 1 to 12
- all powers of 3 from 1 to 6
- all fraction and equivalent percentages from 1/2 to 1/11
- tables from 2*10 to 20*10

Most of you want to do an MBA so that you can do high-quality, high-paying work. If that is the case, then you should approach the duration of the CAT in such a way that you do only quality work during the test.

- Do you want to be calculating 29^2, if it is the answer to a TITA question?
- Do you want to be calculating the value of 2 raised to 8 by starting with 2 raised to 5 in the middle of a problem?

All of these values should already be *fed into* and so deeply *embedded* in the system, that there is no gap between retrieving and executing the solution. In short, you need to be the calculating equivalent of a T20 big-hitting beast.

Converting ones into twos—Reduce the number of steps you write

A few years ago, a student came to have a chat with me; he was retaking the CAT and needed a plan. He said he was really good at maths but could not solve more than twenty-two problems out of thirty-four on the CAT, but that paper had an easy Quant section and turned out to be a high-scoring one. He was working with a well-known consulting firm, had a good profile, and was thus looking at premier schools that needed high percentiles.

My first instinct was to give him a piece of paper and a problem just to watch how he solved it. He wrote down around ten steps on the paper and solved the problem—that was the exact reason why he was able to attempt only twenty-two questions!

Writing and executing the entire solution of a problem is the biggest speed breaker or decelerator in front of you. Each one of you will have varying degrees of dependence on writing. Sometimes, the more diligent the aspirant, the more steps he or she will write (systematically and without clutter) while solving a question.

The problem is that this method will result in fewer attempts and, when coupled with a few mistakes, will end up in a percentile that is perennially hovering in the 85 range.

So, if you are among those who write diligently, then you need to drastically change your approach to increase your percentiles and understand that:

- you are used to writing because you are used to submitting homework
- you are used to writing because missing steps can mean fewer marks being awarded
- you are used to writing neatly because so far, good, clutter-free writing fetched you higher marks

None of the things listed above apply to CAT maths—just like none of the rules of test cricket apply to T20 cricket—no marks for handwriting, no marks for steps.

How do you decrease the amount of writing you do? Start with the following steps:

- Do not duplicate information from the screen on to your rough sheet

    o If it says 'a man does a piece of work in 20 days', then do not write 20 or t = 20 on your paper; you are just executing robot-like steps without getting any closer to solving the problem

- Do not write what you need to execute

  o if you need to calculate the average of five numbers, then there is no way you are writing 5 numbers with a plus sign between them, drawing a line underneath them, and writing a five; you need to just get adding and dividing without writing anything

- Start to skip writing down each step by executing intermediate steps mentally

  o if you have to solve $1/(x+1) + 1/(x+2) = 2$, then maybe the next step you should write is $2x + 3 = 2x^2 + 6x + 4$

In short, write only if you cannot process the information in your head!

This is a question in one of the SimCATs that I solved purely mentally when an aspirant who was working with us in the content team came to me and asked me to solve a paper live to see how I approach a problem.

Q. The function F is defined as $F(k) = 2k^3 - 3k^2 - 5k + 7$ and the function G is defined as $G(k) = 2k^3 + 1k^2 + 7k + 15$. Find the product of all values of 'k' for which F(k) and G(k) are equal.

I knew that I had to equate the two since that is when they will become equal. The cubes cancel themselves out and if I take the remaining terms to one side, it becomes a quadratic $4k^2 + 12k + 8$, which gets reduced to $k^2 + 3k + 2$, whose roots will be -1 and -2, making their product 2. This took about sixty seconds or fewer mentally.

Even if you take more time, the key is that there is no need to write. Some of you might say that if I do it this way, I'll be making mistakes. It is like saying if I drive faster, I will crash, but then you won't win the race—it is about driving the fastest you can without crashing.

This is easier said than done since we have been conditioned over the years to equate writing with thinking and solving, so like the legendary dogs of Pavlov, we start writing the moment we start reading a problem.

To practise the above steps consciously, you should try a few special sessions.

- Take a section test or an area test or the Quant section of a take-home SimCAT with your hands folded or your palms locked in front of you
- Have a pen and paper handy on the table to write only if the need arises
- Force yourself to execute a few steps mentally
- Do not be bothered about time running out; do not be bothered about the score

If you do not try out these things during practice, you will keep doing the same thing over and over again and keep expecting different results, which alas is a non-sequitur (CR enthusiasts should check what this means).

Improvisation—Approximation, Backsolving and other tricks

The biggest innovation in batting, thanks to T20 cricket, are the scoops, ramp shots and reverse sweeps. Why did this come about? The only way to hit boundaries is to send the ball to where fielders are not there, even if it involves a risk. The place where fielders are never present? Behind the batsman! Cue the scoops and the ramps.

Batsmen who are not blessed with the power of the big hitters to hit down the ground chose this route instead. One of the reasons why India has not won as many T20 World Cups as other teams is that, apart from Surya Kumar Yadav, we do not have players who naturally play behind the wicket. Even the most traditional batsmen such as Joe Root have managed to make scoops and reverse scoops a low-risk shot. What seems on the face of it to be a high-risk shot has become a low-risk high-return shot.

What do I mean by improvisation in CAT? In the first question we discussed, we saw how number-crunching muscle was used along with approximation. Let us look at another question.

Q. **Two cars travel from different locations at constant speeds. To meet each other after starting at the same time, they take 1.5 hours if they travel towards each other but 10.5 hours if they travel in the same direction. If the speed of the slower car is 60 km/hr, then the distance travelled in km by the slower car when it meets the other car while travelling towards each other is?**

(1) 120   **(2) 100**   **(3) 150**   **(4) 90**

If you read the problem carefully, it can be seen that question is asking you how much distance the slower car travelled. When moving towards each other, each car took 1.5 hours. If the slower car travelled at 60 km/hr, then it travelled 60*1.5=90!

If your radar is always on like that of a T20 batsman to stay still and score boundaries, then you will have seen this. But usually, we are in test cricket state of mind, so we always try to form equations. We take the distance to be D. We take the speed of the faster car to be S.

So, when they are travelling towards each other D = (S + 60)*1.5. When they are travelling in the same direction D = (S-60)10.5. Equating the two, you find S and D, both of which are not necessary!

These are just a few examples of improvisation. For you to get a proper hang of it, I will devote the next chapter to improvised solutions that become elegant solutions.

4

The Elegant Solution: Think Without Ink

The first person whose solving methods showed me the possibility of elegant solutions was my mentor when I was preparing for the CAT. His USP was using ratios to solve TSD. I learnt that but my skills were limited to that one topic.

When I had just started working with IMS, I met the man who is officially the GOD of CAT—my colleague Scrabbler, who has more than ten 100 percentiles on the CAT. And many a time it meant hundreds on each section and also getting the highest score among all the hundred percentilers!

While I personally know a few other 100-percentilers, I can attest that he is head and shoulders above all the rest. Why do I think so? Because he does not leave a single question! Over all the iterations of the exam over all of these years!

How does he do it? Because he says he hates writing and thus is always solving the entire paper in T20 mode.

I once sat with him and saw him solve question after question without putting pen to paper. Most students see his stuff with the statutory warning: these stunts are performed by professionals, do not try this at home!

While I was amazed at the beauty and elegance of the solutions, I had a feeling that it was not tough. I did not see his solutions as stunts performed by professionals; I felt I should try them myself. We left that session with a set of problems and a plan to meet each other a week or so later with elegant solutions of the same.

When I sat with the problems, I was always thinking, is this fast enough? He will surely have a better solution. And I kept turning the problems over and over again. When I met him, I found that he had found elegant solutions to quite a few; on a few we had the same answers, but on one particular problem, I managed a better solution! It was a great high. A high I would not have felt if I had thought of him as a god, which he is, and myself as a mere mortal who should not compete with the gods!

The problem was an actual CAT problem.

Q. **Total expenses of a boarding house are partly fixed and partly varying linearly with the number of boarders. The average expense per boarder is Rs 700 when there are 25 boarders and Rs 600 when there are 50 boarders. What is the average expense per boarder when there are 100 boarders?**

(1) Rs 580   **(2) Rs 540**   **(3) Rs 570**   **(4) Rs 550**

The regular way to solve this problem is by framing equations using variables F and V and solving for F and V.

F + V*25 = 700*25
F + V*50 = 600*50

It is a regular problem with a regular run-of-the-mill solution. But if we look at it with fresh eyes and understand why this average cost changes, we can solve it in a very elegant manner.

Why does the average cost come down as the number of boarders increases? Because the fixed cost gets shared over a larger number of people. Just like the rent will come down if it is shared by more people. The variable cost is like the fixed rate per plate of food. It increases as the number of people increases. So, this drop in average cost is nothing but:

F/25 - F/50 = 700-600 = 100.

When the number of boarders increases from 50 to 100, the average cost will drop further, which is nothing but:

F/50 - F/100 = (F/25 - F/50)*½ = (100)*½ = 50

So, the average cost will drop by a further 50 from 600, which is 550!

After this, I figured that it was more about my ability to let go of my conditioned responses and less about my ability to find alternate solutions. And sure enough, over a short period of time, looking for the fastest route to the goal by looking at questions through an alternate lens became second nature to me as well.

With Quant, it was almost like it was with cricket for me. I have never thought of myself as a natural sportsman (like I never thought of myself as a natural QA guy) and got by with grit and competitiveness. So, while I opened the batting for my department team, it was more a function of my ability to stay at the crease and maximize whatever I could with the limited but effective range of strokes I had at my disposal and the limited talent in our department, rather than high-quality skill.

We managed to play almost every day (back in the day we had annual exams so we could afford to chill all year and study at the end) and it is only at the end of three years and that too during a practice session that I stepped out of my crease and smoked the bowler (a gentle medium-pacer) over his head for a six. It had taken me close to ten years of playing cricket to do it (and I can still step back into that feeling).

This video shows the alternate approach to a series of problems across different areas and not just arithmetic. Some of the methods are mine, some my colleagues came up with, and some my students!

This video is available on the Bell the CAT YouTube Page. The QR code on page 332 will take you to the same.

What are the things one can consciously do to make viewing problems through an alternate lens a habit?

The term 'alternate lens' might make it seem as if there is a standard lens and there is an alternate lens. In fact, nothing could be further from the truth. What always matters is the most optimal solution to a problem. Why do we not find the optimal solution?

Reject the formula-first approach

Our gut reaction to solving a problem is to try to immediately fit it into a formula. In fact, when faced with a question, we immediately ask ourselves: What formula do I know that can help me solve this?

A formula is only one of the tools that you will use to reach the solution that you have devised; they are similar to a surgeon's or a mechanic's tools. A surgeon does not decide on the kind of surgery to be done based on the tools he has, neither does a mechanic decide on how he is going to fix a vehicle based on the tool he has! So, do not make formula-fitting your first step.

Do not algebraify a problem by force

If we do not go to a formula, we then start taking the first thing we encounter as X and we try to form an equation. We feel that if we can convert English into algebra, we have done our job but algebra is just another language like English. What you have to convert it into is a logical language, which can still be in English but uses words or algebra that uses symbols. Do not convert all problems into algebra, especially the arithmetic ones.

Move to the question first approach

Put the question and what is finally asked as the first and most important thing. Work backward from there to determine what you really need instead of trying to build towards the answer from the first bits of information. Information is never given sequentially and usually, the most important piece of information is given right at the end, and that might make your whole job easier.

Do not treat the given information passively

On most good questions, the given information itself holds more than meets the eye, provided you are willing to at least turn it over in your palm to see a small latch that you can pull.

If you take it just the way it is and do not try to even squeeze a wee bit or cut it, a lemon is as good or bad as a stone or softball (in fact, not even as good as those).

5

How to Increase Your Accuracy on QA

You have read the previous chapters and have been practising for a while now, but you are not able to translate your conceptual clarity into your target scores, you accuracy is stuck below 80 per cent. You are wondering whether you should solve more questions faster or whether you should slow down and increase your accuracy.

The first thing you need to do is to fix the machine or rather ensure that the machine churns out a very high percentage of items within the quality standards. While achieving 6-sigma levels of accuracy is a very high benchmark to set, you should strive to have an accuracy rate of at least 80 per cent.

Irrespective of how many concepts you know, if your machine has an error rate of 35 per cent, then you are always going to be performing below par.

- 65 per cent accuracy versus 80 per cent accuracy

  o 12 attempts: 19, 26
  o 15 attempts: 24, 33
  o 18 attempts: 29, 40

What should you focus on—attempts or accuracy—given that you are taking the CAT to enter the world of business?

Obviously, accuracy since you will always look to squeeze the maximum out of every rupee invested (unless you run an e-commerce business and have investors to watch your back, albeit not for perpetuity).

What do you think is easier to achieve?

- An increase in attempts from 12 to 15, or
- An increase in accuracy from 65 per cent to 80 per cent

If your accuracy is low, then trying to dramatically increase attempts will only further bring down your accuracy. If at your current speed you are prone to crashing three to four out of ten times, then at a higher speed you will only crash more often! So, fix the machine to get the most out of it.

Diagnose the reasons behind your low accuracy

Good accuracy is a function of two things—your **solving technique** and your **choice of questions**. Since we will take up selection ahead, here we will just deal with solving technique.

Since we have undergone the induction process of learning solutions during the long formative years of our education, we don't really know the technique of problem-solving as such. So, we usually attribute our mistakes to that worn-out phrase: 'silly mistake'. If we continue to use that phrase, then neither can I nor can anyone else help you out since the only solution is to stop being silly!

Even if you tell yourself that you will be serious, that you will concentrate hard, it is not going to work since they are just words or attitudes and not process changes.

To improve your accuracy on CAT QA, you need to first stop viewing your mistakes through the silly-mistake lens, and view them through the process-mistake lens.

These are the big process mistakes to which most errors can be attributed:

Missing crucial information in the question—Misreading

We are always in a tearing hurry to read the question, so it is not a surprise that we tend to misread the parts of the question, usually the first parts (if *n* is an integer) or the last part (if they work on *alternate* days).

Since we are always trying to map a question to a pattern we have previously learnt or to a formula, we tend to ignore the unique aspects of the question in front of us and tend to selectively pick out information that either matches a pattern or can be put into a formula.

Taking your eye off the ball while calculating—Miscalculation

Keen followers of cricket will know how Sunil Gavaskar always gets agitated when a batsman gets run out because of not grounding the bat. For him, it is unpardonable since grounding the bat is part of the process of batsmanship and more importantly, it is a case of throwing away one's wicket. He is known to have been such a stickler for correctness—he always took an extra run before celebrating after reaching a 100 since the manual scorer could have made a mistake—no wonder he gets so incensed!

Just like running between the wickets is the hard (or donkey) work in cricket, the calculation part is the hard (or donkey) work in the CAT QA. You can either choose to just run without really being alert and present or be vigilant and fast at the same time a la Dhoni and Virat.

If you watch those two, they don't just run blindly, they have their eye on where the ball has gone and on the fielder; that is what makes them exceptional. They are as alert during the running phase as they are when they are facing the ball and playing a shot.

Missing the complexity of the question—Misjudgement

Sometimes you make a mistake, not because of the above two reasons but because you have underestimated the complexity of a question.

This underestimation can happen at two stages:

- One during the initial stages when you have unknowingly simplified the problem. The reason for this though is again related to mapping a question while reading itself to a previous pattern in your head and thus missing the extra knot that makes the specific question a tad tougher.
- The other is during the execution stage in the rush to solve the question and move forward to the next question.

Such errors tend to occur in questions involving permutations and combinations or probability.

So firstly, do a diagnosis of the process mistakes you commit. Make a list of all the mistakes you have made in the preceding SimCATs in an Excel sheet. Next to each mistake, write down the process mistake you made for the questions that you could have solved but ended up messing up.

You will come to know which process mistake is contributing how much to your errors; for example, **Misreading (40 per cent), Miscalculation (25 per cent) and Misjudgement (35 per cent).**

How to eliminate errors due to misreading

If you are making quite a few errors because of misreading the question and if these questions are not towards the end of a section, which means that the misreading was not due to time constraints, then you should:

Drop your pace of reading

It might seem as if you will solve far fewer questions by doing this but dropping the pace does not mean that you should read at a snail's pace. It just means that you will read without rushing. While you might see a marginal dip in the number of attempts, it will be more than offset by the increase in score.

Read the question in front of you, not the pattern in your mind

Do not always map the question in front of you to a pattern or a formula as you read it. This is a big reason why even though you read at the right pace, you skip information—you selectively pick and exclude information.

How to eliminate errors due to miscalculation

Different questions will require you to concentrate at different levels; some might take up 20 per cent of your mind space, some 80 per cent, but the key is that within the solving time of the problem, the same level of concentration has to be maintained throughout the solving of the problem. You should not view the execution of a solution as a burden or take your eye off the ball during the calculation phase.

Even when you are approximating, which means that you are cutting open something with, say, three slashes of your sword and not ten, each of the three slashes has to be made with concentration and precision.

To keep it simple, look at the ball and the fielder before taking off and always ground the bat.

How to eliminate errors due to misjudgement

Firstly, these are higher-order errors where you are not entirely to blame. The test-setter might have managed to cleverly slip in a trap but that cleverness sometimes relies on you making a process mistake.

So, to start off with, do not start solving as you start reading. By starting to solve as you read, you are setting yourself up for a host of errors:

- Taking the wrong thing as X only to calculate it and find it in the answer options, moving on to the next question thinking you are right, and being shocked when you see the score
- Assuming the question to be simple and setting up a simplistic structure to solve and not accounting for the build-up in complexity as you are reading the question, leading to having to reformulate the problem with different variables and equations

While reading, only evaluate how the solution will unfold, what you have, what you do not have, etc. Before you jump to the solving, just pause for a moment to think about:

- the complexity of the problem or possible cases if it is a P & C problem
- what will be convenient—taking X or taking a 100
- what will be convenient—taking a 100 or taking a number that is a multiple of the ratios (*if two things are in the ratio 7:8, and you need to assume the total as some value, it is better to take the total as 15 or 150 and get the two values as 7, 8 or 70, 80 instead of taking 100 and getting 700/15 and 800/15*)

Improve your solving process

If you see, most of our inefficiencies occur because:

- we are always in a rush, operating all of the time out of a fear of time running out
- we do not read the question properly, so without figuring out the problem, we want to deliver a solution
- we do not think about how to solve the problem, we just jump into solving; aren't we supposed to think, isn't this supposed to be a test of reasoning in different contexts?

It is not possible to make these process changes just like that; you need to programme your brain to slip out of its current grooves and create new pathways. To do this, talk to yourself before every practice session about the changes you need to make—all the great sportsmen do it.

So, before every practice session, tell yourself to:

- read the question properly till the end without panicking
- concentrate hard and never take your eyes off the ball
- think, think and think and not just regurgitate old solutions

Part V

The Data Interpretation and Logical Reasoning (DI-LR) Section

1

Why is DI-LR the Toughest Section on the CAT?

Without a doubt, the Data Interpretation and Logical Reasoning (DI-LR) section has become the toughest section on the CAT over the past decade. While many test-takers who are strong in maths might consider the verbal section to be the toughest, I still feel, given the range of skills and concepts tested, the DI-LR section is the toughest section on the CAT.

It is not DI-LR but MR

The title of the section might make it seem that it involves calculation and logical reasoning. Nothing could be more simplistic than that assumption. Over the last decade, one of the reasons why the section has become the toughest of the lot is that it tests Mathematical Reasoning (MR) more than anything else.

MR involves solving hardcore reasoning puzzles that are built on the base of concepts across different areas in maths.

In traditional DI, knowledge of graphs, charts and percentages coupled with calculation skills are more than enough to tackle most sets. The reasoning skills required were not very high.

In traditional LR, pure logical reasoning skills without any knowledge of maths was sufficient to solve most sets.

In MR, the range of concepts tested increases vastly. So, before we go ahead, you should be clear that you need to develop a solid grasp of the following concepts:

- Numerical reasoning: plugging numbers into equations
- Ratios, percentages, averages, weighted averages
- Statistics: mean, median, mode
- 2-factor, 3-factor and 4-factor Venn diagrams
- Probability, permutation and combination

Where MR differs from Quant is that it requires a higher level of logical reasoning skills than required in Quant. So, the first thing you should have is a great working knowledge of all the concepts listed above.

DI-LR is a big test of your reading speed as well

The big unsaid challenge of DI-LR is that without reading speed, you will always fall one set short of cracking the section. Each set has so much reading and decoding to do that if you do not have great reading speed, you will end up taking a good fifteen minutes to read and solve one set. But to choose the right sets to solve, you will have to read all the sets!

In effect, this section ends up testing your reading comprehension skills in a different context, it tests your knowledge of a wide range of maths concepts, and it tests your logical reasoning skills. In effect, it tests three sections instead of one.

One bad set and your entire exam is more or less done!

On a maths question or a verbal ability question, if you are unable to crack the question, you will know it within two to three minutes or at max, five minutes. If an RC is getting very tough to read, you will quit it in two or three minutes. But because of the very nature of a DI-LR set, you will get sucked in for ten minutes and not even realize that you are getting nowhere. Why does this happen?

- Two to four minutes are lost in understanding and representing the set on your rough sheet
- Every set has at least five conditions and once you start interpreting them, you will spend at least five minutes trying to determine the missing information
- If you are stuck, you will start re-reading the set
- Since you have already spent so much time, you will start re-drawing the set all over again!

Whether the section is forty minutes or sixty minutes long, if you lose fifteen minutes on a set, you will have more or less jeopardized your chances of cracking the section. The worst part is that since the DI-LR section is the one right before the Quant, a poor showing on that more often than not translates into a poor Quant section if you are not mentally strong.

A clear prep strategy for DI-LR

Over the years, I have seen that aspirants do not have a clear-cut strategy to prepare for DI-LR. They end up practising a lot of sets and then hit a plateau. They end up thinking that this is the limit of logical reasoning skills or they end up practising obsessively.

I feel that, irrespective of their level, all aspirants will benefit from going through the step-by-step plan outlined in the following chapters. Once you finish all of these chapters, you can practise sets from the courseware you have subscribed to.

We will start with a prep and practice plan to develop the core reasoning strength. We will follow that up with the standard operating procedure to solve a DI-LR set. Once both of these are in place, we will discuss all the mathematical reasoning concepts required for DI-LR.

2

Developing Your Core Reasoning Strength

Now that you know why DI-LR is the toughest section of all, let us dive into how you can start building the core skills required to crack this section.

Logical reasoning seems like the most self-evident term if there ever was one. But I feel that a lot is actually left to the 'natural' capability of the student. We can always suggest doing Sudoku and it is mighty helpful. But it is similar to the gym work put in by athletes. How do you actually build the specific technique required to score from free kicks or hook bouncers?

What core reasoning strength do aspirants need to crack DI-LR and how can they develop those skills through a particular kind of targeted practice.

The reason I thought about core strength is that I have been doing yoga, strength training and breathing exercises quite regularly over the years and I realized that there is no point in trying to do a few asanas and kettlebell moves unless one had a certain amount of strength in the key areas—core, legs, lower back—and mobility—hips and back.

The current trainer that I am working did not even make me do many of the asanas for close to eight weeks or more, asanas that other instructors start from day one, which one keeps doing for years hoping to get better. This guy spent months just working on strength and mobility so that when he finally made me do an asana, it just felt right—both the strength and the flexibility were there to go into and hold the pose (which never happened in years of practice before).

That is what led me to think about exercises to build core strength for DI-LR. Can there be a specific way to practise and specific sets to practise that can impart the desired strength and speed to the LR muscle in the head?

In the process, I jogged back to my first teaching assignment when I had just finished my engineering (mechanical)—teaching analytical reasoning (AR) to GRE students.

I managed to download the ETS GRE Big Book (it is no longer in print) that has twenty-seven full-length tests with two AR sections per test. Each section had twenty-five questions to be answered in thirty minutes, with approximately eighteen to nineteen LR questions spread over four sets and six to seven CR questions.

I started doing a few sections just to gauge their utility from a CAT prep perspective. I felt that compared to the CAT LR sets, they were way too easy, I could solve the questions within time and I made two or three silly mistakes every single time. Every section had only one or two questions that were tricky (back in the day all of my peers got a perfect score, 800, on this section). But the sets felt like good practice since they were well-designed and needed you to think a bit.

I felt that these sets could be a good starting point to develop LR skills but to yield maximum benefit to the **entire spectrum of students,** I needed to add one bit of complexity: *solve it without putting pen on paper unless absolutely necessary.*

What this meant was that on an A4 size paper, I wrote down numbers one to twenty-five (to note down the answers) and had the rest of the space available for rough work. I would consider myself good only if I solved the entire section within the time limit with barely anything written on the paper and with no more than one mistake.

The moment I set this restriction, I felt that a twenty-five question practice session could serve as a great LR core conditioning exercise since I never solved LR sets mentally. I felt that these sets were at the right difficulty level to solve without putting pen to paper.

To solve these mentally, I had to strengthen four core skills:

- Remember the conditions and the set better
- Decode the logical implications of the information provided in the set and the questions better
- Always find the most optimum route to answer instead of random trial and error
- Concentrate harder

Each of the above is a core LR strength that is needed to solve any LR set and the first three also apply to QA as well, and the last one for the entire test.

I realized that just by setting this simple constraint, I was forcing myself to get better. I forced myself to sharpen that tip of the pencil to a finer point and sometimes, that is the difference between a *great* sketch and a *good* sketch.

Let me take a set and demonstrate what I mean by solving a set mentally. This would mean that all of you would have to imagine things visually.

Solve the set below on your own first and then go ahead and read my solution.

Q. A museum curator must group nine paintings—F, G, H, J, K, L, M, N and O—in twelve spaces numbered consecutively from 1–12. The paintings must be in three groups, each group representing a different century. The groups must be separated from each other by at least one unused wall space. Three of the paintings are from the eighteenth century, two from the nineteenth century, and four from the twentieth century.

- Unused wall spaces cannot occur within groups.
- G and J are paintings from different centuries.
- J, K and L are all paintings from the same century.
- Space number 5 is always empty.
- F and M are eighteenth-century paintings.
- N is a nineteenth-century painting.

1. **If space 4 is to remain empty, which of the following is true?**

   (A) Space number 10 must be empty.
   (B) The groups of paintings must be hung in chronological order by century.
   (C) An eighteenth-century painting must be hung in space 3.
   (D) A nineteenth-century painting must be hung in space 1.
   (E) A twentieth-century painting must be hung in space 12.

2. **If the paintings are hung in reverse chronological order by century, the unused wall spaces could be:**

   (A) 1, 5 and 10
   (B) 1, 6 and 10
   (C) 4, 7 and 8
   (D) 5, 8 and 12
   (E) 5, 9 and 10

3. **Which of the following is a space that CANNOT be occupied by a nineteenth-century painting?**

   (A) Space 1
   (B) Space 6
   (C) Space 8
   (D) Space 11
   (E) Space 12

4. **If J hangs in space 11, which of the following is a possible arrangement for spaces 8 and 9?**

   (A) F in 8 and M in 9
   (B) K in 8 and G in 9
   (C) N in 8 and G in 9
   (D) 8 unused and H in 9
   (E) 8 unused and F in 9

5. **If the twentieth-century paintings are hung in spaces 1–4, which of the following CANNOT be true?**

   (A) Space 8 is unused
   (B) Space 9 is unused
   (C) F is hung in space 6
   (D) M is hung in space 12
   (E) N is hung in space 9

6. If the first five paintings, in numerical order of spaces, are F, O, M, N, G, which of the following must be true?

(A) Either space 1 or space 4 is unused.
(B) Either space 7 or space 12 is unused.
(C) H hangs in space 11.
(D) Two unused spaces separate the eighteenth-century and nineteenth-century paintings.
(E) Two unused spaces separate the nineteenth-century and twentieth-century paintings

Solution

A museum curator must group nine paintings—F, G, H, J, K, L, M, N and O—in twelve spaces numbered consecutively from 1 to 12. The paintings must be in three groups, each group representing a different century. The groups must be separated from each other by at least one unused wall space. Three of the paintings are from the eighteenth century, two from the nineteenth century, and four from the twentieth century.

- Unused wall spaces cannot occur within groups.
- G and J are paintings from different centuries.
- J, K, and L are all paintings from the same century.
- Space number 5 is always empty.
- F and M are eighteenth-century paintings.
- N is a nineteenth-century painting.

Make it a point to remember:

- Twentieth—4 paintings, nineteenth—2 paintings, eighteenth—3 paintings
- J, K, L—same century, N—nineteenth, F and M—eighteenth

INFERENCES from the information as I am reading the conditions from the first to the last one:

- J, K and L are from the same century—cannot be nineteenth century since it has only two
- J, K and L are from the same century—cannot be eighteenth century since eighteenth century has three paintings and F and M are from eighteenth. If J, K and L are from eighteenth, the total will go to five.
- J, K and L—twentieth century.
- G is eighteenth or nineteenth (since it is from a group other than J)
- H and O can be from any century

1. If space 4 is to remain empty, which of the following is true?

This is a *must-be-true* question and hence, I can derive the answer before going to the options.

- If 4 is empty and 5 has to be empty as per the conditions, then the spaces 1, 2 and 3:

  o cannot have twentieth century since there are four paintings
  o cannot have nineteenth-century paintings since there are two paintings, which means that from 6 to 12, seven places, the rest of the seven paintings from the other two centuries have to be placed without a gap, but a gap has to be there between two sets of paintings
  o must have the eighteenth-century paintings

Now I will go to the options and search for an option that says eighteenth must be in 1-2-3.

(A) Space number 10 must be empty.
(B) The groups of paintings must be hung in chronological order by century.
(C) *An eighteenth-century painting must be hung in space 3.*
(D) A nineteenth-century painting must be hung in space 1.
(E) A twentieth-century painting must be hung in space 12.

2. **If the paintings are hung in reverse chronological order by century, the unused wall spaces could be:**

This is not a must-be-true but a *could-be true* so, after drawing a basic inference, I can go to the options.
   Reverse chronological order means twentieth, nineteenth, eighteenth.
   Space 5 is empty, and after that, there are seven places, so we cannot place all nine paintings after space 5. The four twentieth-century paintings have to be in places 1-2-3-4. Now I will go to the options to check which one can be the set of unused spaces.

(A) 1, 5 and 10
(B) 1, 6 and 10
(C) 4, 7 and 8
(D) **5, 8 and 12**
(E) 5, 9 and 10

The first three options can be eliminated since spaces 1 to 4 cannot be unused, the twentieth-century paintings hang there.
   I try out option D—5 and 8 are unused, 6 and 7 are occupied, reverse chronological order so the two nineteenth-century paintings are in 6 and 7. Three eighteenth-century paintings in 9, 10 and 11, and 12 is unused; no rule is broken and hence, this could be true. I will not try to substitute option E unless I want to double-check.

3. **Which of the following is a space that CANNOT be occupied by a nineteenth-century painting?**

Since it is a *cannot-be-true* question, in a way the opposite of the must-be-true question, and since there is no additional information, I have to jump to the options and proceed.

(A) Space 1

If a nineteenth century is in space 1, it has to be in space 2 as well since there are two nineteenth century paintings, and since there has to be a gap between one group and the other 3 have to be empty, 5 is anyway empty, and nothing can be kept in space 4, so all the 7 paintings from twentieth and eighteenth have to go into the seven spaces from 6 to 12 without a space between the two periods, which is not possible and hence, this is the answer. I do not even need to check the rest.

4.   If J hangs in space 11, which of the following is a possible arrangement for spaces 8 and 9?

It is a *could-be-true* question, so I should deduce whatever I can before I jump to the options.

J is a twentieth century painting and it is in 11, so the other three have to be in a group along with J, so the twentieth century paintings can be:

- In 8, 9, 10 and 11 (with J being the last) and unused spaces in 7 and 12
- 9, 10, 11 and 12 (with J being the third) and unused space in 8
- Both cases put together, 8 has to be filled with a twentieth century painting or unused and 9 has to be filled with a twentieth-century painting

Now to the options.

(A) F in 8 and M in 9
(B) K in 8 and G in 9
(C) N in 8 and G in 9
(D) **8 unused and H in 9**
(E) 8 unused and F in 9

A, B, C and E can be eliminated since they all have paintings that are definitely not from the twentieth century in 8 or 9. Hence, option D.

5.   If the twentieth-century paintings are hung in spaces 1–4, which of the following CANNOT be true?

As I mentioned before, a cannot-be-true is another version of a must-be-true. Since they have given some additional information in the question, I can make deductions before I go to the options.

Twentieth-century paintings are hung from 1-4, which means that from 6 to 12, there are seven places and five paintings to be hung. The two blanks can both be between the two groups, or one between the two groups and one at 6 or 12.

I can now jump to the options.

(A) Space 8 is unused

8 is unused, means the free spaces are 6 and 7, and 9-10-11-12, where the nineteenth and eighteenth century paintings can go respectively, so this can be true.

(B) Space 9 is unused

If 9 is unused, then the free spaces are 6-7-8 and 10-11-12, where eighteenth and nineteenth century paintings can be hung.

(C) F is hung in space 6

F and M along with another painting form the three eighteenth century paintings and can occupy 6-7-8, 9 has to be unused and then the two nineteenth century paintings can follow.

(D) M is hung in space 12

If M is in 12, the other two eighteenth-century paintings have to be in 10 and 11, 9 has to be empty and the two nineteenth-century paintings can be hung in spaces 6 to 8.

(E) **N is hung in space 9**

Since all the above options are possible, this has to be the answer.

6. **If the first five paintings, in numerical order of spaces, are F, O, M, N and G, which of the following must be true?**

All of these paintings are not from the twentieth century, so they cannot be the first five in this order after space 5, since there will not be any space for all nine paintings, including the twentieth-century ones.

So, at least a few have to be before space 5. F and M are eighteenth-century, so F-O-M have to be together—1-2-3 (with 4 and 5 unused), or 2-3-4 (with 1 and 5 unused). I can now jump to the options.

(A) **Either space 1 or space 4 is unused.**

All of this reasoning was done and has to be eventually done mentally without putting pen to paper. If you think about it, the reasoning is always a mental process; all you need to do is decouple it from writing.

Practising with a plan and purpose

There are only fifty-four section tests in the book, so you have to make the most out of each session.

1. Keep a separate notebook to practise these sets.
2. One page to note down the answers and the following ones to solve.
3. Your first goal should be to solve the questions in the desired time-limit (with writing).
4. Only if you are able to solve the twenty-five questions within thirty minutes comfortably should you try to solve without putting pen to paper
5. Do not try to go the whole hog mentally, start by decreasing the writing while increasing the thinking.

6. After every set, do a proper analysis of the wasted effort or moves during each set and the reasons for the mistakes, if any:

    i.   Did not remember information
    ii.   Did not draw deductions and directly jumped to the options

7. Consciously make changes while solving the next set.
8. Do not ever do two sections in a row without analysing the first one and setting goals for the next.
9. Do not solve more than two sections in a day, since you will just run through them without getting any better.
10. Ideally, you should dedicate twenty-seven (two sections a day) or fifty-four (one section a day) straight days of practice to see a substantial improvement (do not practise if you are low on mental energy just because I said you have to).

When I started, I used one page for the answers and maybe scribbled on a page and a half, and made around four mistakes. By the seventh set, I barely wrote anything; and even that little I felt was not necessary, I could have reasoned my way through. My mistakes had come down to one per set. All the mistakes boiled down to not remembering information from the set or misremembering it.

This can be useful for test-takers at all levels:

- Those who have never done LR need to develop the ability to solve a section of this difficulty in thirty minutes; if you cannot solve four sets of this level in this time, then you cannot solve four sets of CAT level in sixty minutes.
- Those who are good can use this to solve cleaner and faster.
- Those who are very good (are gunning for a 99.50 plus) can use this as an ideal warm-up.
- And at any level, if you have a silly-mistake problem, this is the practice to fix it.

Keep a track of how your book is looking as you are progressing; it should keep getting cleaner and cleaner with only the numbers and answers remaining.

3

How to Solve a DI-LR Set

In the first chapter, we discussed how one bad DI-LR set can make or break your whole exam. The only way to prevent this from happening is to have a foolproof process to solve a DI-LR set.

Step 1: Determine whether you need to draw a table or not

Our first impulse when we see a DI-LR is to start drawing a table! If the set already has a table, then we start drawing the table on to our rough sheets. Stop. Do not start with duplicating everything that is there in the set on to your rough sheet for the following reasons:

- You might be able to just use the table given on the screen and do the calculations with the least writing possible. (If you did the practice outlined in the preceding chapter, you would have developed this ability.)
- You might need to draw a different table from the kind given in the set.
- A table might not always be the most optimal way to represent information.

Once you resist the impulse to not copy the set on to your paper or draw a table as soon as you read the set, you will be able to spend the time reading the set with more understanding.

Only after you read the set and conditions, think of how best to represent the set. But don't put it on to paper yet. Just have it in your head and put it on to your rough sheet only after the next step.

Step 2: Read the questions to identify whether the set is an open set or closed set

All DI-LR sets are built the same way—some information is given and some information is missing. We start with the assumption that all the missing information can be determined!

But this need not be the case. In most sets, you will be able to find out only some of the missing elements. How can you figure whether you can determine all the missing information? By looking at the questions.

Closed Sets versus Open Sets

Closed sets are sets where you can determine all the missing information. You read the information, represent the information and determine all missing values. Open sets are sets where you cannot determine all the information, your table will have some blanks (if you need to draw a table that is). The table below shows the type of questions that fall into the closed category and the type that are open.

Closed Questions	Open Questions
Provide NO additional information • Who is the person staying in Room 104?	Provide SOME additional information • If Ravi is the person staying in 104, who is staying in 105?
Asks for ONE answer • Who is the person staying in Room 104?	Asks for MULTIPLE ANSWERS • Which of the options lists the people who could be staying in Room 104?
Is a MUST-BE-TRUE question • Must be true means that there is only one value that can fill the information.	Is a COULD-BE-TRUE question • Could be true means that there can be more than one possibility to fill the information
Never has permutations and combinations	Involves permutations and combinations • How many people can be placed in Room 104? • In how many ways can the rooms be allotted to the group?

If *all* questions are *closed*, it means that you can determine all the missing information.

• In this case, you know that you have to determine all the missing information and then proceed to the questions and answer all of them.

If most of the questions barring one or two are *closed*, it means that you cannot determine all the missing information.

• In this case, you should spend some time drawing inferences from the given conditions
• Your table gets partially filled
• Without wasting any more time, you move to the questions
• Answer the closed questions using the information you have determined
• Answer the open questions using the information given in the question

If *all* of the questions are *open*, it means that you cannot determine any missing information; you can only draw a few inferences.

• In this case, you should spend very little time drawing inferences and move on to the questions to use information given in them.

If you do not make this a habit, you will always end up wasting time trying to fill tables that cannot be filled in the first place!

If you make this a habit, even on tough sets you will use the information in the question to answer one or two questions and move on to another set.

Step 3: Find the best way to represent the given information

A table need not be the only way to represent the given information. Sometimes, it takes a lot of ingenuity to figure out the best way to represent the given information and this is what might make your job very easy.

Before we started developing video solutions, paper-based DI-LR solutions were always table-based and horrible. This is because drawing and printing images seemed clumsy and time-consuming. Tables seemed professional. But nothing could be worse than a table to solve a set. The advent of video-solutions is a boon because we can treat the slide like a piece of paper and draw whatever we want to best crack open a set.

Please solve three CAT sets given below on your own, trying to find the best representation. Each of these sets gets progressively non-standard and difficult in terms of representation.

Set 1: The Pizza Set (Easy)

Funky Pizzeria was required to supply pizzas to three different parties. The total number of pizzas it had to deliver was 800, 70 per cent of which were to be delivered to Party 3 and the rest equally divided between Party 1 and Party 2.

Pizzas could be of thin crust (T) or deep dish (D) variety and come in either normal cheese (NC) or extra cheese (EC) versions. Hence, there are four types of pizzas: T-NC, T-EC, D-NC, and D-EC. Partial information about proportions of T and NC pizzas ordered by the three parties is given below:

	Thin Crust (T)	Normal Cheese (NC)
Party 1	.6	
Party 2	.55	.3
Party 3		.65
Total	.375	.52

1. How many thin crust pizzas were to be delivered to Party 3?

    (1) 398   (2) 162   (3) 196   (4) 364

2. How many normal cheese pizzas were required to be delivered to Party 1?

    (1) 104   (2) 84   (3) 16   (4) 196

3. For Party 2, if 50 per cent of the normal cheese pizzas were of thin crust variety, what was the difference between the numbers of T-EC and D-EC pizzas to be delivered to Party 2?

    (1) 18   (2) 12   (3) 30   (4) 24

4. Suppose that a T-NC pizza costs as much as a D-NC pizza, but three-fifths the price of a D-EC pizza. A D-EC pizza costs Rs 50 more than a T-EC pizza and the latter costs Rs 500. If 25 per cent of the normal cheese pizzas delivered to Party 1 were of the deep dish variety, what was the total bill for Party 1?

    (1) Rs 59,480   (2) Rs 59,840   (3) Rs 42,520   (4) Rs 45,240

Set 2: A Cup of Tea (Moderate)

A tea taster was assigned to rate teas from six different locations—Munnar, Wayanad, Ooty, Darjeeling, Assam and Himachal Pradesh. These teas were placed in six cups, numbered 1 to 6, not necessarily in the same order. The tea taster was asked to rate these teas on the strength of their flavour on a scale of 1 to 10. He gave a unique integer rating to each tea. Some other information is given below:

1. Cup 6 contained tea from Himachal.
2. Tea from Ooty got the highest rating, but it was not in Cup 3.
3. The rating of tea in Cup 3 was double the rating of the tea in Cup 5.
4. Only two cups got ratings in even numbers.
5. Cup 2 got the minimum rating and this rating was an even number.
6. Tea in Cup 3 got a higher rating than that in Cup 1.
7. The rating of tea from Wayanad was more than the rating of tea from Munnar but less than that from Assam.

1. What was the second highest rating given? (TITA)

2. What was the number of the cup that contained tea from Ooty? (TITA)

3. If the tea from Munnar did not get the minimum rating, what was the rating of the tea from Wayanad?

    1. 3
    2. 5
    3. 1
    4. 6

4. If cups containing teas from Wayanad and Ooty had consecutive numbers, which of the following statements may be true?

    1. Cup 5 contains tea from Assam
    2. Cup 1 contains tea from Darjeeling
    3. Tea from Wayanad got a rating of 6
    4. Darjeeling tea got the minimum rating

Set 3: The Dormitory Set (Difficult)

At a management school, the oldest ten dorms, numbered 1 to 10, need to be repaired urgently. The following diagram represents the estimated repair costs (in Rs crore) for the ten dorms. For any dorm, the estimated repair cost (in Rs crore) is an integer. Repairs with an estimated cost of Rs 1 crore or Rs 2 crore are considered light repairs, repairs with an estimated cost of Rs 3 crore or Rs 4 crore are considered moderate repairs and repairs with an estimated cost of Rs 5 crore or Rs 6 crore are considered extensive repairs.

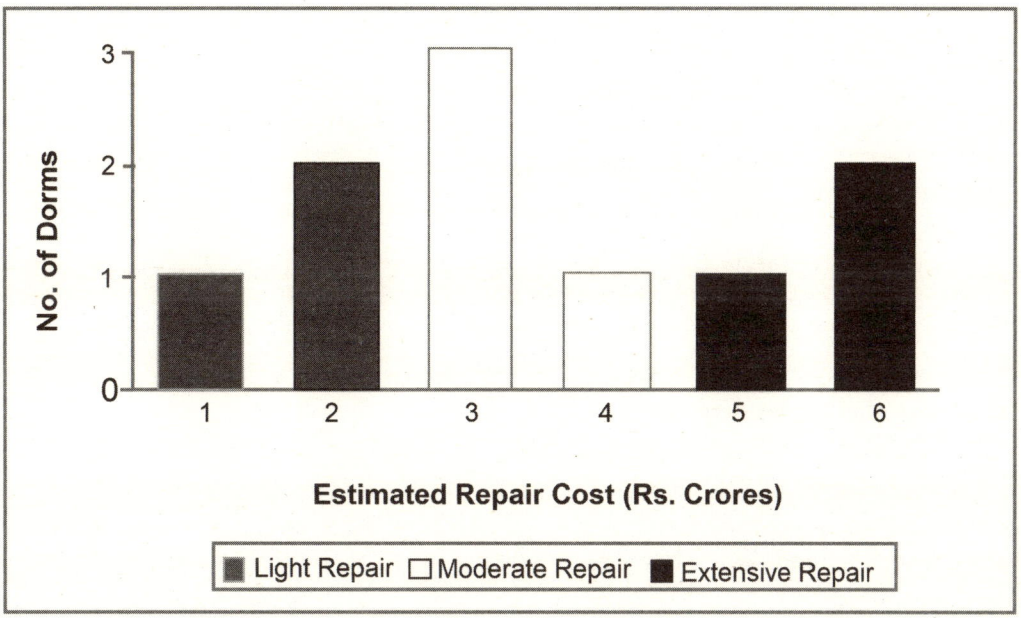

Further, the following are known:

1. Odd-numbered dorms do not need light repair; even-numbered dorms do not need moderate repair, and dorms, whose numbers are divisible by 3, do not need extensive repair.
2. Dorms 4 to 9 need different repair costs, with Dorm 7 needing the maximum and Dorm 8 needing the minimum.

1. Which of the following is NOT necessarily true? (TITA)

    1. Dorm 1 needs moderate repair
    2. Dorm 5 repair will cost no more than Rs 4 crore
    3. Dorm 7 needs extensive repair
    4. Dorm 10 repair will cost no more than Rs 4 crore

2. What is the total cost of repairing the odd-numbered dorms (in Rs crore)? (TITA)

Further information for questions 3 and 4:

    1.   Four of the ten dorms needing repair are women's dorms and need a total of Rs 20 crore for repair.

    2.   Only one of dorms 1 to 5 is a women's dorm.

3. What is the cost for repairing Dorm 9 (in Rs crore)? (TITA)

4. Which of the following is a women's dorm?

    1.   Dorm 2
    2.   Dorm 5
    3.   Dorm 8
    4.   Dorm 10

A video is available on the Bell the CAT YouTube Page. The QR code on page 332 will take you to the same.

Step 4: Find the anchor condition

In every set where there are conditions, some conditions, usually one, at most two, become the anchor conditions.

What is an anchor condition? There are usually two types of conditions—Plugin Conditions and Deductive Conditions.

Plugin conditions are those that give direct information about one detail that you can plugin into your sheet into a cell.

- Ravi scored 2 goals in Match 2

Deductive conditions are those that you cannot directly use to plugin information into a cell. You have to interpret them to make logical values, eliminate some possibilities and then fill up a cell.

- Rajesh did not score a goal in every match that Ravi scored a goal

Anchor conditions are usually deductive conditions that give you information about more than one cell:

- Every even numbered match resulted in an odd number of goals in total.
- No two matches had the same number of goals.

Usually, while solving, every one ends up using the plugin conditions to fill up the table and they do not interpret the deductive conditions, especially the anchor condition. This is because the anchor condition seems most generic. For example, using the anchor condition given above, you have to go to each match, estimate what total goals could have been possible, and use the rest of the data about the match to eliminate possibility.

Remember, as long as you have not decoded a condition, anchor or deductive, you will not be able to solve a set.

Step 5: Keep cycling through the conditions

Sets on average have seven or eight conditions. One key thing to ensure that you are not stuck and are moving forward is to keep cycling through the information.

- Let us say there are ten conditions.
- Start from 1 and once you finish the plugins, go back to the start of the list and interpret whatever are left.
- If some conditions are still unused, start from the top again.

Why should you do this?

- Remember that they are not giving you information in the sequence that is most useful to you!
- Remember that they will give you information that makes sense or yields additional findings only after you have some other information first. For example, condition 2 tells you something, but you can make sense of it only after you see the information given in condition 5.

By consciously cycling through the conditions, you will ensure that:

- you do not forget about some conditions, and
- do not get stuck to the rough sheet

Solve the CAT set below to understand how to use the conditions.

Set 4: The Archery Tourney (Moderate)

Six players—Tanzi, Umeza, Wangdu, Xyla, Yonita and Zeneca—competed in an archery tournament. The tournament had three compulsory rounds, Rounds 1 to 3. In each round, every player shot an arrow at a target. Hitting the centre of the target (called the bullseye) fetched the highest score of 5. The only other possible scores that a player could achieve were 4, 3, 2 and 1.

Every bullseye score in the first three rounds gave a player one additional chance to shoot in the bonus rounds, Rounds 4 to 6. The possible scores in Rounds 4 to 6 were identical to the first three. A player's total score in the tournament was the sum of their scores in all rounds played by them. The table below presents partial information on points scored by the players after completion of the tournament.

In the table, NP means that the player did not participate in that round, while a hyphen means that the player participated in that round and the score information is missing.

	Round 1	Round 2	Round 3	Round 4	Round 5	Round 6
Tanzi		4		5	NP	NP
Umeza				1	2	NP
Wangdu		4		NP	NP	NP
Xyla	5	5	5	1	5	
Yonita			3	5	NP	NP
Zeneca				5	5	NP

Every bullseye score in the first three rounds gave a player one additional chance to shoot in the bonus rounds, Rounds 4 to 6.

- There are nine bonus shots in Rounds 4, 5 and 6—total number of bullseye shots in R1, R2 and R3 is nine or nine 5s to be filled in the first three rounds
- Wangdu did not hit the bullseye and hence did not score a 5, R 1-2-3
- Xyla scored three 5s
- Tanzi, Umeza and Yonita had the same total score
- Total scores for all players, except one, were in multiples of three
- The highest total score was one more than double of the lowest total score
- The number of players hitting a bullseye in Round 2 was double of that in Round 3
- Tanzi and Zeneca had the same score in Round 1 but different scores in Round 2

A video is available on the Bell the CAT YouTube Page. The QR code on page 332 will take you to the same.

The five steps outlined in this chapter are key to solving sets cleanly and quickly. By cleanly I mean without having to go over information back and forth and by efficiently, I mean by solving it only once.

Step 1: Determine whether you need to draw a table or not
Step 2: Read the questions to identify whether the set is an open set or a closed set
Step 3: Find the best way to represent the given information
Step 4: Find the anchor condition
Step 5: Keep cycling through the conditions

If you worked on developing your core reasoning strength outlined in the previous chapter and you practise solving sets by executing these five steps every single time you are faced with a set, you will set yourself up to clear the cut-off and do well on the DI-LR section. But not before you master some key Mathematical Reasoning concepts, which we will cover in the next chapter.

4

The Key Mathematical Reasoning
Concepts You Need to Know

As discussed in the previous chapter, there are some key Mathematical Reasoning concepts that you need to have a solid grasp of to ensure that you are prepared to handle any type of DI-LR sets.

Numerical Reasoning

Sets involving you to plug possible numbers to make up totals. Sometimes, you might even have to frame an equation and see which numbers fit the equation. While this does not require you to learn any special concepts, you need to switch into a plugin numbers mode to crack these sets open.

Arithmetic Reasoning

These are sets that are based on a strong knowledge of the concepts of averages, weighted averages, ratios and percentages. In a way they are extended Quant problems.

Statistical Reasoning

These are sets that are based on your understanding of various statistical concepts: mean, median, mode, range.

Venn Diagrams

A perennial favourite of CAT test-takers, you need to be extremely comfortable solving sets that involve 2-factor, 3-factor and 4-factor Venn diagrams. Once you know how these concepts work, the reasoning itself will be relatively easy. On some CAT sets involving 4-factor Venn diagrams, all you need to do is addition and subtraction!

Non-Standard Graphical Reasoning

While everyone is familiar with bar graphs and pie charts, the CAT throws up some non-standard graphical representations such as spider graphs that at first sight can seem crazy. Your comfort level with decoding non-standard graphs can end up being the difference between a great score and a par score.

Permutations and Combinations

While sets completely based on P and C are not very common, a working knowledge of P and C is necessary since you might find one question in a set or two based on P and C that requires only a very fundamental understanding of P and C.

I have covered most of the concepts listed above in a video, which is available on the Bell the CAT YouTube Page. The QR code on page 332 will take you to the same.

5

Notes on Data Interpretation and Logical Reasoning

Reading Comprehension needs very few concepts but perfect technique and lots of practice to ace. Quantitative Ability needs lots of concepts, decent technique and limited practice to ace. Data Interpretation lies exactly in the middle—a decent set of concepts, perfect technique and a moderate quantum of practice.

This might be one of the reasons why test-takers find DI-LR very tough to prepare for. They practise more than required but without the perfect technique and concepts required.

As a section, it is the toughest because you cannot play the percentages, prepare partially and get away with it.

What do I mean by this? On other sections, you can go in with a limited preparation strategy of focusing on a few things and if you are lucky, you might get away with it. For example, you might decide to focus on arithmetic and algebra on Quant and ignore other areas, and it might work out. Or you might decide to focus only on VA and just solve one RC and get away with it. Unfortunately, you cannot play the same kind of percentages with DI-LR.

Your task is to successfully solve two sets out of all the sets, which is usually four. These four can turn up from any of the areas and can be of varying difficulty levels. So you decide to leave graphs and prepare for arithmetic reasoning but the latter turns out to be the difficult set and the former the easier one. Unlike the other sections, you do not have too many fallback options since the total number of sets is limited and the time invested per set is very high.

Given this, it makes a lot of sense to ensure that you develop your skills across all the different areas on which sets are based and not limit yourself to just a few areas. This temptation is huge in this section since some of you might hate certain types of sets from the bottom of your heart. But you have no way out; you need to look past your hate and learn to score.

How to improve your DI-LR Efficiency

DI-LR is the only section I look forward to solving when I solve the papers from all three every year. This is because it is the only section that forces me to be completely switched on. If the intensity of my concentration, the sharpness of my logical reasoning skills and my mental stamina waver even one bit, I will not clear the cut-off. That much I am sure. And whenever I perform poorly I realize that it is the reason of the same few attitudinal mistakes over and over again.

Whenever you find your performance dropping on a test, check whether you have a tendency to consistently commit any of the mistakes below.

Or if you find yourself stuck on one set during the exam, quickly check if you are committing any of the mistakes listed below.

I. Misreading: *Misread or ignored key information due to speed-reading or skimming*

Before writing this section of the book, I solved all three sections of last year's paper. One set was very straightforward but for some reason, though I could solve which person took which ride—it was a set about three people visiting a Disneyland sort of park—the timings were not tallying. I don't mean tallying with the answers but my solution was clashing with the conditions. I thought the set had some logical flaw.

When I did it for a third time, I realized I had made a fatal mistake—I speed-read what seemed like the most basic piece of information—the time each ride took: I took it as thirty minutes instead of one hour! It was almost as if my mind had superimposed thirty minutes from the outside as I read the set.

Those of you who have been practising for a while or have taken the CAT in the past must have experienced this at least once. It is no different from trying to run down stairs and tripping. I know time is at a premium, so place reading the set properly at a premium as well. It is wise to spend 1.5x the time reading it slowly than reading at 1x twice.

II. Mis-solving: *Started solving without reading the whole set, ignored the anchor conditions*

The temptation to start drawing or solving as soon as you read half of the set is the most dangerous one. Even I am not immune to it. The reason you must wait is very, very straightforward. DI-LR sets are tough because they give you information in the most non-linear format possible.

For example, imagine a 5x5 table with partially filled cells. Let's say ten out of twenty-five cells are given and fifteen are empty. To fill these empty cells, the most important values are the totals of the rows and columns. Using those totals, you know that the number of options for the cells comes down drastically. You plug those options and eliminate.

The problem is that the clues to the totals of the rows and columns are hidden in the anchor conditions. Some anchor conditions are given in the initial description—paragraph—and some are hidden in the total numbered list of conditions along with clues to the values of the cells.

Until you get information about totals, you will not know what is the best table to draw. If you start solving before you finish reading the set or get a hold of the anchor conditions, you will always end up choosing the wrong approach.

III. Unused Conditions: *Did not interpret some conditions, or forgot about some conditions because of not cycling through the conditions*

This is another mistake that creeps in over a period of time. Some conditions seem super deductive and thus we leave them uninterpreted, failing to extract anything from them. At others times, the list of conditions is long and you fail to go back to the ones you could not use earlier. You keep solving using the later conditions in the list.

So whenever you are stuck, always ask yourself: Are there conditions I have left unused?

IV. Misjudgement: *Set should have been left alone in the context of a test*

One of the biggest rules in the DI-LR section of the CAT is to choose the right sets. And the skill to choose the right sets is developed during practice. When you look at the solutions of sets you have failed to solve, you need to always ask yourself the question: Is this a set that is better left alone in a test context?

I will describe the strategy to decide which set to solve and which one to leave, after reading, not solving, in detail in the test-taking strategy section. But your ability to execute that strategy will become very precise if you start judging sets after solving during your practice.

What does solving a set efficiently mean?

Solving a set efficiently means nothing different from solving a Quant question correctly—reading a set once, finding the right representation in the first go and getting most of the questions right.

So, if you find yourself most of the time:

- having to re-read sets
- having to restart solving by re-drawing everything
- not making any progress after doing some basic deductions

then sit and analyse which of the four mistakes listed above you are making.

Once you know the mistakes you tend to make, make a conscious effort to be more deliberate in your solving. For example, if you have many chances to sharpen a pencil with a penknife, you might do it carelessly. If I told you that you had only one chance, you are likely to ensure that you get the job done in one go. All you will do is be more deliberate. It will seem like you will take more time but it will be only marginally more. But what is more important is that you will be conscious of every step.

Similarly, to solve more sets efficiently, it will not be enough to take more time. What matters is how deliberate you are in each of the steps you execute.

Part VI

Test-Taking Strategy

1

Do Not Wait for Your Prep to Be over Before Taking the First Mock

One of the biggest challenges I faced while designing courseware is that, unlike the IIT-JEE or NEET, the planning of the timing of the CAT prep is left to the aspirants. What do I mean by this? Graduation, unlike post-graduation, is not a luxury but a necessity. So, people start preparing for JEE and other exams very early. The prep formally starts for all aspirants in a particular month at the beginning of Class XI and ends in a particular month in Class XII. Everyone has to take admission by a date and no one can get in after that. This means that everyone follows a strict regimen. For those designing programmes, it makes everything easy since everyone, irrespective of their level, has completed the same syllabus and has gone through the same number of different tests.

Since post-graduation is a luxury, everyone decides to join whenever they feel like. Also, they are joining this after their graduation where for the first time, they experience a certain freedom. The stakes of the exams are not as crazy as those of Class X, Class XII and entrance exams. They happen once a year and can be aced by preparing just before the exam. It is with this background that they embark on CAT prep.

A certain proportion who join early do not attend classes or become serious about the prep since the exam is months away. A lot of people keep postponing their joining since they feel the exam is far away. So, we have a situation where every student is at a different level of syllabus completion when the SimCATs begin in April. A large proportion of students join in May–June when the SimCATs have already started. Most people do not take the SimCATs because they are around three or four months away from syllabus completion.

If you cannot take a mock with no prep, you do not have the mindset required to crack the CAT

The CAT is not like your college exam or any other non-aptitude exam that you have taken. It is also not like the JEE since even that requires a lot of concepts. There are no 'concepts' tested in Verbal Ability. In DI-LR, the concepts tested are Quant concepts. The concepts tested in the Quant section are those that you have already learnt by Class X or at the maximum by Class XII. Then why is the test so tough? Because it is a test of strategy.

Cracking the CAT is only 50 per cent about knowing concepts; 50 per cent is about knowing how to take a test—managing the time limit of a section, gauging the difficulty of questions and choosing the right questions to solve.

If you go by the standard approach of fully completing the syllabus and then taking a few mocks, it will be similar to practising cricket only in the nets and directly going to the World Cup after playing a free game.

Test-taking, just like match-play, is a skill that can be honed only through taking as many SimCATs as possible. So, if you decide to skip a few SimCATs till you have covered the concepts, you might still perform poorly whenever you take your first SimCAT since you do not know how to take a test!

So, even if you feel you do not know a thing, go ahead, take the test and solve whatever you can.

I Do Not Want to See a Poor Score

There is nothing called a poor score, only percentiles matter.

Those who are re-taking the CAT or are aware of CAT folklore, would know that there have been years when a test-taker with a score of 0 would have secured the 55th percentile. Imagine, even if you slept through the whole test, you would still have done better than 55 per cent of the test-takers!

So, even if you attempt only eight to ten questions in each section and get six to eight questions right on SimCAT 1, you will still get a respectable percentile on your first outing.

CAT is tough and I am aiming at other tests

Most students want to do an MBA from a decent school and are probably looking at cracking tests that have a reputation to be easier than the CAT.

If you imagine all the MBA entrance tests in India to be stacked up on a dartboard, then CAT is the bullseye. And anyone who has ever tried their hand at darts would know that you should always practise by aiming at the bullseye.

By giving your best shot at CAT, you automatically put yourself in a position to maximize your chances on the non-CAT tests for there are very few people who prepare for the CAT alone.

Serious aspirants would be aiming at the IIMs and taking other tests as a back-up, so even if you do not aspire to ace the CAT, you will be competing with those who do, and having prepared for it, they will give you a run for your money on the non-CAT tests.

If there is one thing that all test-takers should keep in mind during the whole test-taking season, it is this—**Never Miss a SimCAT.** SimCATs offer you the best possible simulation of the CAT in terms of test structure and level of difficulty, so you should always be not just ready but greedy to take a SimCAT.

If you solve half the paper with 75 per cent accuracy, you will score 95 percentile

This has been true since I first took the CAT aeons ago! If anything, in some years, even less than half would have gotten you a 95 percentile. What does this mean?

This means that your job is not to answer all the questions but to leave the right questions. If you do not play the Jasprit Bumrah balls, you will do exceptionally well in the exam.

So, your job right from the first mock is to be absolutely clinical like an M.S. Dhoni and focus dispassionately on leaving the tough and even some time-taking moderate questions and solving only the sitters.

I will discuss the selection and rejection strategies in detail in this section, but for you to execute that, you need to take a lot of mocks over a period of time rather than a few mocks packed into the last two months before the exam.

The strategies will make a lot of sense when you have understood the importance of rejection and have approached the SimCATs with that mindset right from the word go.

But I do not know maths at all; won't I be wasting a mock?

Even if you do not know maths, you can do your best on Verbal and score around 25–35 marks from there. You can try to select and solve only one set from DI-LR in the whole duration of the section and score 12–16 marks. If you get an overall score in the 40–50 range, you will score an 80–85 percentile!

Every year, we provide students around forty SimCATs. How many do students take on average? Eight! So, there is no risk of you running out of mocks!

I will not give the same advice for the GMAT

The GMAT, for example, is not a test of strategy but competence. You have to answer all questions! So test-taking strategy does not come into play at all! Your test-taking stamina and conceptual clarity are all that matter!

I hope this makes it clear that, irrespective of when you join, start your test-taking journey from the first mock itself and not later in the season.

2

All About CAT Scores and Percentiles

The single most frequently asked question is this: Sir, how many questions should I answer to score XX.XX percentile? The answer to that question is given in the tables below.

Table 1: Overall Score

	80 percentile	85 percentile	90 percentile	95 percentile	98 percentile	99 percentile	100 percentile	Total marks
2020	49	50	63	77	92	102	163	228
2021	45	51	60	72	87	97	155	198
2022	36	41	50	60	74	84	142	198
~Average score	~40–45	~45–50	~55–60	~65–70	~80–85	~90–95	~150	
~Average percentage	~20 per cent	~22 per cent	~25 per cent	~30 per cent	~40 per cent	~50 per cent	~65 per cent	

Table 2: Verbal Ability Score

	80 percentile	85 percentile	90 percentile	95 percentile	98 percentile	99 percentile	100 percentile	Total marks
2020	22	24	28	33	38	42	65	78
2021	22	25	29	34	42	47	63	72
2022	17	20	23	29	35	39	60	72
~Average score	~20	~22	~26	~31	~38	~43	~61	
~Average percentage	~30 per cent	~32 per cent	~35 per cent	~40 per cent	~50 per cent	~60 per cent	~90 per cent	

Table 3: Data Interpretation and Logical Reasoning Score

	80 percentile	85 percentile	90 percentile	95 percentile	98 percentile	99 percentile	100 percentile	Total marks
2020	15	18	20	25	30	34	62	72
2021	15	16	20	24	31	34	53	60
2022	11	13	15	19	26	29	51	60
~Average score	~13	~15	~18	~22	~28	~32	~52	
~Average percentage	~20 per cent	~25 per cent	~30 per cent	~38 per cent	~45 per cent	~53 per cent	~85 per cent	

Table 4: Quantitative Score

	80 percentile	85 percentile	90 percentile	95 percentile	98 percentile	99 percentile	100 percentile	Total marks
2020	16	19	23	29	38	43	72	78
2021	12	14	18	24	30	36	63	66
2022	12	14	17	23	29	33	57	66
~Average score	~12	~14	~18	~24	~30	~35	~60	
~Average percentage	~18 per cent	~21 per cent	~27 per cent	~36 per cent	~45 per cent	~53 per cent	~90 per cent	

The format might change but the percentage score does not change

Over the years, the pattern of the CAT has changed dramatically. When I was preparing for the CAT for the first time, I was taking mocks that had 200 questions, 120 minutes, four sections and no sectional time limits. The CAT I cracked had 150 questions, 120 minutes, three sections and no sectional time limits. While the number of questions has always come down, the time limit has kept changing from 120 to 140 to 170.

Irrespective of the pattern across the years, if you score 50 per cent of the total marks in a section, you will get a 99 percentile! So, all you need to do is get half the questions in every section correct!

The most important thing, though, is to select the right half!

3

Why Test-Taking Strategy Is More Important than Conceptual Clarity

Every question posed in the CAT is like a ball bowled in cricket. One of the big psychological barriers when it comes to test-taking is not very different from what batsmen face when they come to the crease—the eagerness to get off the mark.

So, right from the start of a section, test-takers are always desperate to somehow score and get some marks under the belt. Given this desperation, what do they do?

Like batsmen who tend to play every ball, test-takers tend to attempt every question. When batsmen do that at the beginning of an innings, they tend to get out caught in the slips, usually playing away from their body.

The best batsmen in the world are comfortable against both types of bowling—pace and spin, are good off both the back foot and the front foot, and know how to play every shot in the book—from cover drives to the pull and the hook.

Does this mean that they will:

- hit every single ball they face to the boundary?
- play every single ball without leaving a single ball?
- never get out?

The answer to all the above questions is a resounding NO!

Similarly, since you need to answer only half the paper correctly to reach the 99th percentile, what matters is your ability to leave the right questions! You might know all concepts across all topics but that does not mean that you have to attempt all questions since:

- like unplayable balls from a great bowler, test-makers will set questions that most people will be unable to answer
- there will be questions that are so time-consuming that solving each will take five to six minutes, which will slow you down considerably

Protect your time spent, the way you are supposed to protect your wicket

In cricket, they say that the best batsmen place a premium on their wicket. If you remember the big problem with Rohit Sharma at the beginning of his career was his inconsistency and most of it was because of the manner of his dismissals. He would more or less gift his wicket away. This was true of many great players at the beginning of their careers and it was more likely to be true of the more talented players. Aravinda de Silva had more than one shot that he could play to a particular ball. This meant that in the early stages of his career, he would throw his wicket away to a wrong choice of shot. The Aravinda who destroyed India in the 1996 semi-final was fully in control of his shot selection. Both Rohit and Aravinda are talents of the highest calibre but even they did not maximize their potential until they mastered shot selection.

So, like great batsmen, great test-takers are not those who know each and every concept but those who know which questions to leave and which questions to attempt. As test-takers, what you need to learn to do is to place a premium on your time. When you attempt a question, you should be getting three marks for it more than eight out of ten times; the rest of the questions should be left alone. Most of the time, you will find that a lot of your time was spent on questions that gave you no return.

How do you go about selecting which questions to solve and which questions to leave?

Over the years, I have lost count of the number of mocks I have taken. And I have had the privilege of working with the best CAT crackers in the country, counting quite a few 100-percentilers among my good friends and colleagues.

Most of the time, the geniuses are unable to explain what goes on in their head in the split second within which they take their decisions. I am not a genius by any stretch but someone who can crack exams and articulate what is usually called intuition. Using all of my experience over the years, I have come up with clear selection strategies for each of the sections. All three are based on one core concept: *Now, Later, Never.*

4

CAT Test-Taking Strategy: Now, Later, Never

You are standing in front of a tree that has twenty to twenty-five fruits hanging on it. Of these, you know that if you pluck anything more than ten or twelve, you will be the winner. So, do you jump at the first fruit in front of you? No. You will grab at the lowest hanging fruit first—the ones that require no jumping at all. After that, you will try to pluck the fruit that will need you to jump and reach for them. Will you even try to jump for the ones that are very far up? No.

With fruits on a tree, the task is easy. It is not the same with questions. Most test-takers see them as all being on the same level. They spend time getting involved with the question or set and letting go only after wasting some quality time.

So, your first task when you see a question or a set is to not rush to solve it. Your first task is to decide whether it should be solved *Now*; whether you should come back to it *Later*, after finishing all the *Nows*, or *Never*.

But this is easier said than done since our default tendency the moment we see a question is to try to solve it! Because admitting that the question is very difficult or that it should it be left alone is for most people letting fear in: 'Oh, my god, the paper is difficult!'

But if you already know that you are expected to solve only half the paper, then you know that you will be rejecting every second question.

Everyone gets questions in a different sequence

To prevent malpractice, the test-setters ensure that the questions are posed in a randomly shuffled manner to every test-taker. So, it can happen that for one test-taker, most of the easy questions can be loaded right at the beginning of the section, while for others, most of them can appear at the end.

If you do not have a strategy to select, then it boils down to sheer luck! If the easy questions turn up in the beginning, you get a great score; if they are stacked towards the end, you will never reach them!

So, can you allow your future to be left at the mercy of the random order in which the system throws up questions? No!

You do not know how to take a test if . . .

There is a simple test to single out amateur test-takers who do not know how to take a test—if you have even one unread question at the end of a section. If you have unread questions at the end of a section, it means that you have invested time in many questions that you should have left alone.

Every expert test-taker solves a section in two or more rounds

Students think that those who get a 100-percentile or score above a 99 are so bright that they can solve every question they see and thus they just go from start to end solving every question as they see it. Nothing is further from the truth. Expert test-takers know that it is not a test of competence but of strategy. The best test-takers solve a section in three rounds.

They first solve the *Nows*; even among the *Laters*, they do the easier ones first, and then only if they have time do they take a look at the *Nevers*.

A different strategy for each section

The next three chapters are dedicated to the strategy required to tackle each of the three sections. The way to select RC passages is different from the process to evaluate a DI-LR set. So, the method to arrive at the *Now, Later* or *Never*, varies from section to section.

These strategies have become second nature to me after all these years. They will seem intimidating and time-consuming at first, which it will be. But over the course of five to ten mocks, you will execute the strategies in a very short period and begin to see the value in them.

Remember, spending a minute to strategize and let go of a tough question is always preferable to spending three minutes in vain trying to solve it.

5

Verbal Ability and Reading Comprehension: Test-Taking Strategy

The biggest challenge with Reading Comprehension is the time that needs to be invested in reading a passage.

You start reading the passage but somewhere realize that it is not really your cup of tea. But since you have already given it some time, you feel that it is not wise to quit midway. You trudge your way through the passage and somehow get through it, take a half-serious shot at the questions and hope it all works out well. Else, you drop the passage midway and decide to take up another one to see if that is easier.

The problem with this approach is easy to see. In a forty-minute section, you are aimlessly flitting about without a plan, hoping that things work out for you. So, the first task is to have a precise method to consistently select passages that will maximize your return on time invested.

Step 1: How to rate RC Passages

Read the first paragraph, or two in case the first paragraph is very short, of each RC and give it a rating out of 10 with **1** for **Very Difficult** and **10** for **Very Easy.**

To break down this rating process, use three parameters:

1. Complexity of Language
2. Complexity of Arguments
3. Accessibility of Topic

Complexity of Language: 1-2-3

Different passages have texts of different levels of language use. Based on the level, you need to rate the language on a scale of 1 to 3; 3 being very easy to understand and 1 being very tough and a value between 1 and 3—1.5, 2, 2.5—for anything that falls in between.

To give this rating, first evaluate how easy the language of the passage is, irrespective of the topic. Are you able to easily understand it and grasp the content or do you feel that this needs to be read slowly?

Complexity of Arguments: 1-2-3

While the language is at one level, the other thing to consider is the nature of the passage with respect to arguments. Is the passage presenting information or arguments? If the text is purely informational, then it is easy and has to be rated a 3. If the text is presenting complex arguments, then it has to be rated a 1. Anything in between has to be rated a 1.5, 2 or 2.5.

Accessibility of Topic: 1-4

The last thing is the topic itself. If the topic of the passage is something that you like or are very familiar with—Olympics, climate change—then give it a 4. If it is something that you really cannot stand, say, British Colonialism, then give it a 1. Anything in between has to be rated a 1.5, 2, 2.5, 3, 3.5.

What do the overall ratings mean?

Solve **Now**: Passages rated 7 and above
Any passage rated 7 and above is a must-solve.
Solve **Later**: Passages rated 6 or 6.5
Any passage rated between 6 and 7 is one which you should return to later, after you solved the VA questions.
Never Solve: Passages rated below 6

Passages rated below 6 should be left alone. Even if you are a champ at Verbal Ability, it is best to solve such passages at the end, after you have maximized your returns from the rest of the paper.

What is the objective of the rating exercise?

It is to help you decide the order in which you need to attempt the passages. Ensure that you rate the passages in such a way that your rating tells you in which order you should attempt the passages. For example, if you find two passages to be of moderate level, do not rate both as 7; differentiate and give each one a rating that helps you decide the order, say a 7 and a 7.5.

If you do the process casually, then you will end up having the same values for all passages, thus defeating the purpose. So, cut out the gut feel and execute the process as strictly as possible.

There can be nothing worse than getting stuck on the wrong passage early in the section. It can affect the rest of the section adversely, given the psychologically fragile beings that we become during a test, especially in a section that is our Achilles heel (if you have taken a few SimCATS, you will have experienced this).

Let us take all the passages of a recent CAT and do the rating process.

Passage I: Pollution, 121 words

The only thing worse than being lied to is not knowing you're being lied to. It's true that plastic pollution is a huge problem, of planetary proportions. And it's true we could all do more to reduce our plastic footprint. The lie is that blame for the plastic problem is wasteful consumers and that changing our individual habits will fix it. Recycling plastic is to saving the Earth what hammering a nail is to halting a falling skyscraper. You struggle to find a place to do it and feel pleased when you succeed. But your effort is wholly inadequate and distracts from the real problem of why the building is collapsing in the first place.

Language: 2

The language, while fairly understandable, still uses a few metaphors such *as hammering a nail is to halting a falling skyscraper.* There are passages that have language simpler than this, hence a rating of 2.

Arguments: 2

The passage is not informative and it starts making a clear argument right from the very beginning about the current solutions to plastic pollution, hence a rating of 2.

Topic: 4

The topic is something that everyone can understand—pollution—and hence a rating of 4.

TOTAL—8/10

Passage II: War Memorial, 92 words

[The] Indian government [has] announced an international competition to design a National War Memorial in New Delhi, to honor all of the Indian soldiers who served in the various wars and counter-insurgency campaigns from 1947 onwards. The terms of the competition also specified that the new structure would be built adjacent to the India Gate—a memorial to the Indian soldiers who died in the First World War. Between the old imperialist memorial and the proposed nationalist one, India's contribution to the Second World War is airbrushed out of existence.

Language: 2

The language, while informative to begin with, lands a big punch right at the end of the paragraph— *old imperialist memorial and the proposed nationalist one, India's contribution to the Second World War is airbrushed out of existence,* so it is better to proceed with a rating of 2.

Arguments: 2

Again, a major argument is made at the end of the paragraph about *imperialism* and *nationalism.* This argument might be explored in detail going forward, and hence a rating of 2.

Topic: 2

The topic is not something that everyone will easily like to read and thus a 2 seems appropriate.

TOTAL—6/10

Passage III: Mice, 98 words

When researchers at Emory University in Atlanta trained mice to fear the smell of almonds (by pairing it with electric shocks), they found, to their consternation, that both the children and grandchildren of these mice were spontaneously afraid of the same smell. That is not supposed to happen. Generations of schoolchildren have been taught that the inheritance of acquired characteristics is impossible. A mouse should not be born with something its parents have learned during their lifetimes, any more than a mouse that loses its tail in an accident should give birth to tailless mice . . .

Language: 2.5
Arguments: 2
Topic: 3

TOTAL—7.5/10

Passage IV: Elephants, 78 words

. . . 'Everybody pretty much agrees that the relationship between elephants and people has dramatically changed,' [says psychologist Gay] Bradshaw . . . 'Where for centuries humans and elephants lived in relatively peaceful coexistence, there is now hostility and violence. Now, I use the term "violence" because of the intentionality associated with it, both in the aggression of humans and, at times, the recently observed behaviour of elephants.' . . .

Language: 2.5
Arguments: 2
Topic: 2.5

TOTAL—7/10

Passage V: Happiness, 92 words

Economists have spent most of the 20th century ignoring psychology, positive or otherwise. But today there is a great deal of emphasis on how happiness can shape global economies, or—on a smaller scale—successful business practice. This is driven, in part, by a trend in 'measuring' positive emotions, mostly so they can be optimized. Neuroscientists, for example, claim to be able to locate specific emotions, such as happiness or disappointment, in particular areas of the brain. Wearable technologies, such as Spire, offer data-driven advice on how to reduce stress.

Language: 2
Arguments: 2
Topic: 2.5

TOTAL—6.5/10

Everyone's rating will be slightly different

The rating I have given above is not universal; your rating can be slightly different on parameters like language and topic. I have done the rating with an imaginary 'average' student in mind. For me, all of these passages will be a 10 (the only RC passages I find painful are the few science passages that turn up on the GMAT and GRE).

Rate on an absolute scale and not on a scale relative to the particular test

When I say the rating is your personal rating, I mean that it should be based on your skills, but on an absolute scale. What do I mean by absolute scale? All the passages you have done so far during your prep. So the more SimCATs and section tests you take, the better your judgement will become.

What about rating the passages based on the questions?

A lot of people ask me about this method and it is a strategy suggested by many capable mentors. If there are more inference questions, better to attempt them later and if there are more direct questions, then attempt them earlier.

Personally, I do not subscribe to this method because what makes an RC question tough is never the question but the closeness of the options. And until you read the text, you will never know how close the options are.

But after a point, it is a personal choice of what works for each of you.

Sometimes I find that tough passages end up having easy questions!

This is another thing that I keep hearing on and off: 'Sir, I left the passage because it seemed painful to read, later when I solved the questions it was easy, what should I do in such cases?'

This is like saying: 'Sir, sometimes the fastest bowler is easier to play, so all I need to do is touch the ball and it will go for four!' So, maybe it makes sense to attempt the tougher passages.

Well, the key word is *sometimes*. You cannot go changing your entire strategy based on a few exceptions.

All of these ideas usually stem from insecurity and a lack of confidence about your core capability with RC, or from your dislike for the whole process of reading itself.

What you cannot run away from is the fact that while all of these test-taking techniques and strategies can be useful, you need to have a core ability to read and comprehend moderate to difficult level text in English and a solid technique to answer questions. Test-taking strategies help you maximize your performance and core capabilities; they cannot compensate for lack of capabilities.

Step 2: Evaluate the difficulty of RC as an area and the sequence to attempt the passages

At the end of my rating, I am left with the following:

- Pollution: 8/10
- Mice: 7.5/10
- Elephants: 7/10
- Happiness: 6.5/10
- War Memorial: 6/10

Based on the classification we outlined earlier, we can see that there are three passages rated 7 and above that have to be solved right away. There are no scary passages rated below 6 that should not be touched. You can come back to the ones rated 6 and 6.5 after solving the VA questions.

The most important takeaway from this exercise is that you will know how good, bad or ugly the RC part is on the whole.

If four passages are rated 7 and above and you normally solve only three passages, you should realize that this paper is easy. If you easily solve your regular three passages and think you have done your job, you will be in for a rude shock when the percentiles are out, since others would have solved more than you.

If four passages are rated 7 and above and you normally solve only three passages, you should realize that this paper is tough. If you force yourself to solve your regular three passages and think you have done your job, you will be in for a rude shock when the percentiles are out, since your accuracy would have suffered and you would have missed out on easy questions in VA!

The rating will tell you the task that is cut out in front of you.

Even among the passages rated 7 and above, always attempt passages in decreasing order of your rating from the highest to the lowest.

Step 3: Decide on the sequence to attempt the entire section

This will probably decide how well your VA-RC section will go—the sequence in which you attempt questions. If you do not have a plan for this and decide to play it by the paper, then as I keep saying, the test is taking you and you are not taking the test. To have a strategy for this process, you need to know where you stand with respect to the VA-RC section.

Type 1: VA-RC is my strength and I get my maximum marks from this section

For those who fall into this club, the sequence is straightforward: RC-VA or VA-RC.

Always solve all VA questions of a single type together. If you have a specific strategy to execute for each VA question type, you are better off solving all the questions of a type at one go.

You can also try out just to see if it works better for you: Summary—Incorrect Sentence—Missing Sentence—RCs—Jumbled Paragraphs.

Type 2: VA-RC is my second strongest area, I might buckle under pressure if the RCs become tough

RCs rated 7 and above—Summary—Incorrect Sentence—Missing Sentence—RCs rated 6–7—Jumbled Paragraphs

This ensures that the tough RCs do not become a speed-breaker and you get the maximum out of the VA question types. Also, do not attempt passages rated below 6 unless you are through with the whole paper and have time left.

If you have rated all the passages 7 and above, then go ahead and solve all of them at the beginning.

Type 3: VA-RC is not easy and I have quite a bit of trouble clearing the cut-off

If you belong to this group, then your main task is to clear the cut-off by maximizing your performance on the easiest RCs and the VA questions. Doing all the passages at a stretch is an absolute no-no since the ability to process text itself might be the biggest problem.

You should follow one of two sequences:

- RC 1—Summary—RC 2—Incorrect Sentence—Missing Sentence—Jumbled Paragraphs—RC 3
- Summary—RC 1—Incorrect Sentence—Missing Sentence—RC 2—Jumbled Paragraphs—RC 3

Obviously, the order of the RCs should be from your highest rated to your lowest rated ones.

Are you really maximizing your marks on the VA questions?

One thing that has always bothered me a lot whenever I interact with students, is that they seem to be very reluctant to let go of their playing-the-percentages attitude to tests. Throughout school and college, we tend to study by playing the percentages—giving importance to topics as per the number of questions that appear from that topic in the exam.

While this might be a great strategy for school and college exams, as far as aptitude tests go, this strategy is suicidal purely because of the fact that the difficulty level and the number of questions across areas do not follow a fixed pattern.

How is this related to Verbal Ability in the current pattern of the CAT?

The increase in the number of Reading Comprehension questions to twenty-four started with CAT 2015 when the CAT moved to a three-section pattern from a two-section one (QA-DI, VA-LR). So until 2015, RC was something that people conscientiously avoided, and solved only LR and VA.

But the moment RC changed to twenty-four questions, people started ignoring VA. Verbal Ability has almost become a side-show relegated to the last ten minutes of the section. Even within VA, the bulk of the time goes to the most useless question type in the history of Verbal Ability question types across tests—jumbled paragraphs.

I think, as a strategy, this is quite misplaced since the CAT is always about picking out the questions that will give you three marks in the shortest possible time and having the technique to hit high accuracy levels in executing a solution.

Most of the VA questions are TITA, and hence carry no negative marking, but that does not mean that you answer them in a cavalier fashion. You should look at them like legitimate deliveries, off which you could score a potential 15–18 marks, rather than treat them like free hits since you cannot get out!

How to divide your time and attempts between VA and RC

You should always divide your time between RC and VA by using a simple rule of thumb: ~two minutes per VA question and in the rest of the time, as many RCs as you can attempt. You should allocate time as per your percentile goals. You might start the season with an initial goal of reaching 85 percentile and then set it at 95 percentile. Reaching higher goals you will see is a matter of first maximizing accuracy and then attempts. I will take this up in detail in a later section.

- **RC: 25 minutes and VA: 15 minutes**
  - o 85 percentile—20–25 marks—50 per cent–65 per cent accuracy
    - RC: 2 passages, 6–8 questions, 4–5 correct—8–12 marks
    - VA: 6–8 questions, 4–5 correct—12–15 marks

- **RC: 25 minutes and VA: 15 minutes**
  - o 95 percentile—30–35 marks—60 per cent–75 per cent accuracy
    - RC: 3 passages, 10–12 questions, 7–8 correct—18–21 marks
    - VA: 6–8 questions, 5–6 correct—15–18 marks

The first and most important question to ask yourself is, are you dividing your time correctly?

Ideally, your time should also be divided in the same ratio—24:10 or 2.4:1. This means that you have to give at least seventeen minutes to VA.

So I would say anything less than fifteen minutes or more than twenty minutes will be a poor utilization of your time. You can allocate more than twenty minutes if there is a super tough RC that is better left alone.

Since easy, medium and difficult questions are usually spread out across the whole section, the least return you should be getting out of VA is fifteen marks. If you are not getting five out of those ten questions right then you really, really need to work on your VA technique or rather get a technique instead of the good ol' gut feel.

Getting a good return out of VA questions reduces the pressure on having to solve all the RCs and gives you the luxury of leaving one or two RCs out.

If you are scoring 24 consistently, then you are set.

Why you should always leave jumbled paragraphs or JPs for the end?

If you noticed, in all sequences I placed JPs towards the end. It is possibly the oldest question type on the CAT and has been around on and off in the 1990s, if I am not wrong.

It is a question type that is most intelligible to test-takers and thus a type that everyone wants to take a shot at. What do I mean by most intelligible?

Let us use a board game analogy. Imagine you know nothing about chess and have never seen a chessboard. Then you see a chessboard arranged for two players and watch them play out a game.

Will you jump in and tell the next guy, 'I want to play, let's go.' You know there is a lot you do not know and you need to learn a lot before you give it a shot.

What if you see a snakes and ladders board with a dice on it? You can figure out how to play it. Even if you do not know what a snake does, you can figure that out to be the opposite of what a ladder does. In the worst case, you can see two people play for two minutes and understand.

To use another analogy, this time from a casino set-up, there's blackjack versus roulette.

In short, JPs are like Snakes and Ladders and Roulette, too easy to understand and thus too tempting to not want to take a shot at. No one ever says my teacher has not yet taught me how to solve JPs, so I will not attempt it!

When it was not part of TITA, JPs were definitely a high-return question type. The options would lead the way and you would test the logic they showed you.

With no options, every paragraph can potentially be arranged in twenty-four ways (assuming four sentences). Even if you fix one, you know that there are six possibilities.

The reason I suggest leaving the JPs to the end is that since there are no options, we tend to double and triple-check, wasting a lot of precious time at the expense of other questions. If you leave them for the end, then you are budgeting lower time for them.

Everything we discussed above cannot be perfected overnight; feel free to tweak my strategies.

One of the things that I know for a fact is that test-takers imagine they will go implement what they read and expect they will immediately feel comfortable with it right from the word go and their scores will jump. Not that it does not happen; it has happened that test-takers have seen overnight changes in scores but it usually takes a bit of time before you get comfortable with executing something new. The attempt sequences I described above are not set in stone; you can modify them, you can try approaches I suggested for a type as well.

But the key is to have an attempt strategy that is aligned to your capabilities and you know how you are going to deal with it and have backup capabilities for different eventualities beforehand— e.g., VA is your strength and you start with it, but VA turns out to be very tough.

Some of you might be scoring well on the VA-RC section and might feel that you do not need to follow any process when your gut can do the job. I am naturally good at Verbal, but I realized a long time ago that having a process or a technique gives me a way to reason my way through tough questions; the easy ones can be taken care of by your gut. But even on the easy ones, having a process ensures that I reach there faster without making any silly mistakes.

Those of you who find your scores in Verbal going up and down or feel that you are unable to move it beyond a particular level should diligently apply these strategies over quite a few questions and tests till they become your natural way of solving them.

This test finally rewards all-round skills—good competence and technique to handle all question types and good test-taking skills to perform on the pitch.

6

Data Interpretation and Logical Reasoning: Test-Taking Strategy

As I have mentioned time and again, this is possibly the toughest section of the CAT and I am not exaggerating when I say that the first set you choose to solve on DI-LR can make or break your entire set.

What is the logic?

When you choose an RC passage randomly, the maximum time you will spend before you realize that this is not your cup of tea is two to three minutes. But what happens in DI-LR? Unlike RCs, you will be trying to make sense of the set by attempting to represent the data on to your rough sheet. In other words, you will be trying to solve the set. The beauty of DI-LR is that you will get lost in a set and will not realize that ten to fifteen minutes have passed by.

What is the probability that you will choose the wrong set if you pick a set randomly or take up the set that you see first? Given that solving only two sets is enough to get a great percentile, you know that there is a 50 per cent chance that the set you pick to solve at random (or without putting much thought into it) will be the wrong set.

If you lose ten to fifteen minutes right at the beginning and have zero marks to show for it, you confidence drops right away. And once that happens, you are unlikely to recover and do well in the section since panic sets in. The most dangerous part about the DI-LR section is that it is right in the middle of the paper. The number of students who mess up the QA section that follows the DI-LR section is huge. This is one of the big reasons why only a small percentage of first-time takers crack the CAT.

The first rule—you cannot have a favourite between DI and LR

Your job is to choose the right sets irrespective of whether they belong to DI or LR. You choose as per the paper but not as per preset rules. There is a difference between playing preset tunes on an electronic keyboard and actually playing the keyboard.

So this straightaway eliminates the problem of how to allocate your time minutes. You scan all the sets and choose the two easiest ones to start with and then pick one more if the time and the level of difficulty permit.

This is very important in the context of the current nature of DI-LR sets. The tougher the DI-LR section gets, the harder it will be for you to say where DI ends and where LR begins; the lines between the two have gotten extremely blurred. Let's take a look at the DI-LR sets from an old SimCAT, which had a DI-LR sectional cut-off of 21, to see how this choice is best done.

How to choose the right DI and LR sets

Just like RCs, there are three parameters on which you evaluate a DI-LR set:

- Type of Set
- Type of Conditions
- Type of Questions

Type of Set: 1-2-3

We know what standards sets mean—these are the staple of most LR sections—linear arrangements, matrix arrangements and the most standard one of them all, the good ol' sports set! It goes without saying that we do not need to define what unique sets are.

The first task is to rate the type of set on a scale of **1-2-3**. To do this, ask: Is this set a **standard** set or a **unique** set?

- I have **seen and solved** very similar sets before: **3**
- I have **seen somewhat similar** sets before: **2**
- I have **never seen such a set, but I understand** it: **2**
- I have never seen such a set, can't understand it: **1**

Type of Conditions: 0-1-2-3

Every set has a list of conditions but not all conditions are alike. There are broadly two types of conditions:

Plugin Conditions that can be directly represented in a table:

- *Ajay was from Bhagalpur* or *Navin is not an architect.*

Deductive Conditions are those that cannot be directly inserted into a table but will yield information when used with plugin conditions that can then be represented in a table. The deceptive conditions can be:

- **purely logical** in nature, such as *no two players scored the same number of runs*, or
- **numerical** as well, such as *the average weight of the five tallest people was 3 kg lower than the average of the five shortest people*

The second task is to rate the type of conditions on a scale of **0-1-2-3**. To do this, ask: How many of the conditions are **plugin** or **deductive**?

- All or most of the conditions can be directly **plugged** into my rough sheet: 3
- Around half of the conditions are **plugins**, the **rest** are **deductive**: 2
- Most of the conditions are **deductive**: 1
- All of the conditions are **deductive**: 0

Type of Questions: 0-1-2-3-4

In the chapter titled 'How to Solve a DI-LR Set', I had discussed that there are two types of DI-LR questions: *Open Questions* and *Closed Questions*.

Closed Questions	Open Questions
Provide NO additional information • Who is staying in Room 104? Asks for ONE answer • Who is the person staying in Room 104? Is a MUST-BE-TRUE Question • Must be true means that there is only one value that can fill the information. Never has permutations and combinations	Provide SOME additional information • If Ravi is the person staying in 104, who is staying in 105? Asks for MULTIPLE ANSWERS • Which of the options lists the people who could be staying in Room 104? Is a COULD-BE-TRUE Question • Could be true means that there can be more than one possibility to fill the information Involves permutations and combinations • How many people can be placed in Room 104? • In how many ways can the rooms be allotted to the group?

To rate the set based on type of questions, read every question and classify it as an open or closed question. If a question is *closed* give it a one, if it is *open*, give it a zero.

So, if all four questions are closed, then you will rate it a 4; if three are closed, then you will rate it a 3 and so on.

If you have understood these classifications properly or in other words, if you have been able to relate these classifications to the sets you have practised, then you will easily agree that the easiest ones will be standard and closed sets with plugin conditions.

As each of these three settings—*standard, plugin, closed*—start to change, the sets will get progressively harder with the toughest ones being unique, deductive and open sets.

So, your first task is to read a set in under three minutes and evaluate it through this lens.

What do the overall ratings mean?

Must-Solve **Now**: Sets rated 7 and above
Any set rated 7 and above is a must-solve. The golden rule is to remember that there will be two sets rated 7 and above for sure. It goes without saying that even between two must-solve sets, you have to solve the higher rated set first.

Could-Solve **Later**: Sets rated 6

Any set rated between 6 and 7 is one which you can take a shot at only after you solve the must-solve sets. If you have time left over, that is.

Never-Solve: Sets rated 5 or lower

Sets rated below 6 should be left alone unless all the rest of the sets are so easy that you could solve them and have time left over.

You can see my execution of the DI-LR set selection strategy using an actual CAT paper. This video is available on the Bell the CAT YouTube Page. The QR code on page 332 will take you to the same.

7

Quantitative Ability: Test-Taking Strategy

While the selection process for the VA-RC sets and DI-LR sets are a bit elaborate, the process is easiest for the QA section. You are supposed to read the question and decide *Now, Later* or *Never* all under one minute.

But there is one crucial difference: on the set-based RCs and DIs, you read all sets, assess the overall difficulty and then proceed to solve sets from the easiest to the toughest. On the QA section, if you classify a question as *Now*, you have to solve it then and there. Some of you might wonder—doesn't it make sense to read all the questions, classify them into *Now, Later* or *Never* and then start solving all the *Nows*? The answer is a big no for the following reason:

You will tend to speed-read and choose questions that are from your favourite topic.

To read and evaluate over twenty questions will take at least ten minutes. Since that is a lot of time, test-takers tend to speed-read and choose questions. This, more often than not, will lead to them assuming things about the questions. What you will end up doing is choosing familiar types from topics you like.

Why you should not select based on the topic

How test-takers normally select, or rather, reject questions:

- I am good at numbers (or I just did numbers last week) so I will do this question.
- *Geometry* is better left alone, it is always time-taking.
- P and C and probability, no way.
- These arithmetic questions are too long and will consume a lot of reading time.
- I haven't learnt and have never liked logarithms and functions, so better leave.

So what happens when you follow this approach? No arithmetic, no geometry, no logs, no P and C, no probability, only basic algebra, no polynomials!

You will be left with very few questions! You will get at least four or five questions from each of the five areas—numbers, arithmetic, algebra, geometry and modern maths.

If you refuse to do questions from more than two or three areas, you will be left with around ten to fifteen questions to take a shot at and will end up attempting around eight to ten and getting six to eight right and have a score of 15 to 25.

Let us assume there are twenty-five questions with five questions from each area and they follow a typical distribution.

Area	Now	Later	Never	Possible Marks
Numbers	1-2	1-2	1	4
Arithmetic	1-2	1-2	1	4
Algebra	1-2	1-2	1	4
Geometry	1-2	1-2	1	4
Modern Maths	1-2	1-2	1	4
TOTAL	**5–10**	**5–10**	**5–10**	
Correct Probability	**80 per cent**	**50 per cent**	**0 per cent**	
Possible Marks	**11–22**	**6–10**	**0**	

I calculated the possible marks, 3 for correct and -1 for incorrect, in both scenarios: Area-wise and difficulty-level wise. It is obvious you are much better off solving all easy questions, irrespective of the area than trying to solve all questions in two or three areas.

So, the first rule is that you shall not discriminate against a question based on area, topic or length! You will use your powers of discrimination to identify whether the question is *Now (Easy)*, *Later (Medium)*, or *Never (Difficult)*.

Some of you might have a different problem:

• I know all topics and hence, try to solve all questions!

Discriminating on the wrong grounds and not discriminating at all are equally punishable with low scores!

How to classify a Quant question

NOW: If you can see the clear steps to the answer, the number of steps are few and the question can be solved in two or under two minutes.

LATER: If you *feel* you can do it but do not know the exact steps; you will know the way only after you start doing it—you cannot see the four steps to the answer right now.

LATER: If you can clearly see all the steps but there are so many that it will take more than three minutes. As a test-taker, I am always greedy. If I solve a four-minute question, I get 3 marks. But if I leave it for later and I find two 2-minute questions, I will get 6 marks.

NEVER: You do not have any idea how to go about solving the question.

So, in effect, your QA score will depend on your ability to:

- make twenty to twenty-five good selection decisions and
- exiting questions without getting stuck

How many *easy* questions will there actually be in a Quant section?

Before we answer this question, I will try to define easy, medium and difficult in a quantitative way.

- **Easy**: 70 per cent or more people will be able to answer it correctly if they attempt it
- **Medium**: 30–70 per cent people will be able to answer it correctly if they attempt it
- **Difficult**: Less than 30 per cent people will be able to answer it correctly if they attempt it

The 2023 CAT paper arguably had the toughest QA section in recent years. Even so, I found at least 8 easy questions. The key was to keep looking for them first instead of trying to solve medium and difficult questions.

On a tough paper, the number of difficult questions do not go up by much, nor do the number of easy ones. What happens then?

If medium is a range from 30 to 70 per cent of people getting it correct if they attempt it, it means that some medium questions are closer to the easy level and some to the difficult level. So, on a tough paper, the medium questions will tend to be closer to the difficult level than to the easy. They will be time-consuming as well.

We will now look at the entire CAT QA section and solve it using the *Now, Later, Never* approach. This video is available on the Bell the CAT YouTube Page. The QR code on page 332 will take you to the same.

8

How to Analyse a Test

One of the things I remember most about my CAT prep days was the time I spent in post-test analysis. The mocks were always held in the first half of Sunday. I would get back, have lunch and then sit for around two to three hours straight.

At the end of the analysis, I accomplished three things. One, what is the best score I could have got at my current level by cutting out mistakes that could have been avoided and choosing different questions. Two, looking at solutions of incorrect and/or skipped questions to learn how to solve questions from topics I did not have a grip on but were actually easy. And three, looking at solutions of incorrect and/or skipped questions to figure out which type of questions to leave based on the length and complexity of the solution. After every single test, I was trying to see how I could improve my personal best. It did not matter how much my friends were scoring.

Without any statistics, just with these three things, I think I maximized my potential on the CAT. And when I maximize my potential, I will get the highest potential I am capable of. The fact that I received calls from A, C, L and K means that I would have gotten a decent percentile.

But these days we have statistics and I will go out on a limb and say that what I need is my score percentile and the solutions and even today I will hit my best percentiles. Not a single statistic matters. Why do I say this?

If it is information about me, then I do not need the machine to tell me what I am good and bad at. I know what I am good and bad at. My analysis will tell me why I am making the mistakes I am making—misreading, miscalculation or misjudgement. I know once I sit after the test where I wasted my time and after a few initial tests, I stopped getting stuck on questions anyway.

If it is information about others, it does not help me. I will never solve a question slower than I can or in a relaxed manner. I am always solving with a sense of extreme urgency with my foot completely pressing down the accelerator pedal. Given this, I cannot go faster than I can just by knowing that someone else or toppers are faster. I am anyway always trying to minimize putting pen to paper and solving as efficiently as possible. That less than 50 per cent of toppers did not solve a question does not mean it will be tough for me. My brain is my brain and the solution will tell me whether I can solve it or not. For example, if my geometry skills are exceptionally better than the toppers', then I will always find geometry easier than the toppers!

How do you get better from test to test by reducing your errors and increasing your attempts?

All you need to do after a test is to know how you could have maximized your score. Evaluate yourself on the following three parameters to determine how to:

- Question Selection—Test-Taking Strategy
- Question Solving—Accuracy and Speed
- Question Range—Concept Coverage

To maximize your score with the same core skill level, you need to master selection and accuracy.

To maximize your score after you have mastered selection and accuracy, you need to upgrade your skill levels—the speed at which you score and the topics from which you score.

Question Selection—Test-Taking Strategy

If you are selecting the wrong sets or questions, then you are losing the battle even before stepping on to the field. So, after every test, you need to ask yourself whether your question selection was *perfect*, *50-50*, or *poor*. It might seem like there is a rating between perfect and 50-50, but since selection is the most important strategy, unless it is perfect, you have to rate yourself 50-50. Ideally, you should make a table like this for forty mocks and fill it up after every mock.

Test#	VA-RC	DI-LR	QA
SimCAT 1	50-50	Perfect	Poor
SimCAT 2	Perfect	Poor	Perfect
SimCAT 3	50-50	Perfect	Poor

If your selection is fluctuating wildly, it means that you are either applying no strategy or are applying the strategy very poorly or it is a mixture of both. Revisit the selection strategy and see if you would have chosen different sets if you had applied the strategy accurately.

At the end of this analysis, you need to write down your selection goals for each section before the next exam.

Accurate question selection is the first step to reducing errors or skipped questions.

Question Solving Efficiency—Accuracy and Speed

The other area to analyse is how efficiently you are solving the questions. You are selecting the right questions but are consistently making errors or getting stuck in the middle of solving and are unable to move forward.

This means that your solving technique is very poor. Revisit the techniques outlined in parts IV, V and VI of this book and ask yourself whether you are executing the best practices to solve a question or are attempting questions without any process. The key symptoms of lack of process will be a tendency to have to restart solving after one false attempt. In some cases, you get questions correct on a re-attempt but on others, you could make an error or make no headway.

Only if you master your process of solving and execute it consistently will you always hit an accuracy of 75 to 80 per cent, which is a good target to aim at.

Your selection is spot on and your accuracy is also great. What you lack is speed. How do you rectify this?

VA-RC: Read at a slightly faster speed, say 10 per cent faster. You will initially find it uncomfortable but you will need to concentrate harder. It is not very different from the concentration you need to have to run a fast single as opposed to a jogging single. The moment you get comfortable at 10 per cent faster, raise your speed by another 10 per cent.

DI-LR: If your question selection is correct and your processes are correct, you should be able to solve two sets. The increase in speed that you will get used to in VA-RC will come in handy here as well.

QA: The only way to increase speed is to write less. Make a conscious effort to reduce the number of steps you write. Write only when you cannot process things mentally.

Question Range—Concept Coverage

Your selection is great and so is your solving efficiency: strategy, speed and efficiency are covered. The only place left to look for more marks is concept coverage. Think of yourself as a T20 batsman. You are stuck with a strike rate between 120 and 140 while others are comfortably crossing 175 and even making 200 seem normal. What will you do?

Firstly, you will look at optimizing score areas by maximizing the shots you can play. Can you play behind the wicket shots? Can you play switch hits and reverse sweeps? Can you use your crease, stepping out or moving laterally to disrupt the lie and length?

Secondly, you will look at putting on muscle so that even your mis-hits will clear the boundary.

Increasing the range of shots you can play is similar to increasing the number of topics from which you can solve questions. Make a list of all topics that you do not solve currently—either because you do not like them or because you have not studied them yet. Get cracking on them. Master one topic at a time based on the time available between two mocks.

Increasing your muscle is nothing but increasing your speed, which we have already covered.

Make a plan of action for what you need to do before and in the next mock

Once you have finished your analysis, you need to make a list of things to work on before the next mock:

- practise RCs at 10 per cent faster speed
- master the technique for jumbled paragraphs
- master the concepts around triangles
- master 3-factor Venn-diagrams

Make a list of things to execute in the next mock:

- Execute *Now, Later* and *Never* with more precision by not classifying *Later* problems as now
- Identify the anchor conditions in DI-LR set
- Start with VA instead of RC

Just because you got it right does not mean you got it right the best way

The biggest mistake you can make in your post-test analysis is to not look at the solutions to questions you have solved correctly! The team that sets the questions and makes video solutions to the same has mentors who are exceptional at cracking the exam. Given this, it is highly likely that the solutions will teach you:

- better ways to eliminate options,
- faster methods to reach the answer, and
- clearer thinking processes

There is no reason to be proud of running four singles when someone is hitting boundaries!

There is no mock question you should not know how to solve

Just like the golden rule of test-taking strategy is that there should not be an unread question, the golden rule of post-test analysis is that there is no unsolved question. So, before you start your analysis you should:

- solve all the incorrect and skipped questions in a section on your own without any time limit but with the same intensity and speed as in a test
- go through the solutions of all these questions, even the ones you solved correctly

Most importantly, do not ignore skipped questions from areas you have not studied yet! Many students think—I have not studied geometry yet, so no point attempting geometry questions in my analysis. You have passed Class X. You know what a triangle is. By looking at the solution, you can at least learn some property of a triangle, learn a new concept and increase your concept coverage!

Trust me, if you analyse your test the way I have outlined, there is no way you will not reach your best percentile.

9

Setting the Right Targets on Your Way to the 99th Percentile and Above

By now we have discussed a lot of things! The right solving technique, elaborate test-taking strategies and detailed analysis methods. How long or rather how many mocks do you think you will need to get a hang of things and be in control? My guess is at least five mocks at the minimum and on average, around ten if you are very diligent. One of the reasons why people crack the CAT in their second attempt is that only then do all the elements come together.

Given this, it is clear that you will face ups and downs during the test-taking season. Aspirants usually start off full-steam, thinking 99-plus percentile—IIM-A—and then, when faced with disappointments in the initial mocks, tend to lose heart and start going through a phase of self-doubt. You will meet your expectations on one mock and think that you are on the right track, only to be brought down to earth in the next one. Such fluctuations happen because both your technique and test-taking strategy are not sealed and locked. A favourable paper and you do well, a seemingly tough paper and you are unable to keep your head above the water.

A few years ago, I attended the Chennai convocation function for aspirants who cleared the Company Secretary (CS) exam (a relative of mine had cleared it). The chief guest was Padma Shri awardee T.N. Manoharan, who is a pre-eminent figure in the banking and accounting sector in the country, with his book being a must-read for all CA aspirants. He was part of the government-appointed team that cleaned up the Satyam mess and paved the way for the transition to Tech Mahindra. His keynote address was leavened with wisdom and had too many punchlines for me to recount here, but one of the things he said is spot on when it comes to the way we should deal with success and failure. He said, 'Celebrate success with all your heart but do not let it get to your head and do not let failure enter and break your heart, use your head to find out the causes and deal with it.'

The key takeaway is that the test-taking season and mocks are not meant to be emotional journeys but intellectual ones. And this intellectual journey starts with setting the right targets.

Set modest goals, meet them, and set modest increments

If you start your test-taking journey in April with the first SimCAT, a realistic month to hit your best scores will be September. But how do you set mini-targets till then to ensure that you are performing at your peak by the time you are about a month away from the CAT?

On average, scores correspond to percentiles as below (the range takes into account the variability in difficulty levels):

- 99 percentile and above percentiles: 100 and above
- 95–99 percentile: 65 to 100
- 90–95 percentile: 55 to 65
- 80–90 percentile: 40 to 55

Those of you who have a percentile below 80 and are feeling bad about the same, try viewing what 80 percentile means from a different lens.

On average, around 45 marks should fetch you 80 percentile and ideally, these 45 marks should get spread equally across the three sections.

What do 15 marks in a section mean?

- Approximately eight or nine attempts with six to seven questions correct.

So, on average, to get to the 80th percentile, you will be *leaving more questions than you will be attempting* or in other words, you will be attempting very judiciously.

A reasonably reliable estimate of how many questions you should get correct out of how many attempts in each section on the SimCATs to scale different percentile levels is given below.

- 80 percentile: 6/9
- 85 percentile: 8/12
- 90 percentile: 10/14
- 95 percentile: 12/15
- 99 percentile: 15/18

If you speak to previous years' CAT-takers, they might say that these numbers are on the slightly lower side but SimCATs have always been tougher than the actual CAT. If the actual CAT is easier, your attempts and accuracy have to naturally go up.

Setting the right percentile targets over the next three months

I know that the readers of this book will be a varied lot—from retakers who are already at a 95 percentile to first-timers who fared poorly in their initial SimCATs. The percentile targets I am going to suggest are strictly for those who are currently at or below 80 percentile, irrespective of whether they are retakers or not. Given below are the percentiles you should target to reach in the coming months. Please note that you need to touch these percentiles sometime during these months, not necessarily at the beginning or the end.

- 85 percentile: July
- 90 percentile: August
- 95 percentile: September

In these initial SimCATs, you should set modest milestones to start with in terms of attempts, accuracy and percentiles, and slowly work your way up the ladder. One rule of thumb can be to aim at increasing your percentile by 3–5 points every month from now on.

Mid-season review: Should you change your target tests and colleges?

Sometimes, it can happen that, despite their best efforts, some students are not able to hit their desired percentiles. Something in the nature of the test—be it the question types or timing or format—work against them. They decide to turn their focus on to a different exam instead of the CAT, say the NMAT and/or SNAP, and instantly start performing well. I have seen this not just with the CAT but even with the GMAT. A student prepares for and takes the GMAT more than once and does not perform well enough, and then decides to try the GRE and does pretty well. Different exams test different skills; some might need more memory, others more strategy, and still others more speed. Each one of us might not be blessed with all three qualities.

It is thus important that after you have taken around seven to ten mocks, you should step back and take a call on whether you want to make the CAT your main focus or another exam. What criteria should you use to decide the course of action?

If you have not hit your desired percentile after ten mocks, then maybe it is time to consider a change in the target exams and colleges, provided you have:

- covered most of the topics across all areas and sections
- executed test-taking strategies across all sections
- analysed and spent time between tests with clear goals for improvements

If, even after doing all the above, you are unable to reach your target percentiles, then it makes sense to start taking the other exams seriously. This does not mean that you will ignore the CAT. You should still work towards doing your best on the CAT. It is just that you will devote the time required for other exams as well.

10

Test-Taking Blues: The Reason
Why Your QA Scores Are Below Par

While the chapter on how to improve your QA accuracy is more than comprehensive in terms of what is needed to push your score north, there are students who are unable to come to terms with QA. They say they have done concepts and enough practice as well but none of it seems to be pushing the scores up and the confidence levels are pretty low.

It was only a few years ago that I figured out the core issue with these students when I was sitting with one—he was preparing for the GMAT and had a decent amount of work experience, and by the time I met him, he was already through with two attempts spread over two years with sub-par scores. He was willing to put in another attempt and a year more if required to get a par score.

I gave him some broad guidelines and assigned a personal mentor to him, and met with him regularly on overall prep strategy, some specific pointers and test-taking strategies. But at the end of another year, the score was the same.

I could not figure it out—the guy was very professional, super-committed (something you would have figured by now), doing reasonably well in his job, and super-positive despite everything.

It was when he came to meet me again that I threw a few questions at him, questions that I had solved in class and he had attended multiple times, and his reaction to them and the way he reacted when I told him the solution—'Oh, ya, ya, ya, ya!'—that I figured the core problem: he was mugging up maths!

Do you learn maths the same way as you did for your Class X and Class XII exams?

This, I realize, is a bigger problem than what is assumed. Students whose only interaction with maths has been for their Class X and Class XII exams, who have never prepared for an aptitude test before, and took extensive tuitions for their school exams, do not even know that the maths they did then and the maths they have to do now is the same, but the way it is tested cannot be more different.

Those papers needed parrots, parrots who could replicate things step by step and with good handwriting. And nothing could be more different from that than a CAT paper.

So ask yourself the question: Do you mug up concepts or do you actually understand why $a^x.a^y = a^{x+y}$?

If you do memorize and have always done so, then you really need to start from scratch and it is not easy; you will definitely need to approach it more holistically.

I suggest doing this free course by Barbara Oakley—she had a BA in literature and worked in the defence services before taking up engineering later than others: https://www.coursera.org/learn/learning-how-to-learn

Read this book by her as well: *A Mind for Numbers.*

Another thing to keep in mind is that even if you somehow mug stuff up, get a bit lucky and manage to get into an IIM, the first-year course will be as tough, if not tougher than CAT maths—you will be graded relative to others and the others are everybody who has cracked the CAT (the only reprieve is that time is not a constraint). A lot of the students who are unable to complete the MBA programme or finish it over a longer period would have failed in the first-year maths subjects.

Do you know basic concepts but have no clue how advanced concepts came about?

Do you know how the formula for the number of total factors of a number—$a^m.b^n$—$(m+1)(n+1)$—came about?

- A factor is number that divides another number.
- Every power of a from a^1, a^2, a^3, a^4 . . . a^m will divide the number.
- Every power of b from b^1, b^2, b^3, b^4 . . . b^n will divide the number.
- So, m powers of a and n powers of b.
- Each of these m powers of a when multiplied by each of the n powers of b will divide the number. For example, a^1*b^1, a^1*b^2, a^1*b^3 . . . a^m*b^n.
- There will be $m*n$ such numbers.
- Apart from all of these numbers, 1 is always a factor.
- The total number of factors is $m + n + m*n + 1$, which is nothing but $(m+1)(n+1)$.

I am sure there are many who know the above formula but yet do not know how to answer the question below:

How many factors of 1080000 are not divisible by 40?

If they happen to read the solution, they wonder why it did not strike them.

It need not be that you have this issue in the whole of QA. It can be that you have this problem only in some areas—numbers and geometry or geometry and modern maths—or only on specific topics such as P and C and logarithms.

If you are in this bucket, then you need to focus on understanding how formulas came about so that you develop the ability to solve such questions.

Do you try to memorize patterns?

The last category is test-takers who are good at maths but their approach to prep is to memorize as many different patterns and endless sub-formulas (formulas derived for an endless list of special cases) as possible.

The problem with the approach is that whenever they are faced with a problem, the first instinct is to try to map it to a formula or a pattern they have solved before.

It is not that there are no patterns; there are patterns and in recent years, the CAT has become more pattern-based than before. But all that needs to happen is for eight to ten problems that do not fall into a pattern but are otherwise solvable to appear in the paper and these test-takers will not be able to handle them. If a few of these problems turn up at the beginning of the section, then the confidence can take a major hit.

Another issue with mugging patterns is that you need to keep a lot of your brain space free for all of these patterns and sub-formulas. Those who have exceptional storage and memory between their ears can afford to follow this approach. I prefer to have only the bare minimum of formulas and patterns in my head and go by pure logic—the lower the fuel in the car, the faster it can go. I think the golden mean between the two where you know the patterns but are willing to look at a problem first up with fresh eyes is crucial.

Always visualize yourself in front of a problem as a doctor faced with a patient. What does a great doctor do? Listen to you fully; ask the right questions; suggest the right tests, if required; figure out the exact problem; and suggest the least medication possible.

The different kinds of mugging listed above are reasons behind you truly not solving a problem.

If you are truly honest with yourself about this part of your prep, then you will be able to make the changes necessary to achieve a good score on QA and as I mentioned before, it is not just CAT QA that is on the line but also Quant in the MBA programme.

You need to always start with the WHAT and move to the HOW

Some students have written to me saying that when they try to not copy-paste patterns, they find that their mind is blank and they do not know what to do.

Imagine an F1 driver going to drive on relatively unknown tracks every time he goes out to drive—the key word is 'relatively', not 'completely'. He or she will draw upon the experiences but still drive as if it were new.

It is exactly like cricket; you practise in the nets but every pitch, every match, every ball is different.

This is exactly what makes the big three matches in tennis so interesting; they have played each other a million times but they know that every match can be won by either of them. This, despite knowing everything inside out.

And what is different?

Each and every time the questions asked of them by their opponent are different.

WHAT is being asked is different.

If Nadal is hitting the ball closer to the lines, Djoker knows he is being asked a different question and he knows that he has to find a response in real-time while drawing on the past.

If Federer is just creaming winners off the forehand, then Nadal knows he is being asked a different question.

The first task always is to figure out the WHAT and then move to the HOW instead of thinking about the HOW.

When students say nothing strikes them, it is because they are thinking that the HOW will come and strike them. Nothing strikes you if you are not looking for it, except lightning!

Let us take a question to see what I mean by figuring out the WHAT and moving to the HOW.

Question 1

If all the factors of 5040 are arranged in descending order, then which will be the fifth factor?

We know that the greatest factor of the number is the number itself—5040.

- WHAT—We need to factorize this first since we need to find the top five factors.
- HOW—5040 – 2^4*3^2*5*7
- WHAT—If this is the highest one, then what is the one after this?
- HOW—I need to remove the smallest possible factor from this
- What is the smallest possible factor that I can remove? 2
- So, the next factor in descending order will be 2^3*3^2*5*7
- For the third one, we remove a 3—2^4*3^1*5*7
- For the fourth one, we remove a 4—2^2*3^2*5*7
- For the fifth one, we remove a 5—2^4*3^2*7—which is what the question is asking us for.

What if the question is tweaked?

Question 2

If all the factors of 5040 are arranged in ascending order, then which one will be the 56th factor?

When I read this with fresh eyes, I know that this seems crazy. Am I really supposed to write all the factors from 1 to 55? Surely, you must be joking Mr Question-man!

There must be another way—they won't be paying an average salary of Rs 25 LPA at IIM-A for someone to do such donkey work!

WHAT—Before I go ahead, I need to know how many factors are there and where does 55 stand?

HOW—To find out the number of factors, I need to factorize the number 5040 – 2^4*3^2*5*7.

The number of factors—what you will know from all of your previous practice—5*3*3*2—60.

There are 60 factors and they are asking me for the 55th; so, instead of going from 1 to 56, I can come down from 60 to 56.

From here, the problem becomes the same as the previous one.

For some, this might be a huge change since you have to undo all your previous modes of dealing with maths; for others, it might turn on a switch that they never thought they had, but for everyone, there is no other way.

The weird part is that even those who have made it to the IITs do not seem to get this. I had a student from IIT Ropar in one of my GMAT classes and he was like—you must know all the patterns by now, so you can answer all questions!

It is like saying Kohli knows to play all shots, so every time he goes out, he will make a 100! It does not work that way.

Yes, teaching helps, but every teacher does not get a 100 every year in QA, right?

On good exams, one gets rewarded for thinking, not regurgitating!

So, stop mugging, start solving!

11

Test-Taking Blues: Why Your Skills Might Not Be as Good as You Think They Are

One of the big takeaways from my teaching experience is that I need to figure out why students are not able to execute what I tell them. What unique things in their practice or attitude hinder them from doing so. And nothing has helped me more in this regard than the problems that students keep bringing back to me over the years. As the important ones get addressed, I keep getting other questions, which, depending on how one looks at it, are either simple or hide more than they reveal to the casual observer.

One such conundrum is this one, a paraphrase of a problem that I have answered in many of my blog comments: *I do not know what happens to me during the test—I do pathetically, sometimes I am even ashamed to mention how much I score—but when I sit after the test, I find that I can answer all questions easily. How do I deal with this nervousness, how do I tackle this?*

You are looking in the wrong mirror—your post-test performance does not really count

The biggest thing test-takers discount is that they are solving the whole paper for the second time!

- You have already spent forty or sixty minutes with twenty-five to thirty-five problems.
- You have already tried half of the problems for at least two to three minutes each.
- You attempted the rest of the questions for at least one to two minutes.
- You have understood all the superficial aspects of the question.
- You have already tried the obvious methods.

When you read it for a second time:

- your brain registers what it missed or took for granted during the exam
- you do not draw the same table or represent the information in a DI-LR set the same way that you did during the exam
- you actually understand the anchor condition because in the exam you did not give it enough thought

- you thus start correctly solving the questions you spent two or three minutes on during the exam
- you gain confidence and then correctly solve the questions you spent one or two minutes on during the exam
- you conclude that your problem is nervousness

You completely and conveniently ignore the fact that in reality, you spent, on average, four to five minutes on every question, or in other words, you took twice the time to solve the same section.

You took two stabs at the question. You are adding the score of the first and second innings into a single score!

Estimating your capabilities by post-test performance creates a vicious cycle

In your head, your actual capability on a section is 45–50 marks because of the way you ace it post-test, whereas your actual scores are in the 15–25 range.

After every successful post-test solving, you approach the next test with the same mindset—I am awesome at this section; this time I am going to score 45–50.

What happens when you go in with this thinking?

- To score 45–50, you have to attempt around twenty to twenty-two questions and get seventeen to eighteen right or attempt four sets or all RCs
- This means that you are going to attempt almost two out of three questions
- More importantly, this means that you have just about two minutes per question
- You feel under the pump right from the beginning
- A few questions go wrong in the beginning and the downward spiral starts
- You desperately try to keep your head above water for the rest of the section—everything but your head is still
- You come back home, pick yourself up, re-solve the section and feel good
- You think your level is 45–50, next time you will nail it
- The cycle, unfortunately vicious not virtuous, continues

Other things also happen because of these misplaced targets:

- All the question-selection strategies and solving techniques are thrown out of the window
- You think that all of these strategies and techniques are not practical in actual test conditions
- You relegate the processes to the background and go back to being you and doing you

Accept your true ability and set realistic goals

I am not saying that you can never score 45; you sure can, but not right now! Right now maybe your ability is somewhere in the middle—not 15–25 or 45–50 but 30–35.

This might be tough to accept:

- You think you are good at VA-RC since you read a lot
- You think you are good at QA since you like maths a lot and have done well in the past

But the fact is that this exam and the question types and the format have nothing to do with your capabilities in general. It has everything to do with performing in the format of the test.

The only true indicator of ability is your performance on the test. That you are a good test cricketer does not mean you will be an ace at T20 and vice-versa. You play exceptionally well in India does not mean you will play exceptionally well in England!

So, this is what you should do.

Set your ego aside completely; put the test above you.

Set a target of your current average score plus 10. If you are currently scoring around 15, do not aim for more than 25.

Solve only as many sets/questions that you need to solve to reach this score.

If you are used to aiming for three sets, it is okay to aim for only two of the easiest and get them right.

If you do this:

- the pressure of the timer disappears
- you have enough time to execute the selection correctly
- you have enough time to execute the processes correctly
- you are more likely to achieve your target

Once you achieve 25 for two or three tests, add another 10 marks, let your score stabilize at 35 and then add another 10.

Some papers might be extremely difficult, but if you are selecting right, then you will clear the cut-off and get a good percentile despite a lower-than-target-score, since your targets were realistic to start with.

Your problem is nervousness only if . . .

Nervousness is a valid problem only if you are scoring exceptionally well in the take-homes and tanking only in the Proctored SimCATs.

Your performance in sectionals is not a valid indicator of your ability since you are not comparing apples with apples; the comparison is valid only in VA-RC since it is the first section and you have as much energy in the SimCAT as in the sectionals.

So, if you fall into this category—great take-home scores but drastically reduced scores in proctored sims—then, yes, nervousness is a problem. The chapters in the next section will deal with this. But in the meantime, you will not do badly to set reduced expectations; that in itself will decrease the pressure.

The goal is not to score 100 but to score a good 35–40 during which:

- only the right deliveries were played at
- every shot played hit the centre of the bat
- every shot was played right into the gap, and
- got you as many runs as the ball deserved

Walk, jog, run, and finally, fly.

12

The Last Leg: Score Improvement, Attempts versus Accuracy, Prep Planning

Unlike the time when I was preparing, we have tons of data that is quite useful to determine what are realistic goals to set and what are realistic strategies to pursue. Once test-takers hit a plateau, they keep coming back with the same simplistic question around how to increase their scores: *Should I increase my attempts or should I increase my accuracy?*

We should start by once again looking at the score-percentile table. The table below takes a wider range of possible difficulty levels into consideration.

Section	85 Percentile	95 Percentile	99 Percentile	100 Percentile
VA-RC	20–25	30–35	40–45	60–65
DI-LR	12–20	20–25	30–35	50–60
QA	15–20	25–30	30–45	55–70
Overall	40–50	60–70	80–100	140–160

From the above table it is clear that at a sectional and overall level, the range of scores is in a narrow band over the last years in all cases, except when it comes to the QA and that too at a 99 and 100 percentile.

The first step is to set the right target section-wise and not aim to move more than one column to the right at a time per section. If you are currently at 85 percentile in QA, then your target for the next SimCAT should be 95 and not 99 percentile.

So, your task before the next SimCAT is to:

- look at your average percentile in a section: last three tests, last five tests, whatever is best indicative (for example, if you were not at all prepared in the initial SimCATs, no point including them to calculate your average)
- look at the next milestone in the table above—for example, if you are 82 percentile, set your next target as 85 percentile
- look at the score required for the same

You need to first reach base-level accuracy

Most people reduce this to a simplistic equation of increasing attempts, but a look at the table below will show that you are better off increasing your accuracy rather than increasing your attempts to reach a higher score.

ATTEMPT/ACCURACY	8–10	11–13	14–16	17–19	20–24
50 per cent	~9	~12	~15	~18	~22
65 per cent	~14	~19	~24	~29	~35
75 per cent	~18	~24	~30	~36	~44

In my opinion, based on the statistics that we have seen with the toppers and the rest of the population, a realistic accuracy target for each area/section is as follows:

- Verbal Ability: ~65 per cent—five out of eight questions
- Reading Comprehension: 65 per cent—8 marks/set
- Data Interpretation and Logical Reasoning: 75 per cent—8 marks/set
- Quantitative Ability: 75 per cent—8–11 marks/set

What is most important is to observe that you get greater gains by improving your accuracy by one slab than by increasing your attempts by one or even two slabs.

For example, at 50 per cent, increasing your attempts from 11–13 to 17–19 will take your score from 12 to 18. This is also under the big assumption that increasing your speed by 50 per cent to increase attempts from 12 to 18 will not dent your accuracy at all!

But with the same 11–13 attempts, increasing your accuracy from 50 per cent to 65 per cent will take your score from 12 to ~20.

So, the first step is to reach 65 per cent accuracy in all sections.

How are you going to get the extra marks to reach your target score—attempts?

'Sir, should I increase the attempts in my next SimCAT?'

Honestly, this question has always amused me. The underlying assumption here is that you can increase your attempts at will!

Imagine a fast bowler asking his bowling coach: 'In the next match, should I start bowling at 150 instead of 135?'

Well, if you can bowl six balls at 150 without hurling beamers at the batter's head or making your wicketkeeper go diving in all directions, why not?

Firstly, increase your attempts only after your accuracy has stabilized at 65 per cent. And how do you go about it?

VA-RC: You cannot directly attempt three passages instead of two in a SimCAT. You should practise three passages with a timer of twenty-five minutes for at least ten sets with a conscious effort to focus harder while increasing speed.

And this is important—if you have to drive your bike faster, say at 60, you have to focus much harder than you would need to drive at 40!

Once you are clear that you can take up three passages in twenty-five minutes while maintaining your accuracy at 65 per cent, then go for it in the next SimCAT. Otherwise, you will find that your score has dropped, and that sets off another crisis of confidence.

QA: In QA, you need to figure out what is stopping you from attempting more questions:

- Speed: You know all concepts in arithmetic, algebra and geometry but are able to attempt only a few questions because of lack of speed.
- Concept Coverage: You have good speed, but you do not know all concepts in all three areas, resulting in you leaving many easy questions.

If the problem is speed, then you need to ensure the following while solving a Quant question:

- Do not start copying information from the question to your paper as you are reading.
- Do not start solving before you reach the end of the question.
- Do not write each and every step of the solution. Skip writing steps by doing them mentally.

If the problem is concepts, then you need to first master them, starting with one area at a time between two mocks.

DI-LR: The same as QA. You need to check whether speed or concepts—3/4-factor Venn diagrams, spider graphs, weighted averages—is the problem.

A possible elephant in the room!

One of the lesser-discussed issues is test-taking stamina.

Your question selection is fine. Your speed is fine. Your concept coverage is adequate. But you just cannot perform at your optimum potential for two hours.

After sixty minutes or roughly towards the latter half of the DI-LR section, your mental energy tends to flag, you get stuck on questions that you later discover were sitters. In short, your brain refuses to budge. This straightaway means that you do not have the mental stamina to perform at your peak for two hours.

When I took the GMAT in 2017, I found that I, too, was not at full testing fitness. My workload was pretty heavy, so I took mocks late at night (and only two at that).

On the actual test day, I had to take the AWA and IR sections, which I skipped in the mocks, so by the time I reached the middle of the last section, Verbal, I realized that for fifteen minutes, my brain had shut down and I was solving questions based on gut feel and not using my own processes. As a result, I got a good score but in Verbal I scored 42, lower than I did in my mock.

The same thing happened in the CAT, the next year. It was a three-hour paper, and after around 140 minutes, my brain shut down for twenty minutes in the QA section. I was unable to solve easy questions and just could not get bat on ball properly. But it did restart and I was able to knock off a few questions.

How do you solve the problem of test-taking stamina?

You cannot develop a skill or a capability directly in a mock. You need to develop it in practice.

- No practice session should be under two hours.
- Every session should be executed in the same conditions as the actual test—phone switched off, no breaks.
- Take tests only when you have the mental stamina to take a test—late-night after a long day's work might not be the best indicator of your abilities.

Planning your prep in the last leg

Set your goals for every week from now until the CAT using the data and the process outlined in this book—section-wise: percentile, attempts, accuracy.

Make a weekly prep plan aligned to achieving those goals.

You need not have improvement goals for every section in every week. This will lead to a little-bit-of-everything every day sort of prep. You need not practise for more than two sections in a week with clear goals for each section, starting with your weakest sections.

Do not worry whether there is enough time to improve. Give everything you have to reach the best percentile you can this year. Even if you do not make it to your dream school, you will have less distance to cover next year, and more importantly, you will know your capabilities in the real sense.

I got through the CAT on my second attempt, a very stress-free attempt with limited but very high-quality prep, because I gave everything I had in my first attempt and knew exactly what I needed to fix.

As they say, with respect to performing in the final stages of different sports—late into the fourth quarter of basketball, for example—*go deep or go home*.

Part VII

Mind over Matter: Mental Conditioning

1

The Cat Is Really Not as Tough as You Think: In Reality You Do Not Need a 99.5

The scariest thing about the CAT for many aspirants is the 99.xx percentiles that are needed to get into the most elite schools. That number itself seems mind-boggling. But in reality, one does not really need such a high percentile if one really breaks the numbers down.

What is a percentile?

It is the percentage of people who scored lower than you. I have mentioned this earlier as well; in some years, a score of zero yielded a percentile of 55. It means that 55 per cent of test-takers got less than a zero. You might take this as a reflection of how tough the test is. No.

Every year, on average, more than two lakh people register for the CAT. But how many actually end up taking the test? Around 1,75,000. So, a huge population does not even turn up for the test. Of those who turn up for the test, how many of them take up preparation of some sort?

If I add up the number of students enrolled with all the major players for at least a test series programme, it would come to around 1,20,000. These 1,20,000 aspirants are like people who have signed up to go to a gym!

How many of these actually complete the course? Less than 50 per cent if we go by our attendance. We give forty mocks, the average mocks taken are around five! So, in effect, out of the 1,20,000, how many aspirants can be considered serious? 50 per cent or 60,000.

So, your real competition is 60,000 students.

The IIMs in total have around 3500 seats. For each set, they call four people for the interview. This means that they will give out 14,000 calls. So, to get a call, you need to be in the top 14,000 out of 60,000. How many people should be below you? 46,000.

What percentile do you need if you need 46,000 people below you out of 60,000? 46000/60000 = ~75 percentile!

By taking everyone who has ever taken gym membership as competition, you will need a 99.99 percentile! By considering only those who regularly work out, you will find your percentile requirements much lower. Long story short, percentile is a misleading number!

You will score much higher than your mock percentile

People taking the mocks regularly are like those who are the most serious, the ones who go to the gym regularly. This number is on average around 15,000. The rest of the more than 1,50,000 who will turn up on test day are not geniuses but everyone who is going to do worse than you, the ones who never turn up at the gym. So, because you will do better than all of them, your percentile on CAT day will be higher than that on the mocks.

There is a ballpark formula for the same as well.

CAT Percentile = (Mock Percentile) + (100-Mock Percentile)/2
So, if you are currently scoring 85, you CAT percentile will be 85 + (100-85)/2 = 92.5.

Even this is a conservative estimate.

So, from now on, think of your ability based on your actual CAT percentile. And those who are aiming only at old IIMs, do not focus on the second two decimals after 99 and get scared. Focus on the number of extra questions you need get correct.

2

How to Manage Your Energy, Stress and Anxiety

Right at the outset, I would like to clarify that I am not qualified to talk about stress and anxiety in general since I am not a professional in the field. But if you are someone who stresses out a lot around exams but is pretty calm and collected in dealing with the other aspects of life, then I can be of some help. This was a session that I first came up with during the pandemic since it was a highly stressful time for all aspirants. The fact that our students could not meet their mentors in person meant that they had no one to discuss their fears with. I thought that since I was aware of all of the stressors through my interaction with students over the years, I might as well do a session dedicated only to managing the stress around the exam.

This video is available on the Bell the CAT YouTube Page. The QR code on page 332 will take you to the same.

3

One of the Many Ways

A few mornings ago, at the end of holding a particularly strenuous yoga pose, my brother let out a gasp and his back slumped back on to the mat. However, it was one of those days when my mind was sharp and still like the tip of an archer's arrow, and I went to the ground with an even breath and a straight spine—it was the first time it had happened in a long time. Straightaway in my ears, I heard the voice of Shaji shouting at me from one end of a really large room: 'I only said relax, back straight!'

The yelling was from a warm morning in 2013—I had just moved to Chennai after taking up the IMS franchise for the city. I was staying close to the miniature beach in Besant Nagar (or Bessie as the locals call it). On one of the very first evenings there, I took a stroll around the beach and came upon this structure or building or rather what I think is the best word for it—space.

As soon as I saw it and took it in for a few seconds, I thought, this has to be *it*—a year before, while in Mumbai, I had read a few articles about the groundbreaking classical dancer Chandralekha and had also seen a video of a piece choreographed by her that had made a strong impression on me. On reading more about her, I had discovered that her studio was in Chennai and when I saw this space, I was certain that this was *it*.

Chandralekha is considered groundbreaking because she re-invented or reinterpreted what Bharatanatyam can mean through the lens of an even older art form, one that is considered a precursor to all the South-east Asian martial arts—*kalarippayattu*. Shaji, a young practitioner and teacher of kalarippayattu, was one of the two people in the piece choreographed by Chandralekha that I had watched, the other was the writer Tishani Doshi. So, when I saw the place, I made up my mind to go in and find out if they taught the laity; it turned out that they did and before long, I was inside.

Shaji was as old-school a perfectionist as one could get for a teacher. He would spend a long time arranging and rearranging students in what seemed to be a random asymmetrical order. Looking back, I am guessing it was to ensure that he could sight each one of the thirty-odd students who turned up at 6 a.m. from places that were as far as two hours away. He rarely uttered a word apart from the instructions for the movement in Malayalam (like it is in the Japanese way, there is very little active teaching; you are expected to watch, follow and execute until you get the hang of it).

The session opened with a thirty-minute, non-stop movement and kicks-based warm-up by the end of which my lungs were ready to explode. It was on one of those initial days after he had said

266

'Relax' at the end of the warm-up that I slumped against the wall, breathing audibly (to myself) that he shouted at me: 'I only said relax, back straight!'

After about fifteen-odd sessions, I gave up because I realized that very few of the students who came there were amateurs like me. Many of the students were dancers who did this for strength and flexibility, while others were full-time students of Kalari who stayed there for the better part of the day. I felt that unless I was serious about pursuing it as an art form, which would take more than the ninety minutes of everyday class that I was putting in, I would be disrespecting the art form. It was obvious that they were not teaching the classes for the money (else they wouldn't have been charging a meagre Rs 500 per month). And given that I had just invested money to get into a business, there was no way I could give any more than ninety minutes a day, which in itself seemed difficult on most days.

But what I learnt from those few sessions was immense. Firstly, commitment to something is not limited to being strong-willed enough to turn up for the mandated session. True commitment means managing one's energies during the rest of the time in such a way that you are fully switched on during the time you are present (people rarely understand this; we think as long as we are turning up for something regularly despite our super-busy schedules, we are committed). But whenever you are late for something, have only somehow managed to reach on time, it is very clear that your commitment to the same is only that much—18-carat, not 24-carat. If you are fully committed, you will always be slightly early, you would have collected your thoughts and are absolutely ready to dive in.

The second learning is completely related to making the commitment happen. I first started reading about, becoming more aware of my breath and practising *pranayama* in the year 2007. I had read a few really good books and practised intensely for close to three years. But I never really made it a part of the rest of my workout routines, be it weight-training or yoga.

Over the years, I have realized that as far as managing our mental and physical energies is concerned, breath is everything. When I was getting into a series of strenuous poses today, I was constantly aware of my breath, or rather my focus was both on the pose and on my breath; the focus was to ensure that I did not take shallow breaths, which for me personally, during a pose, has always meant exhaling fully rather than inhaling very deeply (unless the pose itself demands otherwise). This ensures that when I have to respond to the instructor's call to hold a pose for thirty seconds, I measure it in breaths—I know that ten seconds more is just two breaths more and my focus goes back to my breathing. It also ensures that the core is tight since you are emptying your abdomen out fully. This results in the spine being straight, and the most important thing—you do not slump and hit the floor at the end.

Each time you slump with a gasp, you expend more energy and more importantly, you release your focus. Each time you go down with an even breath and straight spine, you are ready for the next pose without releasing your focus; you do not give up before the end of the count.

Do you slump at the end of a section or a DI-LR set?

Is your focus as sharp and as still as the tip of Karna's arrow or Achilles's spear for the entire duration of the CAT?

If you have seen the eyes of swimmers when they step out, during the period before they bend down to get on to their marks, you will know that their gaze is always elsewhere, they are not looking at anyone or anything, as if their body and mind are fused into one.

This has to be the case with all sports that require sustained unbroken energy and concentration from start to end, say sprinting, swimming or archery, unlike longer-format sports like say cricket or football where you can afford to take breathers and recoup. But even in those sports, teams and players are most likely to falter after scoring a century or a goal, a tennis player is most susceptible in the game after he or she breaks serve, because they let the focus drop, let the breath go, let the spine slacken.

Have you seen the video of Maradona's gaze before the start of the 1986 Final (or SF or QF) as he makes the sign of the cross? Did you see how Stokes went about his iconic test innings, how he cut everything out and did not celebrate after the century? Have you seen Djokovic go into monk mode? All of these point to the same thing—focus—even breath, tight core and straight spine, and that is why in all martial arts, they tie a cloth around the waist.

Some of you might have trouble concentrating for the entire duration of the test. Some of you might be able to easily concentrate but are leaking energy during the process. Some of you might be hitting your desired scores. I feel that no matter where you are, developing an awareness of your breath through breathing exercises (which will mean that your spine will have to be straight), and learning to manage your mental and physical energies through that awareness, will always give you a jump in scores. And if the paper gets tougher, you will have enough fuel left in your tank and a few more gears left in the mind.

I found that while I learnt this years ago, I have not always applied this diligently. I did it for some years at a stretch and for some, I let go, and unfortunately, I let go when my schedule was the most hectic, which was when I needed it most. All of us can work out, do yoga and eat right when our schedules are light. It is when we manage to do the right things in the middle of a storm that the storm itself becomes manageable.

So, my advice going into the last few months of the CAT prep is that you need to focus on making your energies one-pointed; you need to add breathing exercises to the beginning and the end of your day; you need to get some form of physical exercise to get your lungs pumping at a rate higher than normal, even if it is a brisk walk, at least a couple of times a week; you need to learn to relax by taking in the right things, say reading *Siddhartha* by Hermann Hesse; you need to remove a few things as well, such as social media apps (including the YouTube app)—there is nothing happening on them that is more important to your life than getting into an IIM (essentially, you need to get rid of all forms of sugary and fried food that you are feeding to your brain).

If you do all of these things and are conscious of the way you expend your breath and your time over the next three months, you will not slump with a gasp, the spine will be straight, and the breath will be even, regardless of the depth—you will always be ready for the next ball. And like Arjuna, you will not see the sky or the trees or the bird, but see only *blackness*, the *blackness* in the centre of the eye of the bird.

4

What Do You See Yourself Doing on D-Day?

One of the biggest questions that you need to ask yourself is, how do you think of yourself with respect to life?

- Do you think of yourself as an individual **who makes life happen** or **to whom life happens?**
- Do you see yourself at the **doing end of things** or at the **receiving end of things**?
- Do you **believe** or do you **hope**?

The answers to the questions above will also reflect what your thoughts are currently as you look forward to taking the CAT this Sunday.

If you fall into the second camp on each question, then chances are that you are worrying about:

- the paper turning out to be tough
- questions from all the areas that you have not touched turning up on the CAT
- the kind of questions you were not able to answer in the SimCATs turning up on the CAT
- what will happen if you do not crack the CAT this year
- how you will face your parents and dear ones

The most counterproductive thing of all

While all of these fears are legitimate, is there anything that worrying can accomplish?

For each of these questions, ask yourself two questions:

1. Should I be thinking about it right now or rather, if I don't think about it right now or over this week, will my life be ruined?
2. If the answer to the above question is YES, then can I do anything to address the worry and solve it?

The only worry that you CAN address is the second one—by covering the most important formulas across all the areas/topics you have not touched so far.

All the rest are NOT in your hands and if you can't do anything about it, then no point thinking about it.

Your future hinges on this test but then, can you let your test performance hinge on your negative thoughts about the future?

Worrying does not result in anything; it is the most counterproductive activity of all things we can think or do.

The power of visualization

The thing about the mind is that its very nature is to attach itself to something, like a bee that is constantly buzzing about. You *cannot* stop it from buzzing (something possible for only short periods of time through meditation).

You will be better-off *directing* it towards a correct, single-point focus.

When faced with big days or occasions, it automatically gets directed towards the enormity of the event. This is not something that is unique to test-takers; this is something that everyone faces in life, especially sportsmen who have to face the pressure of performing at the highest level.

The most successful sportsmen and sports teams have learnt to direct their minds towards a particular goal and channelize the power of visualization. Why just sportsmen, don't we do it as fans as well? Haven't we visualized our favourite sportsman leading their team to glory in the toughest of times?

Do we visualize them doing it in the easiest of situations? We always want them to battle and win in the toughest of situations. This is exactly what the biggest sports stars themselves do—they visualize themselves performing at the highest level during clutch time.

Michael Jordan was known to rehearse the entire game as it would play out. He would visualize specific players in the opposition trying to tackle him a particular way and he would work around it. Guess who read this in a book about Jordan, visualized and executed an innings that is now rated as the second-best test innings of all time by Wisden?

In early 1999, Brian Lara returned as captain from South Africa, from a 0–5 drubbing. Before the tour was a pay dispute, after it there was just general despondency. Lara was put on probation as captain for the first two Tests against Australia, and Webster worked closely with the team, and Lara in particular.

Webster describes what Lara was going through then as 'a process of self-sabotage'. Champions can sometimes go through such phases; every conceivable pressure piles up on them and bottles up the ability. It is medically proven that the stress affects vision and makes the reflexes more sluggish.

West Indies lost the first Test of the series, in Lara's hometown, Port-of-Spain, by 312 runs, after having been bowled out for a humiliating 51 in the second innings. Basically, West Indies cricket was crumbling around Lara—which means, also, that he was at the centre.

Around then Lara was exposed to a technique called Visualisation. Think of Visualisation as a mental rehearsal; like writing the plot—and the end—to a story that is still unfolding. At about the same time, Lara remembers, an old friend from school, Nicholas Gomez, presented him with a book on Michael Jordan. 'He had an entire page on how he went about visualizing what's going to happen in a game,' Lara recalls. In the series against Australia, an inspired 213 from Lara's blade had won the second Test at Jamaica to square the series.

In the last innings at Barbados, the venue of the third Test, West Indies were chasing 308 for victory against McGrath, Gillespie, Warne and MacGill. Of course, it was going to be desperately hard. Lara played one of the great Test innings.

Lara had seen it all before it happened. 'I remember calling Gomez at six o'clock in the morning, the last morning of the Test match, and we went about planning this innings against the best team in the world. It was amazing to see how it just came to fruition. You know, a partnership with someone—it happened to be Jimmy Adams—and the innings ultimately evolving into a match-winning one.'

—excerpted from Rahul Bhattacharya, 'Brian Lara: Body,
Mind and Soul', ESPN Cricinfo, 26 December 2003.

It is a great video to watch, chasing 308 after being 105/5 with the last runs being scored in the company of arguably the worst #11 in cricket—Courtney Walsh.

What should YOU visualize?

The important thing to note is that in planning the chase with his friend in the morning, Lara kept it realistic. He knew that his team was prone to collapsing and the support of one other guy would be crucial. He did not imagine for himself a path strewn with flowers; instead, he imagined a road full of potholes and hoped for a good set of shock absorbers.

So, over the next few days, you should visualize yourself doing the right things and overcoming obstacles instead of hoping and praying for an easy paper that falls to your strengths.

Talk yourself into doing the right things

This is what Martin Crowe, who was highly regarded by his peers both as a player and as a captain, had to say about how the power of visualization can be harnessed to maximize performance:[*]

From my own perspective, my mind was often filled with thoughts, coupled with underdeveloped emotions. It wasn't a great mix in which to take on the art of batting at the top level. My footwork was sure and a priority, yet I quickly realised that footwork and mind-work go hand in glove. I needed some mental crutches and so I sought out the new phenomenon of sports psychology to deal with an overflow of desultory musing.

I learnt techniques of visualisation, of playing the future out in the mind first, using pictures.

Most of all, I learnt to repeat affirmations one after the other ('Head still, head still, watch the ball, watch the ball'), slowly and deliberately, to block out any unforeseen random thought ('What if I get out?') that might jump into my head and trip me up again.

He did not visualize himself hitting Allan Donald for a six on a fast pitch; he did not set himself visions of grandeur. He focused on the small things he should do right and the thoughts he should avoid.

Solving questions is very similar, since every ball is similar to a question and solving it successfully is about doing all the small things correctly.

---

[*] https://www.espncricinfo.com/story/martin-crowe-to-bat-right-get-your-mind-right-728587.

What should you see yourself executing?

- Visualize yourself executing all the selection strategies you have decided upon—not jumping to solve the question but taking a call whether to solve it or not.
- Visualize yourself executing the techniques to solve specific question types.
- Visualize yourself reading the question carefully instead of skimming the question and misreading data.
- Visualize yourself doing the calculation part with the calmness required to not make silly mistakes.
- Visualize yourself dealing with the unfavourable turn of events that we listed previously.
- Visualize yourself solving questions in the way you solve it at home—with relaxed nerves.
- Visualize yourself staying calm in the face of a tough/adverse paper.

In the same article, Crowe summarizes things really well.

The key, from what I have learnt, from what I now believe, is that no matter your experiences and circumstances, your reality is in the present moment - what you are living in the feeling of your thinking in the present moment. That's your truest reality.

It is not the memory of what went before, or the concern of what may come in the future, that is real. In batting, it is the clear-minded thinking of watching and moving to the present ball being bowled that is real.

Fear of getting out is really an illusion, a negative thought with feeling added to it, about past failures and / or future ones. It needn't be there at all. The fact is, you will get out, so there is no need to fear it; simply delay the inevitable for as long as possible.

You can succeed if you clear away everything that's not to do with the present moment, the next ball, if you remove old baggage or concern about what might happen in time. Just think about watching the ball leave the bowler's hand. That's it.

Simplicity.

Perhaps Mahatma Gandhi says it best: 'A man is but the product of his thoughts. What he thinks, he becomes.'

Forget the pressure to perform, it is an opportunity to perform

The crucial thing that we should never lose track of is this: you have an opportunity to perform.

Most of you have had the privilege of decent food, decent education, decent shelter. Some of you, I know, have had to struggle for these things. So, now you have the opportunity to build a better career.

Real pressure and real lack of opportunity—migrant labourers waiting at various junctions during the morning hours, hoping that someone would bundle them into a truck and give them an opportunity to just earn their daily bread, just to exist with dignity.

Most of us are lucky to have this opportunity. It is up to us to think the right things and make the right things happen. This is not something that applies only to CAT-day. It will apply even more after you enter a premier B-school—summer placements, final placements and most importantly, life.

The biggest battle is always won in the space between the ears and you have to visualize and talk yourself into doing the right things and succeeding.

5

Are You Ready for a Real Test?

From very early on in our lives, we are exposed (or subjected) to this word called 'test'. As we enter the higher grades, the role that tests play or are supposed to play in our lives steadily increases. If we look back, for most of us, tests have always been part of a trinity, they have always been concomitant with two other things—*fear* and *prayer*.

At some point in time all of us, when faced with a test (including yours truly), have felt at the least a sliver of fear running through our bodies and even the most unbelieving of us has muttered a tiny little prayer under our breaths.

What a test has come to mean

For most Indians, given the supply-demand asymmetry, the word TEST has come to signify something larger than a set of questions. It has become:

- a marker of where one stands in society or rather how one is evaluated (our Class X marks have the potential to become the first chip on our shoulder or the first albatross around our neck)
- a marker of how far one can go in life (if one gets into an IIT or an institution of great national repute, it is assumed that one will go very far in life)
- a door that opens opportunities that might otherwise remain closed forever

A test thus becomes something external to itself; the things that clearing a test can give us become more important than what a test actually is and thus from a very early age, we carry a very distorted view of what it is.

Our fears and prayers were always centred around the same thing—*may the paper have only what I have learnt*. I still remember crying into a plate of food after the physics paper when my Class X board exam threw up questions worth more than 10 marks from exactly the one page that I omitted in my prep.

So, when as children we were asked how the test went, our reply would be: 'I did well, it was very easy!'

What a test really means

The word itself means an examination or being called to give an account of oneself when faced with certain problems that can be related to academics, that can be posed in any format or related to real life itself.

When we came back home happily after a paper and said the test was easy, the fact is that we were not tested!

Why have the word 'test' before the five-day format of cricket? It signifies a test of skill and strength to perform over five days, not over a few hours or even a day but over five days. Why the hesitation over granting test status to associate countries or weaker teams? Apart from commercial considerations, the fact remains that it will be a test only for the minnows and not for the established teams.

Why do we so eagerly await a clash between two great teams? We know that the players will have to play at their best, we know that their ability and their attitude will be tested to the fullest.

So, before we go any further, we need to accept and embrace the fact that the test is supposed to challenge you and one of the prerequisites of triumphing in a challenge is to first enjoy or relish the prospect of a challenge.

One of the reasons that Virat Kohli and MSD perform(ed) so well in pressure situations is that they know that *that* is where the crux of a contest lies; the real test of competing is when you are in a *pressure cooker* situation, that the game has been building up to *this* point; the real stage is the biggest stage and all of the greatest players are measured against their ability to deliver on the biggest stage, be it the World Cups or the Grand Slams.

So wanting an easy test is wanting to not be tested at all!

The CAT will not be the last big test you will take

Given the inordinate amount of importance we place on tests, we tend to think of tests as phenomena that stand apart from life, as interludes that have an outsized impact on life but are not really a part of life.

In reality though, whether we like it or not, we are going to be continuously tested. It will start right from the moment you enter an IIM or any B-school with the summer placements. The placement interview will be a test, your summer project will be a test, your first job will be a test, love is always a test, bringing up children will be a test, managing your post-retirement life will be a test, and dealing with your mortality will be a test.

Unfortunately, we see only some aspects of life as tests and not others; we might actually fail miserably at them and might not even notice until is too late.

So, the CAT will not be the last test you will take and it might not be the toughest test of your life; your biggest hurdles still await you.

This does not mean that we have to live in fear but rather it means that we are constantly being summoned to give a good account of ourselves as individuals. We might succeed at some and fail at some but we need to be aware and view things in the right perspective at all times.

What is life without a test?

I have always been guided by the light of the myths; be they Indian, Greek or Christian, there is a learning from them that can hold us in good stead.

All the great demons or anti-heroes from the myths, be it a Ravana, a Medusa or the Minotaur, are complete in themselves even before the god or the hero arrives on the scene—with superhuman strength or powers accompanied by an evil act or an oppressed people. Even a contemporary demon like Hitler was complete in himself.

The hero, though, needs the demon, needs the anti-hero, needs the villain. The slaying of the demon is what makes a goddess, a goddess; a hero, a hero—Lord Rama, Perseus or Theseus. The centrepiece of the story of their lives will always be the slaying of the demon.

Even America today takes on the role of the righteous saviour waging the just war only because it played a crucial role in overthrowing Hitler; only because of Hitler can it go on creating newer evils with imaginary WMDs that need to be vanquished.

To use an example from contemporary sport—what would Roger Federer, Nadal or Djokovic be without each other to compete with? Would their legacy have been the same if they played everyone else but the other two? Would they have had the motivation to play for this long?

The demons we need to slay to become the heroes of our lives are not always outside of us; they can be the fears residing in our heads, the unique circumstances that each of our lives will throw up in front of us.

Those who succeed in life are those who are willing to embrace the tests life will inevitably set for us.

It does not mean that fear and prayer need to be banished. We will always have a bit of fear, the proverbial butterflies in the tummy, but we should also know that it is natural; we should relish the uncertainty and not let it overwhelm us.

One should pray, but not for an easy test or for there to be no struggle, but for the emotional fortitude to handle all the hurdles and challenges that we will encounter on the way, knowing that they are inevitable and form the very warp and weft of life.

6

Zen and the Art of Test-Taking

Every year, I take a session somewhere towards the end of the prep season that condenses most of the important aspects of this book along with some new anecdotes. The reason the session works well is that different things stick in our heads through different mediums. One student said that one sentence from the session came ringing back to their ears in the middle of the exam at the right time. While the words might be the same, it reaches us differently when the words find a voice.

This video is available on the Bell the CAT YouTube Page. The QR code on page 332 will take you to the same.

7

Getting Ready for D-Day

Everything else that we have discussed is on one side and there are a whole new set of questions not at all related to exam-prep that will be swirling around in your head. These minor niggles will not prevent you taking to the field but they are a bother that you can do without. They range from the randomness of your test slot to the kind of diet you should have.

Is there a chance you might have burnt out or are running solely on adrenaline?

Those of you who have attended all of my webinars know how much store I set on having optimal mental energy. So, for me, a lot of issues can be traced back to the quality of our mental energy. Some of you might not realize that you have depleted your energy sources and are running solely on adrenaline.

Ask yourself the following questions:

- Do you feel fresh and mentally alert throughout the duration of the test?
- Do you tend to flag after DI-LR?
- Do you feel as fresh as you felt months ago when you began the prep?
- Do you need to pump yourself up and motivate yourself to gather enough energy to take a test?

From the answers to the questions above, you will know the state of your mental energy right now. Ideally, you should be feeling alert and light from the time you wake up until the time you go to sleep.

Even if there are about ten days left to the test, it is not too late to shift your focus from practising crazily to building up energy reserves to handle D-Day, which as you know will demand more energy than a mock taken in the comfort (or discomfort) of your room.

I have covered everything about how to manage your energy, stress and anxiety in an earlier chapter. It would not hurt to go through the same again.

I got the worst slot—the early morning slot!

For some, the early morning slot might be a blessing in disguise since that is the time when you usually prepare; for night owls, it can be their worst nightmare come true.

Either way, you need to start tuning your biological rhythms to ensure that you reach the exam centre by 7 a.m. and by 8:30 a.m., you are absolutely fresh and raring to go.

If I were you, I would do the following until D-Day:

- Have a light dinner by 8 p.m.
- Ensure that I turn in by 10 p.m.
- Wake up at 5 a.m. and get fresh by 6 a.m. (all you need to do before leaving for the exam centre is to put on your clothes)
- Do a small round of breathing exercises and meditation for a total of around ten to fifteen minutes
- Read a chapter of any spiritual book or text that helps you go into the right frame of mind (five minutes)
- Have a breakfast involving one or more—bananas, soaked almonds, oats, eggs (if your centre is in a different city, then soaked almonds and bananas are the easiest option)
- Get ready to leave (during the run-up to the test, start your preparation)

Obviously, you need to modify this to account for the travel time to the exam centre.

I do not know if 12.30 p.m. is a good slot or a bad slot

If I have to choose a slot among three to take the test, I would choose 12.30. It is a bit later than the time at which I am at my optimal, 11.00 to 14.00, but I would not complain the way I would about 8.30, which is way too early for me, and 4.30, which would mean getting out in the afternoon (something I hate 😊).

The thing with the 12.30 slot is that, like the early morning slot, you have to slightly alter your biological rhythms. Your body is programmed to feel hungry between 1 and 2, and over the next ten days, you need to reprogramme it.

The following would be my plan until D-Day:

- Wake up at whatever my usual time is but not later than 8 a.m. and get fresh in an hour (all you need to do before leaving for the exam centre is to put on your clothes)
- Do a small round of breathing exercises and meditation for a total of around ten to fifteen minutes
- Read a chapter of any spiritual book or text that helps you go into the right frame of mind (five minutes)
- Have something super-light at whatever your breakfast time is (maximum before 9) to trick your body into believing that everything is the same—I would suggest two bananas and some soaked almonds
- Start your prep or log in to work
- Have a proper breakfast just before the time you need to leave for the test centre on D-Day to reach there by 11 a.m.—oats, eggs, upma, whatever floats your boat but nothing too heavy
- Resume your prep or work

I got the 4.30 slot, I think I should not be complaining

Those with the 4.30 slot need to do nothing different! Just go about things the way you normally do since it is neither a feeding or a digestion slot for the body! It goes without saying that everyone should try to take SimCATs in the time slot of the actual test.

Insomnia induced by test day nerves

I am sure there are those of you who know that you will not be able to sleep the night before the CAT. The sheer nervousness, you are sure, will have you tossing and turning all night.

Even in this case, the best option is to pull an all-nighter two nights before the CAT and not sleep during the day that follows so that the night before the CAT, fatigue will overcome nervousness and your body will crash to sleep. Do not leave this for the end; try it once or twice before.

Managing your diet in the lead-up to the test

I was surprised to get a query around the kind of diet one should have but then I also remember talking to my colleagues about physical fitness for test-taking; so in a way, the question is very relevant.

I will try to answer the question from whatever little reading I have done and whatever experiments I have done with respect to diet, and I will try to keep it simple. This is something that everyone can take up irrespective of the slot.

Food can help you feel two ways, one—extremely happy, satisfied, heavy and ready to hit the sack, which is what happens when you have food that you and maybe most people really like such as biryanis and desserts (you get the drift). The state of body and mind after this is perfect for watching something silly while lying down and going off to sleep. As someone who really likes food and can eat a lot, I have done a lot of this in the past and treat myself to this feeling of satiation twice a month (usually immediately or the day after a webinar 😊).

The other thing that I have also done is have phases where food made me feel another way— nourished and light, exactly the way one feels after eating some fruit.

Given that all of you want to crack the third or fourth toughest test in the world (JEE, UPSC, Gaokao), I suppose you know which one of the two options you are supposed to choose.

Just eat a certain amount of fresh foods (fruits and nuts) and food that is not fried, overtly spicy and oily (the non-vegetarians, please savour the meat and eat smaller portions)—basically home-cooked food in moderation (delete the food apps on your phone).

Also, stop eating when you are just about three-fourths full. Do not crave for the feeling of heaviness. I have found that even milk makes me feel heavy or rather makes me aware of my gut and so I cut it out of my system; you should try it as well.

And yeah, no snacks, at all, nothing out of a plastic packet; they don't just make you feel heavy but bloated and make you crave strong flavours.

Ensure that you include some amount of light exercise every day

One thing that is least talked about is the importance of exercise for mental activities such as test-taking and I cannot vouch for this more. Whenever I sit at my desk for a long time, after a point I feel stale, as if my brain is not working. All I need then is a good short walk to get the blood flowing through my body again. Movement is what gets oxygen into our system and makes us feel fresh.

It has been proven that sitting for long periods of time has many harmful effects and I know professionals who have desks that can be adjusted for height so that they can stand and work. You do not need to get one now, but you need to counter the effects of sitting for a long time at your desk to prepare for a long time with college or work.

All you need to do is a light exercise at an intensity that only at the end of thirty minutes will make your breath reach your mouth and perspire slightly. You should not be panting, and your T-shirt should not be drenched. I would suggest a walk or a jog early in the morning or late at night or yoga or (light) weight training for those who are already doing it.

As I have said before, I cannot think of a better thing than adding a few breathing practices to your day.

Some of you might be thinking: 'Is all of this really necessary?'

Well, yes and no.

If you are my friend who is a twelve-time 100 percentile or one of his students who had a 100 the year before last and scored just a mark or two fewer than him, you do not need any of this. These guys are at a level way beyond the test and the test doesn't need them to stretch. If these guys have to compete on a different exam with many more people at their level, I am sure they would also benefit from being in prime physical shape. But everyone else, including yours truly, can get better by being really fit.

Magnus Carlsen, the current world chess champion and the player with the highest ELO rating ever, does a lot of exercise work as well; he works out every single day, basically a lot of aerobic training. He says it is crucial to be able to sit and think for hours at a stretch. So yes, if Carlsen does it, you and I should as well.

Part VIII

Preparing for WAT-GD-PI

1

How to Prepare for WAT and GD

On the face of it, it might seem like WAT, GD and PI are different beasts altogether and besting each one of them requires different skill sets. Well, at some level, they can be equated to the different formats in cricket—test Cricket, ODIs and T20s (not in any order). While the format is different and there are specialists in each format, the core skills tested are cricketing skills.

Over the years, the core skill tested in each of GD, WAT and PI is your awareness of current affairs.

That GDs and WATs test general knowledge and current affairs is something that need not be stated. But even in PIs, interviewers want to test how aware you are of the world around you. For example, they might ask you to:

- name all the districts in your home state as you travel from north to south
- name the CEOs of leading companies in your sector
- give your view on recent political events in your state or sector
- give your view on events of national importance or policy

Your knowledge of people and essential trivia about what you call your hobbies (it is trivia because it is just a statistic, but it is essential because you have mentioned something as your hobby). So, what you need to understand first is that at some level, the second stage is closer to preparing for the Civil Services, albeit a very watered-down version.

In this chapter, we will deal with how to go about preparing for GDs and WAT.

What kind of topics crop up in GDs and WATs?

The topics for GDs and WATs broadly fall into three categories:

- Policy-based
- Issue-based/Topical
- Lateral-Abstract

Policy-based WAT-GD topics

These are the kind of WAT-GD topics you do not want to encounter in the second stage since their focus is on important policies or legislation that has been in the news in the past year. For example, what were the big policy-based debates in the last year?

- The Rise of AI—How to regulate?
- The Climate Change Conference: Time to phase out gasoline cars slowly but surely around the world?
- Policy lessons from the Cryptocurrency fiasco

Some institutes, such as IIFT, tend to favour topics based on economic policy such as the last one in the list above.

Issue-based or Topical WAT-GD Topics

Every year, there are a few issues/events that capture both public and media imagination, generate a lot of debate and hence, become topics worthy of discussion in a WAT or a GD. The IIMs and other premier B-schools would like to see how prospective students view this issue, what sort of a perspective they have and how well they are able to put forth their arguments.

What have been the significant issues over the past year? To name a few:

- The Israel-Hamas War: Is there anything called a right and just war?
- The future of work: office, hybrid, WFH forever?
- What language should shop signboards be in: Can metropolises be thought of as local any more?

It is important to note that the topics might not always be presented in a straightforward manner. The topics above would need you to know not just about what is happening nationally but also about what is happening internationally, both in terms of issues and in terms of politicians.

While these are specific issue-based topics, there are other topics that are based on broader debates of a more topical nature. For example:

- Can India overtake China in terms of GDP?
- Economy versus Ecology
- Should capital punishment be abolished?
- Entrepreneurship and India

Lateral-Abstract WAT-GD Topics

Then there are topics that do not test your knowledge of current affairs or policies. For example:

- It is better to trust a woman's instinct than a man's reason.
- If there was one invention/discovery from the past (recent or distant) that you would have liked to have made, which would it be and why?

- A true traveller is never bothered about the destination and is not intent on arriving.
- Space.

How and where does one start preparation for WAT-GD-PI?

Well, if there was a pill or an injection or a book that would deliver all the information you would need neatly packaged, I would give that to you.

But from this point on, the point after you have cleared the written test, your success in life will not rely on your ability to reproduce things from books or the ability to solve problems that have nothing to do with the real world. The road to success is not paved with MCQs and past papers; it will be harder to win.

So, I would want you to start your WAT-GD-PI Prep by putting in the effort to gather information/opinion/analyses from various sources. For articles on issue-based topics, you can look at ThePrint, Scroll, Open and *Caravan*.

Please understand that you will face similar GDs three months into your study at a B-school when faced with summer placements, so your preparation now is going to come in handy then.

Start your WAT-GD-PI preparation by:

- Reading the newspaper inside out every day, including the business, world news and editorials sections
- Researching the policy-based topics listed above
- Reading articles from the sources mentioned

All test-prep firms also offer detailed prep guides for WAT-GD-PI. If the specific programme you have enrolled for does not offer one, then please upgrade or enrol for one. It will save you the trouble of finding information on your own.

2

How to Prepare for the Personal Interview

The Indian B-school interview is maybe the most random of all interview processes that you will ever face in your life. Going by student testimonials and transcripts over the last few years, barring IIM-B, none of the schools seems to have a fixed yardstick for asking questions.

If panels have one thing in common, it seems to be their mistrust of candidates and the claims they make. Most panels start with the premise that the only thing the candidate wants is to make more money, and hence, it might be useless to start asking them the Big Five Standard Questions:

- Tell us something about yourself
- Describe your work experience
- Why do you want to do an MBA?
- What are your long-term and short-term goals?
- List your strengths and weaknesses

They would instead test your mettle by grilling you on the things you mention in the form or on current affairs. They will use the standard questions as a surprise element when you are least prepared for it, or they might not use it at all.

So, how do you go about preparing for this randomness, apart from the current affairs prep outlined earlier?

Draw the largest circle with yourself as the centre

The PI is primarily a test of the stuff you are made of. So, right at the centre of it—a lamb to the slaughter or a gladiator in the Colosseum (though it is best you don't think of yourself as either the latter or the former)—is you.

Draw a circle with you as the centre and divide it into four quadrants.

Quadrant 1: Your Personal Background

This quadrant contains all the information that is relevant to you as a person:

- The meaning of your name
- The number of districts, rivers, Lok Sabha seats, recent events, future elections, famous personalities, anything and everything to do with the state you are from or the state you were born and raised in
- Your parents' professions in case there are questions there; for example, a defence kid might get asked about the services

Quadrant 2: Your Educational Background

This quadrant, as the name suggests, deals with all questions that can be relevant to your educational background—yes, your engineering subjects will haunt you one last time.

Usually, the questions can fall into two types:

- Lowest hanging theoretical concepts in your discipline: The panellists might not be from your discipline. Still, they will have enough top-level knowledge about many subjects to ask you basic questions from any area. For example, students with a commerce background might be asked the difference between single-entry and double-entry accounting, a mechanical engineer might be asked questions on thermodynamics, and an electrical engineer might be asked about Kirchhoff's laws. So, you must revise the basic concepts across the most critical subjects in your graduation.
- Practical applications of your discipline: This applies more to engineering and science graduates. Panellists may ask an electronics and telecommunications engineer the difference between 3G, 4G and 5G or how Bluetooth works or what the Internet of Things is, a mechanical engineer about how CVT or automatic transmission works, etc. IMS students will get an e-book with all the previous year's questions; scouring through that is the best way to find out the kind of questions that have been asked in the past.

Quadrant 3: Your Professional Background

Working professionals will be expected to know more than the projects they are working on. So, everything ranging from the turnover of your firm to those of your major competitors, the CEOs of the big firms in your industry, the recent controversies or happenings in your field (for example, if you work in banking, then you might be asked whether you have heard of Sam Bankman-Fried; if you work in the auto sector, you might be asked about electric cars, and Tesla and Musk) and the major trends shaping your industry.

Quadrant 4: Your Hobbies and Interests

Whatever you mention as your hobbies and interests, you need to have an in-depth idea about the same. What do I mean by in-depth?

If you say you love football, then you need to know everything from the weight of the football, the circumference of the football, the dimensions of a football field, the dimensions of the goalpost and everything about your favourite team. If you say you love trekking, then you need to know what the highest mountains in the world are, what the highest motorable road in the world is, etc.

This would technically be the largest circle you can draw around yourself that you need to fill with every GK or CA question that can be asked within this circle.

It goes without saying that you might not be able to learn everything about football. For example, a panellist might ask you, do you remember Zidane's Champions League volley? You might say yes, very much, it is one of the great goals in football; the panellist might ask which team Real was playing against in that final. Some of you might know, and some of you might not. So, do not freak out thinking about the most random things that can be asked.

On any topic, there is a circle that denotes your knowledge and a circle that denotes the panellists' knowledge. Your job is to maximize the chances of overlap.

Remember, the harder you work, the luckier you will get.

3

Why Everyone Should Write the IIM Bangalore SOP

One of the things about preparing for a B-school personal interview, especially that of an old IIM, is that one struggles to find a structure to prepare for what can potentially be the most random twenty minutes of one's life. I am sure my previous discussion, despite my intentions, would have scared readers rather than reassured them. So, let us see how you can bring some structure into your PI prep.

One-half of the prep is what I wrote previously—doing a 360-degree survey of different aspects of your profile from a GK and CA perspective.

The other half is answering The Big Five questions:

- Tell me something about yourself
- Describe your work experience
- Why MBA?
- What are your career goals—short-term and long-term?
- What are your strengths and weaknesses?

Answering these questions individually can be a painful task since there might be an overlap in the answers you have framed for each one of them. Also, most people end up mouthing *clichés* and *platitudes* when they look at these questions in isolation.

The IIM-B SOP prompt asks, more or less, the same five questions:

Prepare a short essay of 600 words on yourself in the space provided below. You may wish to talk about your background, significant events, accomplishments, extracurricular activities, relationships with friends and family, career plans and how the Post-Graduate Programme in Management from IIMB fits into your dreams and aspirations. Please make sure your essay forms a coherent whole.

I think this prompt gives you clues about what goes into a good SOP.

Firstly, an SOP and a *Tell Me About Yourself* need not be two disconnected things. Aspirants tend to look at an SOP as a literary exercise and think of a template that best allows them to write one.

So, they employ the usual worn-out formulas—*start with a quote.*

Quotes are good, but good quotes that are relevant to an SOP are few. So you start searching frantically for a quote that few people are likely to use or you take a quote from a famous person and then try to show that your whole life revolved around that.

There can be quotes that we live by or use as guiding lights or touchstones in our life, but we cannot explain everything about ourselves through a quote unless we have been actually living our life based on one.

If you look at the IIM-B prompt, what it is essentially saying is this: *Tell us the story of your life*.

How to best tell the story of your life

We divide this story of your life into four parts: Formative Years, Graduation, Work Experience, MBA and beyond. To make these parts most impactful and honest and to give a narrative arc to your story, you need to use the hooks in the IIM-B SOP prompt. Let us take a few words and phrases from the IIM-B SOP prompt and try to see how best you can use them to frame different parts of your story.

Formative Years: Your background, significant events, relationships with friends and family

When you look back at your childhood, what is it that you want to talk about? Ask yourself the following questions:

- What role did your parents or their occupations play in your life?

  - Did your parents' transferable job mean that you travelled to different places and hence, know different languages?
  - Does your parents' occupation stand out in any way for it to have an impact—business, police/defence, a senior government official who achieved a lot?
  - Your parent was none of these but was a great source of inspiration for you; it can be the way they built their life or the values they passed on to you.
  - It can be that they played no significant role; they were, well, just parents, so there is no need to include anything about them.

- What role did your school play in your formative years?

  - Did your school have any role to play in shaping your personality?
  - Did it have a particular focus on sports or academics that led you to focus on a specific area, or did it make you an all-around talent?

- What was the big spike growing up, or what did growing up revolve around?

  - Were academics a significant focus, and did you always do well?
  - Were sports or other extracurriculars, say music, the most significant part of your life while growing up?

- Were there any financial hardships, personal setbacks or emotional challenges that you had to face as a family or as an individual that have really shaped you?

  o It is essential to search for what was most important and what impact it had on you. For example, suppose your parents are divorced; there is no point mentioning that if it did not have any major impact on you then or on your world view now.
  o You cannot mention things just to elicit sympathy; you have to show how they shaped you as a person. For example, a student told me that having lost his father early, he became financially independent at a very young age. He did not take a single rupee from his family during the whole of his graduation and supported himself by doing part-time jobs, and it is no wonder that he has a start-up now.

This is also the place where you mention your relevant accomplishments. Accomplishments are like data to support an argument. In themselves, they make no sense if they are recited or presented as they are on a resume. The argument should be the frame within which they should be presented—*I was and am very competitive*, so I did really well throughout school and stood first or in the top three right from KG to Class X or *Maths was a major passion* and I participated in various Olympiads.

Graduation: *Significant events, accomplishments*

Use the same method for graduation as well:

- What did it primarily revolve around?
- Did the stature of your graduation college give you opportunities you did not have until that time?
- Was it a time of personal growth for you?
- Were you part of any clubs and teams that participated and/or won events?

Work Experience: Significant events, accomplishments

One of the big things about the way you present your work experience is to change the perspective or vantage point. Instead of looking at your role from the inside out, zoom into it from the larger point of view.

Instead of describing your KRAs right away, you should lead there from the larger organizational structure. For example:

I work as a sales engineer in XYZ. The organization is divided into three segments: passenger vehicles, trucks and HCV. I work in the HCV department. I am part of a network of sales engineers whose job is to do XYZ. I handle the ABC region and I handle XXX clients with a turnover of YYY. My role is to do XYZ. In my stint, I achieved ABC.

Or for the most common job role—IT.

I work in the BFSI domain of ABC. I have worked with X client(s) so far as part of a team of YY members. We help the client with ABC business solution by providing them with XYZ tools. My role is to do ABC. In my stint, I achieved XYZ.

MBA and Short-Term Goals: For those with work experience

For those with eighteen months or more of work experience, an MBA has to be about career growth—moving from the functional side to the business side within the industry. For example:

- From coding and maintenance in IT services to business development, pre-sales, product management, data analytics, or IT consulting
- From technical support or product design to sales and marketing roles in the same industry (from automobile design to sales and strategy for the same)
- From handling a small part of R&D or quality or logistics to larger roles in operations in XYZ firms

Do not make MBA a route to a full-fledged industry shift from IT to finance or automobile to FMCG. Even if you are sure that you want to leave IT, even if MBA is the parachute out of IT that you are dreaming of, do not mention it. You can try for the same once you make it to a B-school.

For the purposes of the interview, you should say that you want to leverage your experience to move into business-side roles in the tech sector at large; it need not be IT services only. Otherwise, what you are saying is 'please ignore my work experience and treat me like a fresher'. Instead of ignoring your work experience and treating you like a fresher, they might as well ignore you and take a fresher.

The only way you can make a case for a domain shift is if you have already taken concrete steps towards the same—IT work experience but have done CFA L1 and want to move to finance.

MBA and Short-Term Goals: Freshers

You have to link your MBA to your:

- educational background—from commerce to MBA in finance, and within finance, you want to build a career in ABC.
- traits and interests—match your traits, interests and accomplishments to a particular specialization and career in the same

Engineers looking to get into marketing or consulting should use the latter route—skills, traits and interests to make a pitch.

MBA and Beyond: I want to become an entrepreneur

I know some of you are intensely passionate about becoming entrepreneurs, and others are harbouring hopes of the same.

In both cases, what matters is how specific the dream is and what work you have already done. Ask yourself whether you have any of these:

- Have you already worked with a start-up or have one of your own?
- Do you have a business plan (numbers, not ideas) for the business you want to build?
- Are you or were you part of E-Cells in your college and have hence developed a strong passion for entrepreneurship through the various activities you organized as part of the E-Cell?

If all you are going to say is 'I will do an MBA, gain corporate experience for some time and then start my own venture', do not say it. It is just a thing you think about occasionally; you have not done one thing about it. No, watching videos of Jobs, Ma and Musk do not count as having done anything tangible towards entrepreneurship.

Your thoughts and your consumption of relevant content do not hold water since it is only actions that count, be it entrepreneurship or spirituality (do you sit and meditate every day?).

Instead, you can mention that, in the long run, you see yourself taking up CXO roles in this industry and making an impact in that industry, like XYZ (if you have anyone in mind).

Why this institute?

This is the answer on which you can spend the least amount of words and time. The pre-eminent colleges won't expect you to praise and glorify them and hence, might not even ask you this question in the interview.

If you can find a link between what the institute is known for and your aspirations, then mention it: 'Since I want to build a career in finance, this college will give me the best courses, teachers and job offers for the same.'

Why it is vital that you write this down

Most aspirants practise or rehearse answers in their heads. They have broad points jotted down and feel that they will be able to express them in front of the panel.

Now, irrespective of your confidence or your communication skills, you need to realize that what you are doing is *crafting the story of your life*.

And stories are:

- written down word by word
- sentence by sentence, and then
- sentences are rearranged, deleted, added and organized into paragraphs
- sometimes, paragraphs are re-ordered before they can deliver what the last sentence of the IIM-B SOP prompt asks for: *Please make sure your essay forms a coherent whole.*

There is no way you are going to deliver a coherent whole if you do not write, rewrite, rewrite, edit and polish.

Some of you might feel: What's the point of writing this if I don't have an IIM-B call?

Interviewers do not follow a fixed sequence. They might ask you a GK question and suddenly ask you why you want to do an MBA or what your weaknesses are.

Once you are ready with your story after spending considerable effort on the same (and you have done the prep I have recommended earlier), you will have the confidence to instinctively take the relevant portions of your SOP and quickly modify it in your head to answer the questions posed.

Think of this as the foundation, like basics or techniques for Test match cricket, which will help you deliver in whatever format the interview goes—Test, ODI, T20 or gully cricket.

A few writing tips to come up with a unique SOP

I have read quite a few SOPs over the years, and one of the common features of most SOPs is that they sound really, really clichéd.

An SOP is not a test of your literary writing skills. It is a test of your ability to tell a good story. Imagine telling, not writing, a great story to an audience. Do you imagine yourself:

- using big words, or
- trying to deliberately introduce formal words, or
- using what you feel are 'corporate' words

So, please avoid aping what you think is corporate-speak—*holistic, corporate ladder* (just so that you know, there is no ladder in any corporate closet), *corporate world, game changer, add value*, etc.

You can use words like *augment* and *bolster*, not to impress but because you use them naturally without having to use a thesaurus to find them.

You are a human being, not a brochure. They want a convincing story, not a literary manuscript. So, use simple words and relatively short sentences. Focus on the overall impact and narrative quality. And yeah, use the Grammarly app to run a grammar check.

I know what some of you might be thinking.

After reading all of this, in your head, you might be going:

- my parents are ordinary and boring; they did not cause me great harm or do me any great good; they are just nice and supportive (not always), so essentially nothing to write based on them
- my schooling from an average or above-average school was just about doing well—no sports, no music, no dancing, nothing, just going to school and coming back
- outside of school, what I did cannot be called sports—mostly gully cricket that yielded no certificates or accomplishments, only sweat and unadulterated joy
- my graduation is the main reason why I find myself reading this book now
- the only growth I experienced during graduation was the weight I put on
- my work experience in the IT firm cannot be called work if one really examines it
- it is because of all of the above reasons and with a wish to make my life better and/or to earn tons of money that I want to do an MBA

Well, I can sympathize, and I have had a student who asked me this question after I took a class: 'Sir, *mere paas kuch nahi hai*, I have nothing worthwhile to say!'

Those of you who feel you have nothing much to write about—focus on your traits, qualities and skills to make a case for why you are suited to do an MBA.

Use stories or minor accomplishments from your life to demonstrate these qualities.

It can be as simple as, it is you who all of your friends turn to for advice; this can be used to illustrate that you are a level-headed and sensible person. You can use an incident or project to show that you can handle and deliver under pressure—you do not crack.

There must be something inside of you that makes you believe that you are a suitable candidate for a career in management and for taking up business side roles after your MBA.

If you feel you have nothing and an MBA is the most logical option right now, then . . . (well, I won't say it!).

B-schools, on average, call four people for one seat, so the chances of conversion are still only 25 per cent, and you can take it from me that a higher percentile has very little bearing at this stage.

And remember, the harder you work, the luckier you will get.

4

How to Approach the Indian B-School Personal Interview

As the interviews get closer, aspirants will be trying to get as many insights as they can right from how to dress for the interview to how to reduce India's fiscal deficit without affecting our growth.

Amidst all of this clutter, how does one go in with the right perspective? What is the state of mind with which one should approach an interview? How you approach an interview will make all the difference.

The interview is not a test

For almost every aspirant, this interview is a test, albeit an oral one, in which they will be interviewed/interrogated and they have to somehow find a way to get through this successfully.

Everything—your answers, your body language, your facial expressions, your composure—is determined by your attitude towards the interview. The panel being this set of two or three gods (benevolent, hectoring or bullying) upon whose mercy your life hangs.

To start with, let us drop the test metaphor and try to view the interview as something else.

Do not become a child again because you want to get into a school

Over the years, I have seen that irrespective of whether they were working professionals or freshers, most candidates turn into children the moment it comes to a B-school interview. I have seen this not just with people with three to five years of work experience but even while interviewing candidates with ten-plus years of getting a call from a PGP-X programme.

While mock-interviewing one such candidate, I asked: 'What will you do if we do not select you?' The moment he heard that question, his face immediately dropped. Instead of looking at it as a professional question about his plan B, he took it as a rejection, as if someone he really looked up to and was desperate to seek approval from just told him that he was not worth it.

The candidate had more than ten solid years of work experience, had spent huge amounts of time abroad at client locations and knew his domain inside out. He had a call from one of the twins among the old IIMs for its PGP-X programmes.

To think of it, the PGP-X programmes at the IIMs are good but not mind-blowing. They are also in a lower league than ISB among one-year programmes in India. In fact, when they do information sessions for their PGP-X programmes, IIMs attract twenty-five to seventy-five students at max, whereas ISB has its halls full. The way I looked at it, the IIM would have benefited more from this guy joining them than the other way around.

But we place education from elite institutions on such a pedestal that we immediately become schoolchildren yearning desperately to be liked and admitted to a school.

He should have just told them that he would aim for a higher GMAT score and apply to international programmes as well next year.

So, the first thing to realize is that the interview is a professional meeting and not a teacher-student meeting. If you do not make this switch in your head, you will have lost the battle between the ears before the interview even begins.

The panel is your prospective client

Why is the panel your client?

Firstly, because they have a problem—they need to fill a certain number of seats. Well, that might not seem like a problem, but it is. It is a problem because they want the *right candidates* for the seat.

Secondly, finding the right candidate is not an easy job because just aptitude won't do. They expect the candidate to have many more traits that cannot always be evaluated objectively. Hence, the IIMs go through the trouble of organizing interviews spread out across the country and across many weeks. Else, they would have shortlisted people based on CAT scores and weights assigned to different aspects of the profile.

If every seat they have to fill is a problem, then each IIM needs about 300–400 solutions.

What is your job?

To convince them that you are one such solution.

Why the prospective client metaphor?

Simply because it determines what attitude you take to the interview. Prospective clients can be very similar to interview panels: generous, expressionless, grumpy, combative, high-handed and many more, as those among you with work experience will attest.

How would you handle a prospective client?

- Would you be walking in trembling and underconfident?
- Will you sit passively across the table and expect them to ask questions and provide answers, or will you try to establish a connection?
- Will you go unprepared, or will you go in with the best pitch you can make about your firm and your product?
- If the client throws a tantrum or is asking you uncomfortable questions, will you sweat and give up or will you handle it with poise to the best of your ability?
- Would you give false information and expect the client to not question or probe further, or will you say 'I am not aware of that, I will get back to you on that one'?

The answers are self-evident, and so are the traits you need to display:

- Self-belief and confidence
- Communication skills and personableness
- Preparedness and purpose
- Poise and ability to handle stress
- Honesty and prudence

A test of potential

You might not have all the above traits in abundance but a few of them like honesty are must-haves. The rest of the traits cannot be imparted through specific courses at an IIM but can only be polished during your stay at the B-school and the internship you will be required to do as part of the programme.

So, at some level, you are supposed to demonstrate these traits to some extent and show that you have the potential to become a business leader if you get a chance to learn at a premier business school like an IIM.

This might seem similar to *selling/marketing yourself*, and maybe it is to a certain extent, but there is a vital distinction you have to make—you are not marketing yourself to an individual like in B2C marketing (business-to-consumer); you are marketing yourself to an institution like in B2B marketing (business-to-business).

So, all the traits we spoke about have to be displayed with the assurance of a solution provider rather than the spirit of a salesman.

If you are able to approach your interview through this lens, I am sure you will be able to give a good account of yourself in your interview.

If you approach the interview panel as you would approach a client, you will end up displaying these qualities.

A few dos and don'ts

It is tough to cover the whole gamut of questions and possible scenarios in which a PI can play out since it largely depends on the profile of the candidate. Be that as it may, we can still look at some general principles that will hold you in good stead to handle a PI.

Be prepared for all the standard questions (tell us something about yourself, why MBA, career goals, strengths and weaknesses).

Be genuine. If you do not know, say 'I am not aware'; if you are making an educated guess, then preface your answer with 'I am not sure, but I think . . .'

Do not throw jargon such as 'I want to do brand management or investment banking' unless you have done quite a bit of research about that and are genuinely prepared to answer questions such as what is your favourite brand and why.

Do not seek affirmation for your performance in the form of visual cues from the panel—smiles and nods. They might stay expressionless, stonewalling you into feeling stressed and losing your composure.

Be prepared to think on your feet to answer questions that you are not expecting—your brain has to be alive and ticking, not frozen.

Be prepared to handle questions from your engineering. I know you want to do an MBA to escape engineering, but you have to for one last time 😊

Be prepared with GK and current affairs.

And wear a smile—it looks good on almost everyone.

All the very best for your upcoming interviews!

5

Believing in Yourself

Every year, around 15,000 candidates get calls from one of the twenty IIMs, and one-fourth of them secure an admission into the premier campuses. I get a chance to interact with a lot of these call-getters across the country when I travel to conduct the two-day workshops dedicated to acing the interviews. I don't find a lot of difference between the candidates on paper since most of them have got calls by meeting a mix of the criteria of various colleges—Class X, Class XII, work experience, CAT score, gender diversity and education diversity.

The difference is mostly in the kind of account they give of themselves during those twenty minutes of the personal interview. My goal in the workshop is to make them believe in and present the versions of themselves. What makes the workshop entertaining are the stories of my own interviews from ages ago.

I am sure this recording will more than help you go into the right frame of mind. It is available on the Bell the CAT YouTube Page. The QR code on page 332 will take you to the same.

Part IX

Plan B

1

What to Do after a Horrible CAT

Be it the day of the CAT or be it when the final admits results come out, it is not easy to be a mentor—on the one hand, you are happy for students who crack the exam and get an admit and on the other, you are also tinged with sadness for those who have had a bad test day or fail to convert. The toughest thing was always to meet a student who was happy, knowing that another waiting outside was sad. So, with the years, one develops a certain equanimity since one cannot be so happy that one is not able to empathize with the ones who are having a hard time and one also cannot get so bogged down by sadness that one cannot partake in the joy of the successful.

In some cases, students just disappear. Somehow they take it very personally—that they have failed even after reading all of my blogs and attending all the sessions; they feel almost as if they have let me down. And I am left wondering, whatever happened to that student? The others thankfully come down to meet me or reach me through the blog comments even if it is just to feel lighter instead of heavy and burdened.

There are two things about clichés—they are dead boring since they have been repeated so often but at the same time, they are also true. So are all the clichés about failure; I won't repeat them but I will attest that they are true.

In one of previous chapters, I spoke about how everyone has to face a test and how heroes in myths are defined by overcoming obstacles. The thing about myths is that they rarely show heroes failing *at a task* spectacularly. But if we look at real-life successes, almost every spectacular success has had a big failure or inability as well. I am not linking failure to success or calling it a pre-requisite.

All I am saying is, everyone fails, so do not go beating yourself up about it.

There is nothing to be gained from self-flagellation

The first reaction understandably is to hit oneself with an emotional sledgehammer and of these the worst one is: I am useless, I am not smart enough, I suck, I do not have the skills to crack this exam, no matter what I do, it will not change a thing.

Firstly, I will be happy if you are telling yourself all of these in anger rather than through a bucket of tears, since anger with oneself can be a very good motivator.

303

But whether you are telling yourself these things through anger or through tears, you need to quickly move from 'I suck' to 'I suck at this particular aspect of CAT', from the generic to the specific, from the emotional to the strategic.

- This was the first time I took an entrance test and I was overwhelmed by it
- My reading speed was the biggest hindrance when the paper became tough
- Before the test, I did not talk myself through what I was going to execute during the three sections
- Before the test, I did talk myself through things but everything went out of the window once the test started
- I did not hunker down and solve two DI sets but flitted from set to set
- I could not solve moderate QA questions from arithmetic; my level plateaued at easy questions
- My technique to solve inferential RC questions was not really up to the mark

My favourite story when it comes to dealing with doubts about one's ability is Brian Lara's answer when questioned about being McGrath's bunny (he has got him quite a few times). Lara did not talk about the number of centuries he scored against Australia or the single-handed manhandling of a peak Australian team over an entire series. All he said was: 'Someone from the opposition has to get me out some time, right?'

Evaluate the extent of damage and your options and view things in proportion

The right lens to view things should not be through your success or failure at CAT but in terms of your prospects of doing an MBA from a premier B-school.

Just like the extent of damage in a war varies across the various battlefronts, the damage, if any, to your MBA dreams, varies across different profiles.

Who are the aspirants who are worst hit?

Those who already have four years of work experience and had a horrible CAT are the worst hit since another shot at the CAT and the two-year MBA is effectively ruled out; they only have the rest of the exams in this season to make it count. (It is not that you will get rejected, you can still get an admit into a two-year programme, but the number of recruiters looking at a five-year profile will be fewer; you will still be able to get the career growth you are looking for in your domain).

Those who have three years of work experience will still have a shot at the CAT next year but to stay close to the average profile in a B-school (having four or more years of work experience will make the profile a bit of an outlier), they should crack one of the remaining exams in this season.

Those who have two years or fewer work experience have nothing to worry about as far their MBA dreams go; they are well and truly alive. You can still get there, not when you wanted to and in the way you wanted to, but you can still get there.

Some of you might wonder whether you have it in you to take another shot. You do not have another option.

What greatness really means

Roger Federer played from the 2012 Wimbledon to the 2017 Australian Open, seventeen Slams, without winning a single slam, being stuck at seventeen, losing to players who were not in the same league as him. At every single Slam during those five years, my friend and I would talk, just before the semis or finals, about how well Fed was playing, the new things that he was inventing—the SABR (Sneak Attack By Roger)—and as usual, the crazy points in the matches until then, only for him to lose again.

There were articles asking why he was still playing. I was supporting him saying that it need not be number one or nothing. As long as he is easily making it to finals and semis and believes he can win, he should play since he is still ranked in the top four and unlike in a team sport, he is not delaying a transition or eating into the prime years of a youngster. In effect, even I had ruled out the chance of him winning again; I was happy that he was competing well.

Federer is great not because he has won twenty Slams but because he believed in himself so much, believed in himself through four years and seventeen Slams of heartbreaking failures, four years of ageing and his body breaking down in 2016, while others were catching up with him.

I am sure no victory tasted sweeter to him than the 2017 Australian Open when he finally won a Slam again. (I have never felt more elation at the end of a sports match than while watching him win the 2017 Australian Open).

The same thing applies to Messi as well. He had to wait until his fifth World Cup to lift it. During all of these years, he was called all sorts of things. So great was the pain of not winning a cup, even the Copa America, that he announced that he was stepping down, only to change this decision. In an interview he said his son asked him why he continues to play for Argentina when people seem to hate him and say all sorts of things. He replied that if he gave up, all the children who are his fans would also think about giving up in life. What is even more admirable is that during all these years of losses, Argentina had poor managers and an average, not stellar, team. His teammates missed sitters in finals but Messi never once said a word about the administration, his team members or the many comments from all the pundits in the world. Not one excuse, not one retaliation.

Gathering yourself before the next exam

All of you are so young, this exam season is still young, you have enough time to acquire the skills to crack the CAT at another shot (if required).

Cut all the negative voices out of your head; your own voice, that of your parents as well, if necessary (since all that most Indian parents seem to care about is the timing of your wedding and how another shot affects that).

They will release the paper with your response soon and based on that, all test-prep brands will release a tool to calculate your score. This can cause another meltdown—it is never easy to actually see the marks. If you know you did not do well, do not try to find out; let the results come out when they come out.

Some of you might be raring to smash the other tests to smithereens, and others might be feeling out of gas and motivation to pick yourself up. The latter, please give yourself a break, do the things you like to do, eat the things you like to eat, and relax for the rest of the week; restart next Monday.

There is little you can do right by pushing yourself without a break or a good rest and being a bunch of ragged nerves.

Getting ready for the next event

It is not easy to crack the test on your first or second attempt unless you are on the top of your game for at least ten to fifteen mocks with additional reserves to handle a tougher-than-usual paper. I cleared the test on my second attempt.

Even those who have set their sights firmly on the old IIMs will be taking a few more tests, at least the IIFT exam and the XAT. Now that you have the CAT monkey off your back, go ahead full-throttle on these other tests.

Even if you have decided on another shot at the CAT and IIM-A, give the other tests you have registered for seriously, crack a final admit to IIFT, NMIMS, SIBM or even XLRI and then reject it. *Achieve something this season and set yourself higher goals for next year.*

Before enlightenment, chop wood, carry water. After enlightenment, chop wood, carry water.—Zen proverb

2

To Retake or Not to Retake the CAT

There are those who do not get admits that they like or get no admits at all, and there are those who get some admits but are not sure whether they should settle for their backup colleges or take another shot at the CAT.

It is not an easy call to take but your task will become easy if you ask yourself the right questions and give the most honest answers you can to them.

A look into the mirror

The answer to the retake conundrum depends on three things:

- Your evaluation of your ability with respect to the CAT
- Your evaluation of your mental state when contemplating another attempt
- Your evaluation of your aspirations

Let us try to make this a bit objective by making it a Q and A situation.

You versus CAT—Ability

The first questions you need to ask: Is this the best shot you could have given? Was this a full-fledged, completely-immersed-into-CAT attempt? Do you believe you have exhausted the limits of your aptitude as far as the CAT goes? Answer all of these questions and then answer the question below.

Question 1

Do you believe that you have maxed out and can go no further in terms of percentile if you give another attempt—YES/NO?

You versus CAT—Stamina

The next question is whether you have enough mental fuel left to go through another year. Do not count the attempts that you made just like that. Is this your first or second or third fully serious attempt?

Question 2

Have your attempts so far taken so much out of you that you dread the thought of another attempt despite knowing that you can get better—YES/NO?

You versus College

What do you think of the options in front of you right now? How do you view yourself vis-à-vis the options you have?

Question 3

Do you believe that all you need is a decent degree and a decent break and will make the most of the opportunities you get irrespective of the brand, or do you believe that your aptitude, your profile and your ambition deserve a better college than the options you have in front of you right now—YES/NO?

If your answer to all the above questions is YES, most importantly the third question, then you should NOT RETAKE and get into a college this year itself.

If your answer is NO to all three, then you should definitely retake the CAT but also evaluate the GMAT depending on your profile and aspirations.

These are not easy questions to answer and I am sure there will be other personal considerations and pressures from different quarters that you would need to factor in. But understand that this decision is purely about your career and hence, the decision has to be taken keeping only that in mind.

Not everyone might be happy with your decision but satisfying all is satisfying none. As far as your career goes, you are the only one who has to be satisfied.

So, you really need to answer these questions for yourself and take a decision.

3

Resetting Your Mind Before You Retake the CAT

I have always been a big believer in the principle that how we approach a thing—an exam, a project, a relationship; the quality of our thoughts around the same—ends up determining the end outcome to a much larger extent than the actual strategies and the things we do since the mindset precedes all of these things.

So, before I discuss how to prepare for a retake, I thought I should talk about the right mindset that you should get into before you set sail once again.

Firstly, count only the 'proper' attempts

I have seen a lot of people talk about attempts as if they were carrying a huge burden—this is my third attempt—as if they have given their lives for this exam and it just does not seem to love them back!

Well, firstly, unless you have taken at least ten mocks, you cannot legitimately say that you have prepared for the exam—it is not *true* love.

You think you do but you do not have a clue about what this exam is, which you would have found out on D-Day.

Stop saying this is your third attempt if you took it in your final year casually, and then in the first year of your job took it semi-seriously, but in both cases, you did not take the minimum ten SimCATs. Tell yourself that is your first attempt at the CAT; it will help you get rid of all the baggage completely.

You might say: 'Sir, but many people know that I have been taking the exam and they might say things like "*kitni baar lega test*"'—just tell them that this is your first *serious* attempt.

And do not forget—those who matter do not mind; those who mind do not matter!

Think like a prospective MBA, not like a worker

Those who are quitting or plan to quit their job to retake the CAT are perfect candidates to fall into a 'donkey-prep' mindset.

309

You have made a commitment to the CAT and for this sake, you have left everything. So now, you are going to prepare eight hours a day for the same.

You are a prospective MBA, so start thinking like one—would you pay Rs 200 for what you can get for Rs 100, or would you spend 100 hours on a project when all you need to spend is 50 hours—just because you really want to do the project well or you really want the product? No. It is all about optimization, right?

Similarly, prep for the time 'you' need to get better and move from score X to score Y and not to show your commitment to put in those eight hours. The law of diminishing marginal returns applies even to working out and prepping for the CAT.

A student had recently asked me how much time out of the planned eight hours every day should be allocated to revision and it just beat me!

Revise what, for god's sake? Practice I can understand—topics, area test, section test, full-length test—but revise?

Do you revise actually riding a cycle or driving a car, every day?

You either know how to drive a car or ride a cycle or not, and you train for a race.

Similarly, you should know what weighted averages are for the rest of your life and you should practise solving problems at the right levels to increase speed and accuracy. But you should not have to revise what weighted average actually is, or the formulas!

To want to be an MBA (maybe not in HR) and have to revise arithmetic is literally the biggest contradiction there is since business is all about arithmetic! The whole world runs on compound interest and if you have to keep revising the formula, god help you!

So, start thinking like the MBA you want to be and this is your first MBA project. Just like you need to maximize revenues for a firm in the future, you need to maximize your marks on the CAT. The difference is that here, you are raw material, you are worker, you are machine, you are manager, you are the CEO—so technically, everything is under your control.

You need to take the right investment calls since no one will know yourself better than you.

Do not let your ego decide your prep needs

A lot of us measure ourselves based on external parameters—the brand of our college, our prior academic profile, and even the intellect of our friends. But you know better than assuming that all or one of the above—big brand college, great marks in non-aptitude tests, super-bright friends—translate into great personal potential on the CAT.

None of the above factors have any bearing on *your* ability on the CAT—only your scores last year (not just the CAT score but also those on the SimCATs you took seriously) indicate your ability on the CAT, and start with the premise that that is your current level.

Do not get into the 'if I had prepared I could have scored higher since my actual level might be closer to my friend's who, with a similar profile, took more mocks and got a 95—mode'. No.

You are what *your* scores say; just accept that.

Do not decide your prep needs based on the assumptions that you might have made about yourself.

Take decisions on whether you need formal prep for the whole exam, for a section, or not at all based on how you are actually faring and not based on whether your friends who cracked it last year took help or not.

If you do this, you will give yourself the best chance to give your best shot at the CAT.

The best source for me to learn was to watch people better than me solve—my teachers, the odd peer—and then want to solve like that. Some people need to watch it once, others need to watch it twice and some others quite a few times before they actually learn to solve like their teacher or peer. So, choose your prep needs based on which category you might fall into on the test or on a particular section.

If you took more than ten mocks last year (without formal prep, only test series) and

- scored less than 90 percentile—you will be better off taking formal prep for the whole test or for a section if your scores are very lopsided
- scored between 90 and 95—you will be better off taking formal prep for your weakest section that stands between you and the 99. You need not do it now, you can do it post-June
- scored above 95 percentile—you will not need formal prep unless your score on one section is very low. You need not do it right now, you can do it post-June

If you took fewer than ten mocks last year, and are *not* confident about your capabilities, then do not wait for this season's test series to start; take up a programme right away.

If you took fewer than ten mocks last year, and are confident about your capabilities, then take up a test series straightaway and take a call post-June—once you have five SimCATs under your belt—on the specific prep needs you have.

I hope you give these things some good thought since many a time a poor result can be the result of ten minor things rather than sheer ability; and if you are doing it one more time, you would want to ensure that you get everything right.

4

How to Prepare for a CAT Retake

Among those who are planning to retake the CAT, for some it might be a case of almost getting there but missing out because of one poor section or just missing out on the overall percentile. For others, the CAT day might have been a bad day at the office and you knew straight away that nothing much was going to happen. On my first attempt, I fell into the latter group—I knew I was out of my depth when I saw the Quant paper; there was no way I was going to clear the cut-offs. This despite consistently doing very well in the mocks leading up to the test. I decided to take another shot since I was very clear that it was not out of my league.

Do not use percentiles to evaluate your ability on a section

One of the ways by which test-takers evaluate their performance on a section is by looking at their percentile on the same. They rate their ability on a section depending upon what percentile they scored in that section. The CAT is a non-standardized exam with question types and levels of difficulty varying wildly from year to year. If we evaluate CAT-23 with respect to CAT-22, there were significant changes: the Quant section was definitely trickier than on CAT-22 as well as the preceding years, making speed and accuracy less of a factor

If you got a 90 this year on Verbal and Quant and lost out on DI-LR, which was as tough as it was in the previous year, then can you rest assured that your VA and QA are strong and you will need very little prep?

What if next year, the RC passages go up a few notches? What will you do if the Quant section poses trickier problems and LR becomes easy? This has happened to quite a few students in the past, with percentiles getting reversed on the second attempt.

Nothing can be more dangerous than evaluating your ability solely on the basis of your percentile when planning a re-attempt! This is especially true when your sectional percentiles are in the 80–95 range. Only those with a percentile above 98 on a section can rest assured that their ability on a particular section is pretty solid.

Make a list of your skills across each section and across all areas

We have discussed in previous chapters that the three levers to improve your scores and performances are question selection, question solving technique and question range.

Question selection is a section-level skill, so rate yourself on your selection skills on each section: poor, moderate, great.

Question solving technique is an area level skill as far as VA-RC goes. Rate your technique (the techniques have been outlined in the book) on each of the question types in the section: poor, moderate, great. On other two sections, it is a sectional level skill. The technique is outlined in the 'How to solve . . .' chapters in the respective sections.

Question range is relevant only to the DI-LR and the QA sections since there are only four or five question types on VA-RC and you are supposed to be able to solve all the types. Make a list of the topics where you lack the conceptual clarity in DI-LR and Quant: Venn diagram-based sets, remainder theorem, etc.

You need to peak at the right time

This is something that is very often talked about in sports—peaking at the right time.

Those who watch sports regularly know that no individual or team performance is at the same level all the time. Within a tournament, we see that a team can start slowly but then manages to hit the peak form at the right time—like Australia in the 2000 World Cup. Within a season, as is the case with leagues across sports, teams peak at different times—with Arsenal always peaking at the wrong time! Even across a career, a sportsman will have a purple patch where they can put no foot wrong—Djokovic in 2015 or Virat last year.

What you need to do is ensure that you peak at the right time for CAT—September.

What usually happens on a retake is:

- you start off full-steam in the March–July period and somehow lose energy or burnout as you get closer to the test
- you decide to go underground till June–July and then straightaway try to go into an intense prep mode

Both are deeply flawed methods. While your practice should start from March and go all the way through to January for XAT, the intensity and focus should vary across the months.

Till June: Be in *learning* mode

From the March–June period, you need to only be in learning mode. You do not need to be pumped up and thinking things like 'this time I won't just crack the test but smash it to smithereens'! You just need to ensure you are being regular in your prep and enjoy the learning process. This should be a happy phase with very little anxiety. Think about this phase as net practice—one is working on learning to get better. My friend once saw Virat practise in the nets in Australia—30 minutes of just playing bouncers!

During this period, nail your question solving efficiency and question range.

July–November: Be in *testing* mode

Right from the first test onwards, you need to be in game mode. Question selection needs to be the main area of focus along with accuracy. This means that you need to be kicking yourself over silly mistakes, working to cut down on the wrong choice of questions and focusing on improving test performance. This will only be possible if you have already covered the learning needs before July. You can't be learning basics and maximizing test performance at the same time!

One size might not fit all—regularity over frequency

The prep schedule outlined above need not suit all aspirants since each one of you will have a different daily schedule depending on your work or your college load. So, you would have to tailor or modify the plan to suit your needs. But what is most important is that you make a plan and stick to it.

What matters more than frequency is regularity. No matter how hectic your day, what is the barest minimum that you can eke out—can you ensure that you at least read the newspaper before turning in to bed on a really crazy work day?

If your weekdays are variable but your weekends are predictable, then can you ensure that you make a weekend plan and stick to it?

Most often we have a clear long-term plan, in this case, cracking the CAT come November, but whenever something else comes up in the shorter-term—a weekend with a friend visiting from out of town, a new movie or a new TV series that is supposed to be insanely good—we end up accepting it. So, in effect, short-term decisions end up jeopardizing long-term goals! You have to say no to a few things, give up a few things (besides deciding to grow a beard till the test).

Whatever plan you draw up, stick to it. Do not be like the guy who draws up a will but refuses to die!

Part X

The Better Problems to Have

1

How to Choose Between the IIMs and Other Premier MBA Programmes

After the first round results of the major B-schools are out, we get regular queries about which B-schools to join. There is rarely any confusion about A, B and C but after that, it seems as if aspirants are having a lot of trouble choosing between the IIMs L, I and K and other top B-schools such as FMS, XLRI, MDI and others. How does one go about making the right choice between the IIMs and other top schools? One of the terms thrown around a lot these days is ROI.

How you should really calculate ROI

A few years ago, an aspirant I was speaking to after an ISB info session said: 'Sir, these days even IIM-A does not offer a great ROI, the average salary and fee are close to each other.'

A lot of aspirants tend to use ROI to evaluate colleges. They use ROI in conjunction with batch size to decide which college to join, where ROI is simply taken to be the average salary/cost of education.

Well, once you do an MBA, you will realize that more than an ROI, the better tool to use will be a cost-benefit analysis since you are not investing in a purely financial instrument or land or gold.

Whenever one does a cost-benefit analysis, one has to consider not just the tangible but also the intangible costs as well as benefits.

The intangible benefits or the benefits to which you cannot put a number are the ones that most aspirants on the verge of joining an MBA programme, those who are doing their MBA and those who have just graduated, are unaware of. The idea is to share all the intangibles that might help aspirants to make a decision.

The three letters I-I-M carry more weight than you can imagine

Firstly, no aspirant should forget that the second most prestigious and valuable prefix that an institution in this country can carry is IIM. When most aspirants start preparing for the CAT, they do not tell themselves that they want to crack XL or MDI or FMS; it is always the IIMs that are on most people's minds.

The same holds true for the rest of the business management fraternity—the word IIM carries a lot more weight than you can imagine. People evaluating you at your workplace are more likely to pull down an IIM grad without the slightest hesitation saying, 'How can this person be an IIM grad?' than they are to say, 'How can this person be from MDI or XL?'

The IIM tag predisposes people to think positively about you

When you introduce yourself as an IIM graduate, people's perception of your ability becomes vastly exaggerated. People will tend to treat you as being good unless you prove them wrong. Whereas those from other brands are viewed neutrally and they have to prove themselves. It goes without saying the same applies when people look at your resume.

An MBA is about a lot more than your first job

The problem with the ROI method is that it places unduly high importance on the short-term result—the first job you get out of campus. Don't you think that is barely any return? Good investments yield returns over a longer time period and a good MBA is also supposed to do the same.

You might not get your dream job even at IIM-A

On-campus recruitments are very unlike recruitments off-campus and this difference is key to understanding the long-term value of an MBA.

During placements on campus, recruiters are constantly comparing you with a huge list of other candidates they have at their disposal. For recruiters, it is like a buffet with many awesome things to choose from but with one constraint—**time** and **competing recruiters**!

So, what do companies do? They start using various filters to ensure that they look at fewer people and somehow get the people they want before their competitors get them. What are the filters that get applied? They vary from company to company but to name a few:

- the brand of the college you graduated from (everybody wants to get into McKinsey but they can't possibly interview everyone, so they use the college brand as a filter)
- leadership positions held (so guys with big leadership roles on campus get filtered in over maybe people with a better CGPA, etc.)

So intense is the competition among companies that this year one prominent consulting firm at IIM-A was even willing to forgo the final interview round if the people who they shortlisted so far were still not picked up by others. Imagine, they were scared that by the time they finished their process, they would have no candidates left!

Compare this with an off-campus process. Firstly, it is not a three-day affair, so companies are not in any hurry to shortlist and interview people as fast as possible. You will end up getting a fairer shot and enough time to make a good case for your candidature.

Companies do not need people only at the time of campus placements. In fact, most fresh MBA graduates quit their first jobs within a year! There is a constant need for people all year round and they scour various portals and recruitment agencies to get resumes.

So, you do not need to worry about the campus placements being the final summit or crowning point to reach. In fact, it is just the beginning of the climb.

What the MBA gives you is a platform to reach the top over the course of your career.

It's your peer network that will get you jobs in the long run

Campus placements last only a few days but your peer network, network of immediate seniors and alumni network will be the ones that will be getting you jobs over a longer period.

When you graduate from an IIM, you graduate with access to a network of people working in the best companies in the country. You will not come to know of openings through Naukri or other portals but from your peers since firms hire a lot through referrals.

Also, you get access to platforms such as iimjobs.com through which candidates and recruiters find each other. A student who just graduated from IIM-A told me that after graduating this March, he was approached by three companies via iimjobs.com.

Can you place a monetary value to the opportunities that this network can open up for you?

If you want to start your own firm, the tag is invaluable to attract investors

Investors are always taking bets on people as much as they are on ideas. Even before you pitch your ideas, investors will be aware of all the hot ideas and opportunities that are present in the market. So, in essence, they are only evaluating the capability of the team and one of the things that goes a long way in boosting your credentials is the IIM tag.

Keeping all of this in mind, how should you make your choices?

IIMs-L, I and K versus FMS, XLRI, S.P. Jain, MDI

Technically, I would always place the old IIMs above all other schools purely for the reasons mentioned above.

The only exception can be FMS, for the almost low fees! How does one break this deadlock? Choose FMS over the others if:

- You have already done your graduation as a fully residential programme from an IIT, BITS, NIT, etc., and/or
- You are sure you want to explore entrepreneurship options immediately after your MBA

What is the rationale behind this?

Firstly, if you have not studied at a premier national-level college, whilst staying on campus in the hostel, an education at FMS or S.P. Jain will be incomplete in terms of the experience.

You will do an MBA only once and the experience of studying in an entire awesome campus dedicated to MBA education, as opposed to one building or a department in a college where the main programme is not the MBA, which is the case with FMS, S.P. Jain, NMIMS, and MBA programmes at IITs is something that you will cherish for life. You are not going to really enjoy life again (maybe for a few years after you graduate). 😊

If you have already experienced the same during your graduation, then you can go ahead and choose FMS, else go for the IIMs.

Secondly, if you want to start working on your own venture straight out of college, then an education loan will always be an albatross around your neck, making FMS the best option.

There is a case for choosing SPJIMR-Ops over IIM-I and IIM-K if you are really keen on getting the full range of core operations jobs to choose from. The IIMs might not offer you such a vast selection since they do not admit based on specialization.

Other colleges versus newer IIMs is a personal choice

When it comes to the choice between new IIMs and other schools, choose other top schools over them since you will get the benefit of the degree only over a very long term, when they are no longer considered new.

Also, everything else, right from campus to college culture and placements will just be beginning to take root and hence leave you quite a bit on the back foot in the short term. There will also be no large network of peers of seniors through whom you can get access to jobs.

This caused a bit of agony to people who were studying at new IIMs. You can find first-hand experiences of people who studied in-person at the new and baby IIMs on my blog thecatwriter.com

You are not investing in a college, you are also investing in yourself

Most view the expenditure on an MBA from the *what-am-I-getting-for-what-I-am-paying* lens, making it the college's responsibility to deliver. Well, unfortunately, the college owes you nothing.

The college deems you suitable for a career in management and has offered you a seat, giving you access to:

- the learning that they can offer, and
- the best firms in the country

You are investing this money to acquire this education and this network to maximize your potential and your career opportunities.

Most of the time what you study during the course will barely be used in the first few years of your life as an MBA. It will only start making sense when you come into big decision-making roles later in life (even those subjects which you will find most useless on campus).

You are not learning subjects that will help you do your first job better. You are learning and developing the skills to lead a company later.

So, it makes a lot of sense to view things not from an immediate placement perspective but from the perspective of maximizing your chances of leading the best firms or starting a successful firm of your own.

If you are still unable to make up your mind, do not worry. All of these colleges guarantee great outcomes; it finally does not matter one way or the other!

2

How to Choose Between an HR Programme and a Regular MBA

India is probably the only country where people will be willing to shell out more than Rs 20 lakh for a product and at the same time be willing to accept whatever variant the seller decides to give them. What am I referring to here? When I ask students who have both BM and HR calls from XLRI what their preference is, or what they would prefer between XL-HR/TISS and IIM-K/MDI, most are very clear—the specialization does not matter, all that matters is the brand; others start bringing ROI into the picture.

I feel people put in more thought when choosing between a diesel and a petrol car! We are so crazy after elite institutions that we fail to even consider whether we will succeed/fail in or like/dislike a particular field. The objective of this chapter will be to give you enough information to choose the right programme when faced with a choice between a premier HR programme and other programmes.

It is not as simplistic as *people skills* versus *communication skills*

People tend to think of the choice between HR and marketing as a choice between liking to interact with people and possessing great communication skills.

Any MBA worth their salt needs to have great people skills and communication skills. I feel that our ability to build a successful career in any area (assuming a particular level of intelligence) is more a function of our innate traits and temperament than our skills.

Let us take two people with great people skills and communication skills starting off their careers in sales and marketing—will both be equally successful in sales as well as marketing? Will both do equally well in the roles of national sales manager and chief marketing officer?

No. A lot depends on the temperament of each individual.

For example, I had a student who, after his MBA, took up a pre-sales role in an IT firm purely because he felt that he just could not do a desk job, he needed to be on the move, he could not just sit and think.

So, how do you decide whether you are made for HR or for any general MBA? There are three things you need to consider:

Are you ready to settle for the award for the best supporting actor?

The big difference between HR and other functions is that marketing, finance and operations are line functions—functions that directly impact the top-line—*the revenues*—or the bottom-line—*the profits*—of a company. HR is a support function, which requires specialized knowledge, that indirectly contributes to the revenues and profits by providing the people and creating the environment required to run the other functions successfully.

What does this mean in terms of career progression?

HR professionals very rarely rise to become CEOs; every other specialization has a direct path to the CEO chair; firms choose CEOs from among the top management—be it CMO, CFO or COO. Also, the curriculum of an HR programme is a very specialized one and not a generalized business strategy geared to build future leaders. The only case in which HR professionals become CEOs is if they are part of the founding team and started with taking up the HR responsibility and later moved on to other roles.

What does this mean in terms of temperament?

Those who are very ambitious, competitive and want to be close to the action—revenue generation and profit maximization—will find themselves to be misfits in HR. While Indian firms have started to give the importance due to HR as a function, by and large the Indian firms still look at HR to not be of core importance. So, if you are ambitious and like to call the shots, you might not fit in at all.

Please keep in mind that this is not a value judgement on people in HR. Just like supporting actors are indispensable to a movie, the same is true of HR as well. It is up to you to decide the role you will excel in.

HR on average will pay lower; are you okay with it?

Salaries of most people working in line functions have a high variable component that is based on the numbers that they are measured against year on year. People working in line functions have measurable targets that also carry a high incentive. The higher the revenues, the higher the incentives that people get to earn.

HR professionals also carry measurable targets but the incentives are not as high as those in other functions. In finance, on the other hand, professionals working in i-banking end up getting a small percentage of the size of the deal, traders have a direct upside related to the profits they make for the firm, so essentially, there is no ceiling on the amount they can earn, making finance a very sought-after field, as well as one with a lot of scams—higher rewards induce people to take higher risks.

Be that as it may, those graduating from the top HR schools earn enough to have great *roti*, great *kapda* and great *makaan*. If at a comparable firm and level, a marketing professional is at around a Rs 75 lakh CTC, an HR professional will be in the Rs 50–60 lakh range. The gap narrows down or rather would cease to matter once you reach the position of head HR. Please keep in mind that what I have written does not apply to each and every HR professional in each and every firm. Anyone at Amazon will have a really high salary and make tons of money through ESOPs.

Are stress-levels and work-life balance major priorities for you?

Given the fact that the monthly revenues and profits are not driven by HR, roles in HR carry lower stress levels—*lower stress levels do not mean lower workload.* My friend in HR travels as much as, if not more, than my friend in marketing and puts in as many manhours but, on average, has lower stress levels, though not all the time.

The end of the month is always a high-intensity time for other functions. Managers keep pushing their subordinates through encouragement or outright swear words to make them boost sales as much as possible.

HR professionals face high levels of stress during mergers and acquisitions when people are let go due to workforce rationalization, or while downsizing during a recession (you should watch the movie *Up in the Air* if you haven't already).

So, if you are someone who by nature seeks less stress, then HR might be the right choice.

In non-HR roles, you have to consciously use stress management tools to ensure that you are able to maintain the balance. You might reach home but if your mind is still carrying the stress from work, then the balance will suffer.

If the answer to all of these questions is a strong YES, then HR is the obvious choice for you.

If you are not able to make up your mind on these questions, then give them a rating from 1 to 10, 1 being a strong NO to 10 being a strong YES. If your cumulative rating on all three questions is higher than 22, then you are probably a better fit for HR.

To sum it up, choosing primarily on the basis of the brand might be too simplistic when it comes to specialized programmes since we are not comparing apples with apples.

The better you know yourself, your traits, your temperament and your skills, the better you will be at building the right career for yourself.

By now it will be clear that you cannot have your cake and eat it too; there is always a trade-off to be made.

3

How to Make the Most of Your MBA Programme

You have made it to your dream B-school and you are super-excited to reach campus. But like with your CAT prep, there are a few things that others who have been there and done that can tell you, which will make you enjoy as well as get the most out of these final two years filled with a lot of work, to make it a lot less stressful and much more focused as well.

This video is available on the Bell the CAT YouTube Page. The QR code on page 332 will take you to the same.

Epilogue

1

What I Learnt from Working Out

A student once asked, 'Sir, I understand this technique, process and stuff but can't I not do this only on tough questions? All the rest I'll solve normally.' The first problem is the assumption that there is something normal and that the technique or process is something special! What we call normal are rather the mindless processes that each individual has figured out for themselves, not those done by experts.

A few years ago, I did the exact same thing that the student asked in my workout regimen, and this is what happened. I started out on a new workout programme called 5*5 Stronglifts, which involves doing just five sets of five reps of three exercises every alternate day. All exercises were compound exercises with an Olympic barbell that needed you to use your whole body. The catch is that you start with an empty bar, and every alternate day, add five pounds to it. So, when I started, I found the empty bar so easy that I did not make it a habit to activate each and every part that needed to be activated to execute an exercise. So, for many sessions, I did not do overhead squats by transmitting the weight from my feet to my calves to my hamstrings to my core and then to my shoulders. I just stood up mindlessly and lifted the weight. After a month, when the bar was no longer light, I could not add more weight beyond a point.

Because of not following the technique, I had not strengthened all the different muscles that came into play to do the exercise right. And once the weight goes beyond a point, one needs each and every muscle group to execute each move perfectly, which is why I hit a wall.

The moral of the story should be clear—one cannot suddenly execute technique when one moves into the knockout stages of a World Cup and is facing the best bowlers in the world—technique is always built ground up.

The more I teach, the more new things I learn to do in life, and the more I reflect on these two things, one thing stands out for me: the paramount importance of technique in everything we do—not just answering a question in an exam, but even driving a car, working out, or something as mundane as simple home cooking.

When I look back at the various things I learnt without anyone teaching me any real technique, I realize that I was and am pretty mediocre at those. If I start with sports, the two I played regularly were table tennis and cricket. In both sports, I thought I knew how to play and was part of a few

327

college teams as well. I made the most of the few things that came naturally and was average on the rest. But when I saw those who were taught formally how to play and had a natural skill for the same, I realized that I knew nothing—everything, right from my grip, was flawed, but it did not matter at the level I was playing.

In other cases, such as driving a car, I was taught but not taught by anyone who really went beyond telling me the basics of how stuff works. No one told me that a great driver, not a racer, is judged by how the rest of the passengers in the car feel—they barely experience a jerk and feel very safe. No one told me how a great driver achieves this until a colleague let me in on a secret shared by a really skilled driver—always drive in such a way that you maintain a fixed distance between your car and the one in front of you. When I thought about the implications of this, it became very clear to me that to do that, one has to ensure that one is not braking or accelerating in bursts; both have to happen in a very gradual manner.

Recently, I saw the big changes that following a process can bring about in cooking! I have been cooking for a long time, but I was never taught anything and knew nothing about any technique. I asked my mother for recipes and relied on instinct until I saw my younger brother cooking after learning stuff from YouTube! I realized that small things like following precise timings concerning cooking rice or even something as simple as frying fish ensured that every single time one hit the bullseye, every single time the dish turned out right. Other things, such as being process-oriented in prepping the ingredients and handling the kitchen counter, made everything smooth and easy. I was not saving any time by my crazy multitasking!

I have outlined various techniques in this book, and all of them will seem laborious to start off with. This is natural since executing a process mindfully always seems harder for quite some time in the beginning. For example, anyone who has lifted a dumbbell will know that your instructor will tell you that you are supposed to lift it fast and lower it slowly. We will find the lifting easy when we do it, but slow lowering seems tough or unnecessary. What happens because of this? You will take twice as much time to see results because you are only using half of the exercises, and, in the case of leg raises, the useless half!

I have been working with a personal trainer for four years now, and I realize that the most important thing is understanding the exercise from the inside out. I make it a point to ask him exactly which part is supposed to get activated with a particular exercise and what is the most important thing to ensure. Even on the odd exercise that I absolutely hate, I ensure that I do not go through the motions but do it right since I know that it is part of the whole process and one cannot cut corners.

I want you to remember this every time you decide to skip a step in the process or ignore it altogether: pausing after reading the question stem and forming a shadow answer is the crux of being great at RC! You cannot ignore it and dream of scoring beyond a particular level. It is like doing a chest press without involving your chest but your arms. You will not be able to increase reps or weight beyond a point.

When you watch a master craftsperson converting a piece of wood into something, you will be amazed at the speed and ease with which they perform. They might seem to be using very few steps to shape the wood into a finished object. In reality, they are using all of the steps—they are doing it so fast that they are not visible to the naked eye.

Technique is *everything*.

2

Motivation Is a Myth

A student once said, 'Sir, I love motivational books; I read them all the time!' I replied, 'When will you get motivated?' He was a bit taken aback since he thought that I write so many blog posts that motivate him, I must be really into it. Nothing is further from the truth. I think of myself as someone who knows about all the technical, strategic and mental skills that go into acing the CAT and other premier exams. I am happiest when students say they used this or that process and got higher scores. I am happiest when they say they remembered my words during the exam when the going got tough and they needed to keep their head calm and not give up. I do not think I succeed when people say they feel motivated because I feel motivation is a myth.

Why do I say this? I say this because motivation, as it is understood, is the drive to achieve something by putting in a consistent effort. And from what I know about life, the drive to put in consistent effort comes from one of two sources: love or fear. I work out regularly because I absolutely love working out. I absolutely love solving CAT questions. I do not know of one successful student who cracked the CAT despite not enjoying a single part of the exam. Not in all of these years. Everyone liked some parts, if not all, and worked through the others.

Many others start working out in their forties because their doctors have told them that unless they do so, they are likely to get hospitalized soon. So, some start working out and continue out of fear, while others begin to enjoy the process after they start seeing results.

The whole industry of motivational literature operates on the periphery rather than the centre. When you are really desperate and ready to make some right changes, a motivational piece can give you a boost. Once you start something new and begin to enjoy it, a motivational coach can be a decent support. But the key is the joy in the process rather than the talk or the words.

We can read all the books we want to on all the philosophies of the world and talk about them very intelligently endlessly, but unless we act in the right way every single time we are faced with a problem, all the knowledge is useless. It is of no use to be able to analyse and understand later what happened. What is important is that the action is right whether one knows the theory or not. The reason I stress this is that we can easily mistake consuming theory for action. We will get sucked into the trap of watching videos on a topic endlessly without doing anything about it. After a point, we move on to a new topic. What we are doing is watching videos, not learning anything. We truly learn only by doing. And we should talk only after doing something sincerely for some period of time, observing the results and drawing our conclusions, not after watching.

Practice is *theory.*

3

Finding Your Centre: A Way of Life

Whenever we approach a task, the outcome will only be as good as our state of being before we begin the task. In the summer of 1984, Malcolm Marshall sustained a double fracture to his left thumb in the last test between West Indies and England. This usually means being ruled out of the match, but he played on with a plaster, took seven wickets for 53 runs, and even scored a one-handed boundary. West Indies won the test and completed a 5–0 rout, which was dubbed a Blackwash!

In the 2023 World Cup, Glenn Maxwell began cramping up after his hundred, and when he limped and fell down while trying to complete a single, he had a back spasm. No one thought he would be able to continue. The skipper Pat Cummins had the number 10 batsman standing near the ropes. Having first received physio treatment when he was on 109, the right-hander went on to hit a further seven sixes (out of 10 in total) and nine fours (out of 21) in a scarcely believable display that finished off the chase. Maxwell struck 78 from his last 33 balls, barely moving his body as he swung at the ball, yet still managing to consistently find the boundary.

How did these two players manage to do this? The extreme situation made them become completely one-pointed. Given the state of their body, every single ounce of mental energy went into just the task at hand, they could not operate on autopilot. Maxwell said the same thing in different words.[*]

> But once I sort of calmed my breathing down, and I had the physio out there and he sort of talked me through it, what it was going to be like. I had one person pushing my foot, one person lifting my leg. It was strange. But that actually probably made the whole job a little bit more simple. I wasn't overthinking the situation. I just knew if I got a ball that I could hit, I'd try and hit it.

What is important is the first phrase—*when I calmed my breathing down*. This sums up everything. When our breathing is calm and serene, when our mind is rested and our body well fed, the outcome of the tasks we approach will always be right.

---

[*] https://www.cricket.com.au/news/3772958/cramping-maxwell-plays-through-the-pain-for-a-world-cup-epic.

When we are not centred, we are like an instrument that is not tuned. Just as a musician always tunes the instrument before playing it, we should always centre ourselves by ensuring that our breathing, our mind and our body are calm and alert.

This applies to every important thing that we need to achieve, including our daily CAT practice, important office meetings and important life events. It is not to be confused with the flow state or being in the zone, which comes later, after the task starts. This comes before you even start.

If I could give you one piece of advice, it would be this: ensure that your mind and body are in perfect condition on most days through pranayama, meditation, exercise and diet. Once you start doing this regularly, you will see a change in the quality of your being; and once that happens, the outcomes will follow.

You should not stop after the CAT is over, after you get into an IIM, or after you land your dream job. That is when everything starts, like getting into the Indian team. You will have to play well—if you have the right skills, you will be made captain, and one day, you will be in the final of the World Cup. If by then you are used to finding your centre every single day, the final of the World Cup will not be something special—you will be ready, as you are ready every single day.

Finding your centre is a way of life.

Please scan this QR code to watch
the various videos mentioned in the book.

Acknowledgements

This book would not have been possible without my long and diverse experience at IMS. I must thank Kamlesh Sajnani, the MD, and Anand Sutaria, the CEO, of IMS, for the immense faith they have reposed in me. The various roles they have entrusted me with have helped me develop a deep understanding of both student and teacher journeys.

The essence of what I have communicated through this book stems from my love for the CAT exam and for guiding MBA aspirants, a love that I have shared over the years with my brilliant peers at IMS. So here is thanking Jose Augusto De Abreu for introducing me to the elegant solution, and Sujit Kumar, Amit Panchmatia, Hemang Panchmatia, Kumud Choudhary, Parmeshwar Sha, Deepak Shukla, Vipul Tyagi, Ujjwal Nagar, Prakash Rajput, Sanjith Nair, Eldo Paul, Sheshanshu Sekhar, Ritesh Sinha and Edwin Devaprakash, to name a few, for their passion and commitment.

Lastly, I would like to thank the editorial team at Penguin Random House India, especially Manish Kumar, who championed the book as soon as I presented it to him, and Ralph Rebello, who spotted things big and small that made the book complete.

Scan QR code to access the
Penguin Random House India website